Challenging

UNIVERSITY OF
GLOUCESTERSHIRE

at Cheltenham and Gloucester

care professionals in training and in practice.

Jonathan Gabe is Senior Research Fellow in Medical Sociology at Royal
Holloway College, University of London and Senior Lecturer in Sociology
at South Bank University, London. **David Kelleher** is Reader in Sociology
at London Guildhall University. **Gareth Williams** is Senior Research
Fellow at the Centre for Health Studies, University College, Salford and
Department of Sociology, University of Salford.

Challenging medicine

Edited by Jonathan Gabe,
David Kelleher and Gareth Williams

ROUTLEDGE

London and New York

First published 1994
by Routledge
11 New Fetter Lane, London EC4P 4EE

Simultaneously published in the USA and Canada
by Routledge
29 West 35th Street, New York, NY 10001

Typeset in Times by LaserScript, Mitcham, Surrey
Printed and bound in Great Britain by
Biddles Ltd, Guildford and King's Lynn

British Library Cataloguing in Publication Data
A catalogue record for this book is available from the British Library

Library of Congress Cataloging in Publication Data
A catalog record for this book is available from the Library of Congress

ISBN 0–415–08816–X (hbk)
ISBN 0–415–08817–8 (pbk)

Contents

Contributors

Michael Bury Professor, Department of Social Policy and Social Science, Royal Holloway College, University of London.

Robert Dingwall Professor, School of Social Studies, University of Nottingham.

Lesley Doyal Professor, Faculty of Health and Community Studies, University of the West of England, Bristol.

Mary Ann Elston Lecturer, Department of Social Policy and Social Science, Royal Holloway College, University of London.

Jonathan Gabe Senior Research Fellow, Department of Social Policy and Social Science, Royal Holloway College, University of London and Senior Lecturer, Legal, Political and Social Sciences, South Bank University, London.

David J. Hunter Professor, Nuffield Institute for Health, University of Leeds.

David Kelleher Reader, Department of Sociology, London Guildhall University.

Jennie Popay Professor of Community Health, University of Salford and Director, Public Health Research and Resource Centre, Bolton, Salford, Trafford and Wigan Health Authorities.

Mike Saks Professor, Department of Health and Community Studies, De Montfort University, Leicester.

Gareth Williams Senior Research Fellow, Department of Sociology, University of Salford and Centre for Health Studies, University College, Salford.

Anne Witz Lecturer, Department of Social Policy and Social Work, University of Birmingham.

For Charlotte

Preface

The medical profession has long been thought of as an occupational group that has considerable power, but one that used its power in the best interests of individuals and society. In a world that often appears to be controlled by experts, the medical profession has been among the most powerful of these groups. As the high priests of modern society, doctors have come to be seen as experts not only on the treatment of bodily ills but also on how to live the good life. From time to time their power and status have been challenged, but these challenges have always been easily brushed aside.

Until the late 1960s most sociologists accepted medicine's definition of itself as a profession, using its expert knowledge and special skills rationally and benevolently. Subsequently, the growth of a more critical sociology encouraged an alternative view of medicine as a dominating profession, monopolising the provision of health services or responding to the requirements of the economic system. Indeed, some even suggested that medicine was responsible for creating demand for its services by medicalising everyday life.

This 'professional dominance' model has been extremely influential over the last two decades but is increasingly being questioned. Initially this was couched in terms of what has come to be called 'deprofessional-isation': the proposition that medicine's professional status has been under-mined as the 'knowledge gap' between physicians and consumers has diminished and new specialised occupations have arisen around bodies of knowledge and skills that physicians themselves are not competent to employ. Within the general backlash against professional society, lay people have been less willing to accept uncritically the judgements of doctors. More recently, it has been argued that the medical profession is being 'proletarianised'. According to this argument its members are being deskilled, losing their economic independence (becoming wage labourers) and being required to work in bureaucratically organised institutions under the instructions of managers. Yet others have suggested that medicine's dominance is being threatened by the growth of new social movements, ranging from feminists to anti-vivisectionists, who have questioned the basis of medical knowledge and the techniques used in its production and application.

Given these developments there would seem to be good reason to reassess the position of the medical profession in contemporary Britain and the extent to which it still dominates the health field. How seriously should we take arguments about proletarianisation or deprofessionalisation, which have been developed primarily with the US context in mind? Is the profession's position of power under serious threat from the new social movements? Or is the prime threat to medicine the economically driven rise of managerialism?

The present book aims to address these issues by inviting a number of well-known medical sociologists to consider a range of 'challenges' currently being faced by the medical profession from within and without the health care system. Each contributor has been asked to assess the significance of his or her challenge in relation to the theoretical arguments outlined above.

We believe that such a book should have an appeal for a number of reasons. First, most of the literature on this issue is to be found in journals or in books whose primary focus is different from the present one (e.g. Gabe *et al.* 1991). Second, those books that have considered the question of medical dominance in recent times have tended to focus on challenges from within the health care system, especially in the United States (e.g. Starr 1982; Freidson 1989), and to have played down or ignored the significance of the range of external challenges to be considered here. Third, this gap in the literature needs to be filled because of the widespread interest in the social relations of health care. It is hoped that this book will appeal not only to medical sociologists but also to a much wider audience including policy analysts, health service workers, medical journalists and interested members of the public.

REFERENCES

Freidson, E. (1989) *Medical Work in America*, New Haven: Yale University Press.
Gabe, J., Calnan, M. and Bury, M. (eds) (1991) *The Sociology of the Health Service*, London: Routledge.
Starr, P. (1982) *The Social Transformation of American Medicine*, New York: Basic Books.

Understanding medical dominance in the modern world

David Kelleher, Jonathan Gabe and Gareth Williams

'And the very lightest diet,' said the important doctor.
'Soups.'
He smiled, and it became a mystic word, dimly steaming upon his tongue.
Mrs Bonner was compelled to smile back. 'So nourishing,' she sighed, herself by now nourished.

(White 1981: 356)

THE PLACE OF MEDICINE

We are so accustomed to thinking of the profession of medicine as a stable institution with considerable power, that it is sometimes difficult to imagine that it could ever be otherwise or that it has ever been different. In the eighteenth century, however, patients and the public had little conception of the medical profession as a collective entity. In this unregulated world of medicine the competence and sound judgement of healers, licensed or not, was highly variable (Stacey 1988). What mattered in the formulation of opinions about medicine in the eighteenth century were face-to-face encounters with individual practitioners in what amounted to a free market in healing (Porter and Porter 1989).

Although these interpersonal encounters have remained an important influence, from the middle of the nineteenth century onwards individual doctors were increasingly incorporated into professions, institutions, and bureaucracies which had definite social and cultural relations to civil society and the State. In this process the occupation of healing changed from being frequently seen as a rattlebag of quacks and rogues (Porter and Porter 1989) to a profession with considerable power, authority and status. Two strands developed. The general practitioner (GP), who was part of the same social world as the patient, often played a key civic role in his or her locality (Tudor Hart 1988). The hospital consultant, meanwhile, was a rare breed to whom the familiar GP occasionally referred patients. He was a distant and recondite figure with access to knowledge which transcended local concerns and was unavailable to ordinary people. These medical men and women increasingly became stabilising authorities in a universe prone to occasional disorder. They were the people to whom one turned at times of crisis, after all other sources of help had been exhausted (Berger 1967). Their self-presentation might sometimes be brusque and aloof, but within the class structure and gender order of the time such interpersonal inequalities were seen as part of the way things were, at least as far as most ordinary people were concerned.

In the first half of the twentieth century some important developments occurred in the delivery of health care, the organisation of the medical profession, and the scientific foundations of medical practice. The growth of research laboratories and the increasing numbers of hospital patients had put medicine in a strong position to capitalise on the growing concern about the public health (Stacey 1988). First, hospital doctors and later GPs found themselves with more money, higher status and greater political power. The Second World War ushered in significant political changes. Doctors were now part of a public service – the National Health Service (NHS) – at a time when the universally blessed goal of such a service and the professionalism of its workers were largely taken for granted. They were exemplary members of a 'professional society' (Perkin 1989) in which everyone wanted to get professionalised (Wilensky 1964).

After the Second World War doctors' power was further underlined by various social, cultural and technological changes. The validity of medical knowledge had always rested on a degree of trade-off between technicality and indeterminacy (Jamous and Peloille 1970), the former emphasising the solid scientific basis of medicine, the latter stressing the interpretive mysteries of diagnosis and treatment. How else could 'soups' come to have such therapeutic potency (White 1981)? The decline of organised religion, moreover, led to doctors being cast more and more in the role of secular priests whose expertise encompassed not only the treatment of bodily ills but also advice on how to live the good life, and judgements on right and wrong behaviour (Zola 1972).

In addition, doctors benefited from being gatekeepers to a whole range of new pharmacological products which were generally perceived as enhancing their ability to save life and minimise personal discomfort. The power and status gained from such pharmacological developments, and the close alliance between doctors and the pharmaceutical industry (Bodenheimer 1984), were further enhanced in the 1950s and 1960s by the introduction of surgical procedures which for the first time facilitated the replacement of diseased organs by transplantation (Stocking 1992).

In the last two decades the position of the medical profession appears to have changed. The corporate power of medicine has been increasingly challenged and doctors, the high priests of modern society, have become increasingly embattled as their position as experts has been challenged from inside and outside the health care arena. In conjunction with direct challenges to their knowledge and expertise have come doubts about the nature of their power, stirred by the secularisation of medical mystique and changing perceptions of the dynamics of power in society.

CHALLENGES TO MEDICINE

One of the major internal challenges faced by doctors in Britain comes from management. In chronological terms this is not the first challenge, but it is certainly the most salient. Before the Griffiths Report of 1983 (DHSS 1983) the NHS was run by consensus teams with doctors and nurses sharing managerial responsibilities with what were then called administrators (Harrison *et al.* 1990). Griffiths introduced the notion of commercial business management from the private sector and turned administrators into general managers who would have overall responsibility for the delivery of health care. One consequence of this has been that managers, by way of information systems and clinical budgeting, have been expected to establish some control over the activities of doctors and their use of resources (Cox 1991). This ability to influence clinicians has been extended by the 1989 White Paper (DH 1989) which stipulated that district general managers should be involved in appointing consultants, allocating merit awards and agreeing detailed job descriptions with consultants on an annual basis (Hunter 1991). At a more general level, the introduction of an 'internal market' into the NHS, with a separation between the purchasers and providers of health care, has set up changes within the system which have major implications for the autonomy of the medical profession (Flynn 1992).

The response of doctors to this challenge has been mixed. While many medical staff in hospitals have reacted critically to the increased powers of general management (Harrison 1988) some have welcomed the opportunity to take upon themselves the responsibility for newly established clinical directorates. For example, while hospital consultants have tended to view developments with suspicion and hostility, those in registrar level positions have seen the new managerial opportunities as a way to evade the bottleneck to consultant posts and escape the traditional power hierarchies (Oakley 1991). Within primary health care the situation is even more complex. The allocation of budgets to general practices has created the possibility of greater autonomy for GPs in decision-making about patient care. While some have eagerly applied for fundholding status others have rejected outright the commercialisation implied by this development, pointing to the potentially adverse implications for practice and patients (Haines and Illiffe 1992). At the same time, the imposition of new GP contracts and the emphasis on audit and management by the Family Health Services Authorities (FHSA) in seeking to 'commission for quality' (Butland 1993) potentially undermine the independence of GPs. The sources of this managerial challenge are both economic and ideological. The period since 1979 in British politics has been characterised by a heavy emphasis on 'liberalising' the economy, abolishing the 'dependency culture' and encouraging business values and the disciplines of the market. From this perspective the crisis in the organisation and funding of the NHS in the 1980s was a direct consequence of the restrictive practices of the medical profession and the failure of the old style administrators to take action on inefficiency and waste. Against this background, developing new policies and targets for health care can be seen as part of a more generalised dilution of the power of those professions and other corporate bodies which had previously been able to provide a counterweight to government policy (Cox 1992).

The introduction of general management is not the only change internal to the NHS that poses a potential challenge to the medical profession. Nursing, or rather the nursing elite, has embarked on a process of occupational development in recent years which is threatening to redefine the relationship between nursing and medicine. The history of nursing is full of accounts of struggles to define the role of nurses as something more than handmaidens to doctors (Dingwall *et al.* 1988). In recent times, the introduction of more patient-centred care in hospital is an attempt to make nurses' work less routinised while at the same time being more sensitive to the needs of patients. This 'new nursing' has been informed by a body of theory which has been developed in the newly established academic departments of nursing in Britain, drawing on US nurses' efforts to redefine their role as independent clinical practitioners (Beardshaw 1992). At the same time, nurses working in primary care have had the opportunity to develop new responsibilities, undertaking health promotion, screening and counselling as well as more routine work which has traditionally been undertaken by GPs (Greenfield 1992; Williams *et al.* 1993). Both these developments have been accompanied by a major reform of nursing education, Project 2000, which links nursing more directly with higher education, increases the amount of theoretical knowledge being transmitted to student nurses, and reduces the time which they spend on the wards providing a service. The appearance of the 'new nurses' on hospital wards has been greeted by doctors with words such as: 'Oh, you're the new thinking nurses, are you?' (Hall 1987). Taken together such changes may be perceived as an explicit professionalising strategy designed to give skilled nurses a distinct sphere of influence and greater autonomy from doctors, who have traditionally dominated the health care division of labour. Alternatively, they may be perceived, as Salvage (1988) has argued, simply as a 'survival strategy' involving an attempt to construct a new model for occupational authority in the face of an unprecedented combination of threats to their already limited autonomy.

The challenge to medicine can also be seen from groups within the health care arena but outside the boundaries of medical orthodoxy. The growth of interest in and support for activities that are often lumped together as 'complementary' or 'alternative' medicine (*The Times* 1983; Fulder and Monro 1981) is indicative of a challenge to orthodox medicine which is simultaneously ethical and epistemological. These alternatives to orthodoxy can be found not only in the clinics of practitioners, but also on the shelves in the health section of any large bookshop. Some suggest that the growth of alternative medicine is a product of the disillusionment many people feel with the dehumanising effects of 'scientific' medicine: the manifest lack of interest doctors display in treating them as persons with identities, roles and relationships, as well as bodies. For others, the key to alternative medicine's growing attractiveness is quite simply the failure of medicine to match up to the expectation (which it encouraged) that it could deal safely and effectively with a wide range of common symptoms.

The specific criticisms of orthodox medicine exemplified in the popularity of alternatives to it have to be seen against the background of wider social and cultural changes which have altered individuals' expectations about their health. Although these altered expectations are not evenly distributed through the social strata of western societies, they may none the less mark changed cultural and indeed 'theological' concerns about what in human life is taken to be valuable and important. In responding to these changes the medical profession has used a number of strategies (BMA 1986). These range from extreme scepticism about the scientificity of anything lying outside its boundaries to attempted incorporation of some of the techniques of alternative practitioners into its own sphere of work (Fairfoot 1987). Just how serious a challenge alternative medicine poses and whether it is best understood as a reaction to changes in society rather than a series of practices that have arisen in response to shortcomings in medicine are serious questions which are now beginning to be addressed (Saks 1992; Sharma 1992).

Threats to medical hegemony from outside the health care workforce also need to be considered. These come both from other professionals and from lay people with an interest in medicine and medical care who have organised themselves collectively in order to fight for change. Of those professional occupations now involving themselves increasingly with the practice of medicine perhaps the most powerful are lawyers and journalists. Lawyers in the UK have benefited financially from the rapid increase in medical negligence claims in recent years, in terms of frequency and severity, following trends in the USA (Annandale 1989; Dingwall *et al.* 1991). Moreover, some have actively encouraged such claims by advertising in local newspapers for prospective litigants to seek their firm's advice about their eligibility to participate in current or possible future class actions. Furthermore, although litigation has traditionally been targeted against high-status medical specialties such as surgery or obstetrics, recent events such as the legal proceedings over the prescribing of benzodiazepine tranquillisers suggest that general practitioners are also being implicated by lawyers. In such circumstances it is not surprising that there should be growing concern amongst doctors about the possibility of being sued for negligence and about the actions of lawyers in facilitating this process.

While medical negligence claims have provided the main reason for activity by lawyers in the health care arena in the UK, the creation of the internal market in health care – and the development of quasi-market contracts to improve the efficiency of service delivery (Bartlett 1991) – has raised the possibility of another niche for legal work. Although the contracts between purchasers and providers of health care in the NHS are not contracts in law (Hughes and Dingwall 1990), it has been argued that competition law theoretically has the capacity to influence practices within British health care, just as anti-trust enforcement has affected the US health industry (Miller 1992).

Journalists, too, have taken an increasing interest in medicine and medical care in recent years, in part perhaps because of the growth of a consumer culture which treats health as a commodity (Crawford 1984), and in part because of escalating health care expenditure and thus the increasing political salience of health (Allsop 1984). Available evidence suggests that not only has media coverage of medical and health matters increased, but the proportion of that coverage which makes use of lay as opposed to medical perspectives has also increased (Lund 1992). It is against this background that journalists have not simply accepted medical definitions (Karpf 1988; Turow and Coe 1985), but have developed a more critical view of medical knowledge, medical technology and medical practice. Although there are still television and radio programmes and newspaper articles which present a narrow, 'technophoric' view of medicine, the creation of a more critical journalistic perspective may be providing a counterweight to medical power, empowering readers, listeners and viewers to challenge medical decision-making and reducing the esteem in which doctors have been held. The medical profession has responded to this by including a 'Medicine and the Media' section in the *British Medical Journal*, which reviews television and radio coverage of medicine in a critical light, often hitting back at what it sees as the sensationalist 'trial by media' characteristic of much reporting. At the same time, it could also be seen more positively as part of a general move by professionals and scientists to use the media for their own ends (Nelkin 1987).

Challenges to medical dominance from outside the health service are not confined to those from other professionals. As we noted earlier, lay people with an interest in medicine and medical care have, since the late 1960s, been increasingly willing to question medical expertise. One illustration of this tendency has been the growth of self-help groups, though their prevalence and rate of growth is difficult to quantify with any confidence. It would be naive to regard self-help as some sort of simple consumer revolt, like the food riots of the eighteenth century. Self-help groups have developed against a backdrop of increasing discontent about the effectiveness of medicine in dealing with chronic morbidity, along with growing political pressure on professionals to be accountable to consumers (as in *The Patient's Charter* (DH 1991)) and on consumers to take greater responsibility for their own health (as in the recent government White Paper *The Health of the Nation* (DH 1992)).

The pattern of self-help activity has complex origins (Williams 1989). Some self-help groups have been initiated by professionals and have stimulated the growth of statutory services (Robinson and Henry 1977; Trojan 1989). Others have acted as an alternative source of advice and care about which doctors are uneasy (Black 1988; Stewart 1990). Many are large, national organisations with easy access to the media and professional bodies; others are local organisations with limited funds and restricted networks. Whether they are antagonistic or agreeable to orthodox medical services, and whether or not they can be said to constitute a new social movement (Gussow and Tracy 1976), their very existence can be interpreted as a developing challenge to professional power (Klein 1983).

Alongside the growth in self-help as a means of responding to the unpleasantness of illness comes a lay challenge to the way in which problems of public and environmental health are defined by doctors in these fields. In the face of contemporary hazards to the public health, groups of people in different localities, both in the USA and UK, are taking action against those individuals or organisations they believe to be responsible for the problems (Brown and Mikkelsen 1990; Martin 1993). For example, families in Grangetown on Teesside have engaged in legal action against ICI for nuisance and negligence in response to what are perceived to be high rates of cancer and respiratory problems in their area which they believe are linked to the toxic emissions produced by local industry (Utting 1991).

What makes this development challenging to medicine is the fact that many groups are doing their own research, sometimes referred to as 'popular epidemiology' (Brown 1992). In developing such 'competing rationalities', lay people have found themselves engaged in disagreements with those experts from orthodox epidemiology and public health who insist that the evidence does not support the claims they are making (Williams and Popay 1993). The direction of this challenge leads to the involvement of lay people not just in the process of doing the research or responding to scientific findings produced by others, but in identifying and conceptualizing the nature of the risks and how they should be studied. In view of the obligations now placed upon purchasing health authorities to be actively engaged in 'listening to local voices', these developments may have considerable political potential.

There are a number of other challenges to medical dominance which can more confidently be described as social movements. These movements are clearly trying by 'collective endeavour to promote or resist change' (Bottomore 1979: 41), and their actions are underpinned by an overt ideology and self-consciousness of purpose (Giddens 1984). One such collectivity, albeit a diverse one, is the women's movement, which has been very vocal in its criticism of the quality and quantity of health services available to women and, in the United States at least, has established alternative services emphasising self-help and minimising professional distinctions (Fee 1983; Ruzek 1986).

In Britain the movement's involvement in health and medicine is said to have changed over time (Doyal 1983). In the late 1960s and early 1970s attention was concentrated on women as 'consumers' and on the treatment they received at the hands of male doctors. Feminists exposed the sexism inherent in much medical practice and sought to take control of reproductive technology (Stacey 1988). Establishing alternative services, however, was not considered economically or politically viable, mainly because of the existence of the NHS, which provides treatment free at the point of use (Doyal 1983).

Subsequently, in the late 1970s and early 1980s, priorities shifted towards attempting to defend the NHS against cutbacks and increasing privatisation. These campaigns involved women not only as users of health services but as producers of health care. New groups of feminist health workers (radical nurses and midwives, and feminist doctors and medical students) joined women's health groups in campaigns to save hospitals, jobs and services (Doyal and Elston 1986). Alongside these changes, some feminists have started to develop an alternative analysis to that underpinned by the biomedical model (Popay *et al.* 1993). Here the aim has been to discover how women's morbidity and mortality can be explained by the capitalist and patriarchal organisation of society, and to develop campaigns to improve their living and working conditions. All this is not to say that earlier priorities have been totally displaced. Recent campaigns around the development and application of new reproductive technologies (Stacey 1988), and attempts to alter NHS Well Women's Clinics to reflect the values of the women's health movement (Craddock and Reid 1993), indicate that the struggles of feminists to challenge medical dominance and the hegemony of the biomedical model continue on a broad terrain.

Another configuration of resistance to orthodox medicine is that represented by the animal rights movement and anti-vivisectionists who have criticized medical scientists for using animals in their experiments and for exploiting such animals for career purposes. The organisations which make up this movement have used various strategies to get scientists and their institutions to stop using animals for research purposes and to recognise these animals' rights by including them within the sphere of social citizenship (Turner 1986). The challenge they represent is not only ethical but epistemological. It threatens the scientific basis of medical knowledge by questioning its reliance on animal models and their relevance to human health. The movement has provoked an increasingly organised, visible response from the medical research community and other interested parties such as the pharmaceutical industry. Educational materials have been produced for use in schools, learned scientific societies have organised petitions in support of animal experiments and there has been a general attempt to 'go public' in the mass media in order to win the battle for the 'hearts and minds' of the general population.

These developments represent major challenges to medicine. They also raise a number of questions for sociology, perhaps the most fundamental of which is: to what extent are the traditional explanations of medical dominance and more recent propositions regarding 'deprofessionalisation' and 'proletarianisation' able to account for the challenges that medicine is currently facing?

SOCIOLOGICAL ANALYSIS OF MEDICINE

Until the late 1960s most sociologists accepted medicine's definition of itself as a profession using its expert knowledge and special skills rationally and benevolently. Thereafter, the development of a more critical sociology stimulated an alternative view of medicine as a dominating profession, monopolising the provision of health services (Freidson 1970) or responding to the requirements of the economic system by narrowly concentrating on sickness and by commodifying medicine (Johnson 1977; Navarro 1978). Indeed, some went beyond this to argue that medicine was itself responsible for creating the need for its services by medicalising the ordinary problems of everyday life (Zola 1972; Illich 1975).

This critique was part of a much larger process during the late 1960s and early 1970s in which the world was, for a short time in certain sectors, turned upside down. In Britain and elsewhere, education, medicine, the law and the police were increasingly found wanting, both in the academy and on the streets. Workers, students and other groups proclaimed the need to be liberated from the shackles of authority in whatever form, and the celebrated tolerance of western liberal democracies was seen to be a 'repressive tolerance' (Marcuse 1969).

Since those eventful days and the initial critique of professional dominance the status of medicine and the medical profession has come under renewed attack, as we have seen, from both inside and outside the health care system. Yet sociological explanations of what has been happening have not been very fully developed. One view that has been put forward by Haug and her colleagues (Haug 1973, 1988; Haug and Lavin 1983) is that medicine is being 'deprofessionalised', as part of a more general trend of rationalisation and codification of expert knowledge and a rejection of professional paternalism. Writing about recent developments in the United States and the consequences for doctoring Haug has argued that the relationship between doctors and patients has changed as the 'knowledge gap' between them has reduced. On this argument the popularisation of medical knowledge by the media, increased literacy and the computerisation of medical diagnoses and treatment are combining to undermine patients' unquestioning trust and increase their willingness to shop around for medical services as consumers in a health care market. In addition, doctors' autonomy is said to have been curtailed as new specialised occupations have arisen around bodies of knowledge which doctors themselves are not competent to use.

With the general backlash against professional society, lay people have been less willing to accept uncritically the opinions of doctors, less happy to grant unquestioning trust and more likely to object to their autonomy, power and rate of remuneration (Watkins 1987). In spite of the continuing 'magic' of medical technology there have been specific challenges to medicine's ethics, politics, and epistemology:

> At the very time when physicians can diagnose the inner reaches of the brain with magnets, disintegrate kidney stones using sound waves instead of scalpels, and command an increasingly impressive techno-logy, the profession is feeling besieged.
>
> (Stoeckle, quoted in Light and Levine 1988: 10)

Other writers have argued that the medical profession is being 'prole-tarianised', in line with the requirements of advanced capitalism (Oppenheimer 1973; McKinlay and Arches 1985; McKinlay and Stoeckle 1988). Not only do people no longer believe in doctors' special status; the very material basis of their work is changing. On this view, the profession's members are being deskilled, losing their economic independence (becoming wage labourers) and being required to work in bureaucratically organised institutions under the instructions of managers. Or, to put it another way, they are becoming technically, economically and organisationally alienated (Larson 1977) in a system restricted by increasing state control of the financing of health care and by the growth of corporate provision of health care for profit (Elston 1991). In the United States, where this argument was first developed, many doctors work in hospitals or health maintenance organisations (HMOs), paid not on a fee-for-service principle, but in terms of a pre-payment plan with a third party payer such as Blue Cross/Blue Shield. The financial interests of these organisations stand above the interests of individual clinicians (however charismatic their authority may be), and the introduction of diagnostic related groups (DRGs) and HMOs requires doctors to tailor treatment to the organisations' contractual responsibilities.

There are different slants on these arguments. First, it can be contended that as medical knowledge becomes codified and routinised and subject to audit, less imagination and less space are required for the autonomous physician to use his or her intellectual powers (Armstrong 1990). Second, the harsh fact is that medicine has simply become too expensive and is being squeezed. In this regard, in Britain at least, the health service and the medical profession are exposed to the same trends towards privatisation that have affected many other areas of public sector activity (Marsh 1991). The fact that several prestigious London hospitals are under threat of closure (Tomlinson Report 1992) indicates that doctors are no longer special; they are no longer part of a ruling elite but are subject to the same market forces as other professions.

Given the developments outlined in the previous section there would seem to be good reason to reassess the usefulness of existing theories in explaining the position of the medical profession in contemporary Britain and other industrialised countries. How seriously should we take arguments about proletarianisation or deprofessionalisation, which have been developed primarily with the American context in mind? Is de-professionalisation a general process, or are we seeing the decline of some professions, such as medicine, and the rise of others, such as accountancy (Perkin 1989; Crompton 1990)? Is the profession's position of power under serious threat from the new social movements, alternative medicine or the media, as a reconstituted deprofessionalisation thesis might suggest? Or is the prime threat to medicine the economically and ideologically driven rise of managerialism, an explanation which fits better with the prole-tarianisation thesis?

Alternatively, should the various developments we have identified be reconceptualised as part of a deregulated, and essentially post-modern world? From this standpoint the challenges to the expert system of modern medicine could reflect the breakdown of legitimised authority, permitting any number of challenges to be made. Thus, the proliferation of in-numerable groups and movements could be understood as part of the freedom of expression possible in a post-modern world in which the exploration of the self and the body in new ways are encouraged as part of a 're-enchantment of the world' (Bauman 1991).

Our objectives in editing this collection are twofold: first, to represent the state of play with regard to the sociological analysis of medicine in society; and second, to illuminate the situation that doctors and other health care workers find themselves in. The book does this by exploring the changes taking place in the relationships between the State, the public and institutions that constitute civil society, the health care system and the medical profession. In this way medicine is seen as part of society rather than simply an institution experiencing internal strains. At the same time, contributors have been asked to write their chapters in such a way that their contents are accessible to a wider public who might be searching for ways of understanding and coming to terms with a changing health care system which seems to be in a state of fiscal crisis (O'Connor 1973), as well as an ideological one (Williams 1991).

In light of these concerns we have invited a number of social scientists to consider the challenges we believe medicine now faces in Britain and to assess whether they parallel developments in other advanced capitalist societies such as the United States. Their contributions should be seen as attempts to develop specifically sociological analyses of complex and rapidly changing situations. For that reason, although the chapters each deal with one substantive issue, they all relate these issues to broader theoretical and political concerns. It is hoped that the volume will contribute to an informed overview of what is happening to medicine and health care in Britain and other advanced capitalist societies at a time that may well prove to have been a watershed in the history of the medical profession.

The first chapter, by David Hunter, examines the strength of the managerial challenge to medical dominance. He describes the rise of managerialism in the NHS from 1974 onwards, and notes that it is of recent origin in health care systems generally. The main purpose of the chapter is to chart the management thrust of the British NHS reforms since 1991 and to assess their implications for medical practice. Hunter argues that for all the plausibility of sociological arguments about proletarianisation, it would be unwise to overestimate the extent to which doctors' influence has been seriously eroded by developments in management. Doctors are perfectly capable of transforming themselves into managers and exerting their power in such a way that no fundamental challenge is mounted to their view of the health service.

The next chapter, by Anne Witz, examines the changes taking place in nursing. Reminding us of the long and chequered history of nurses' attempts to establish a distinct sphere of competence within the health care division of labour, she advocates a cautious stance to the challenge which nursing poses. Witz suggests that recent changes in the organisation of the NHS may offer some nurses the possibility of higher professional status, but this will be at the expense of the majority, who will be deskilled. She argues that the main difficulty faced by nurses in challenging doctors is that while the former may claim caring as the centre of their profession, caring is traditionally seen as women's work and accorded low status. The problem *for* nursing, therefore, has been and continues to be the problem of gender.

In the third chapter Robert Dingwall considers the effect that working within a culture which defines relationships in legal terms has on doctors. He begins with a review of the formal legal environment within which the medical profession operates and, in particular, its experience of tort litigation. He argues that this litigation is a problem for the profession rather than for the NHS and that it is part of a wider shift in the status of the professions rather than being unique to medicine. From this perspective the medical profession's response is best understood as a status protest and as a symbolic expression of its discontent with other social and cultural changes. Dingwall goes on to argue that the real challenge to the medical profession is not from law but from governmentality, which favours law as its operative strategy of social control.

The next chapter, by Michael Bury and Jonathan Gabe, considers the way in which the medical profession and medical work are portrayed on television. It starts by outlining the argument that medicine has come to dominate media coverage of health and illness. On this view, any challenges to medicine's knowledge base and power as a profession have largely been absorbed and therefore neutralised. The authors then proceed to test empirically the assumptions behind this argument by considering three examples of television's portrayal of medicine, employing different programme formats: the exposé (*The Cook Report*), the documentary (*Operation Hospital*) and the drama serial (*Casualty*). Their analysis suggests that the proposition that the 'box is doctored' is difficult to sustain in its original form when exposed to empirical tests. While it is still possible to find television coverage which displays clear ideological support for the medical profession and medical practice, it is also clear that the media are acting as carriers and amplifiers of a more challenging position.

In Chapter Five Mike Saks explores the challenge that the increasingly popular alternatives pose to orthodox medicine. He examines the occupational strategies employed by the medical profession in defending its position against external competitors and the ideological arguments that are deployed to underpin these strategies. Saks argues that the authority of the British medical profession has been thrown into question by the growing public demand for alternative therapies, and that the creation of the internal market in the NHS may provide openings for some alternatives to be incorporated into the health service. The main conclusion of this chapter is that while alternative therapies pose important challenges to medicine, they have not yet significantly reduced its dominance.

In the next chapter David Kelleher examines the challenge of self-help groups to modern medicine. He starts by describing some of the activities of self-help groups, using the distinction between 'inner focused' and 'outer focused' groups. This demonstrates that groups often engage in both kinds of activity to varying degrees, and that while much of what goes on can be interpreted as complementary to medicine, there is nevertheless a subversive readiness to question the status of medical knowledge and assert the value of lay knowledge. Kelleher then goes on to explore the ways in which the relationship between self-help groups and modern medicine has been influenced by changes in contemporary culture. Against this background it is suggested that self-help groups can also be seen as part of a new social movement, resisting the dominance of medicine's instrumental-cognitive rationality and, by valuing experiential knowledge, retaining the possibility of seeing things differently.

In Chapter Seven Gareth Williams and Jennie Popay examine the challenge posed by lay perspectives in the field of public and environmental health. They note how, in recent years, there has been an increase in lay challenges not just to those institutions seen to be responsible for causing environmental health problems, but also to those experts whose role it is to explain and suggest solutions to these problems. Beginning with an examination of lay knowledge about health issues, they go on to consider the phenomenon of 'popular epidemiology' using the events surrounding the contamination of the public water supply at Camelford, North Cornwall in 1988 as a case study. They argue that such community responses to environmental health problems pose a challenge to the dominance of conventional biomedical perspectives that is both epistemological and political.

In the next chapter Lesley Doyal considers the feminist challenge to medicine. She starts by describing briefly the range of feminist critiques of medicine. This leads on to a consideration of the evidence of gender inequalities in the control of the formal health care system and the consequences for women's subjective experience of care. Doyal then considers the male bias in the production of medical knowledge and its relationship to medical treatment, before turning to whether there have been any changes in practice as a result of feminist analyses and the campaigns they have generated. Overall she suggests that while women have collectively mounted an important challenge to the medical profession they have not been powerful enough to bring about any major change in medical practice.

In Chapter Nine Mary Ann Elston considers the extent and the nature of the challenge to medicine from the anti-vivisectionist movement. She begins by outlining the links between the rise and fall of the movement and the medical profession's rise in status from the 1870s to the 1960s. Against this backcloth she considers the marked revival of anti-vivisectionist activity over the last twenty-five years. She notes that initially the emphasis was primarily on the moral status of animals and their alleged widespread use in laboratories for non-medical purposes. During the 1980s, however, the focus switched to making the kinds of claims about the morality and value of animal experiments for human health that had been voiced in the late nineteenth century, providing a renewed challenge to medical science. Medicine's response, she suggests, has been much more vigorous than in the past, and has involved mounting a campaign to win the 'hearts and minds' of the public in the face of the perceived success of the animal rights movement in integrating some of its concerns into public consciousness and political life in Britain.

As an alternative to a conventional conclusion, the editors bring together some of the main themes of the book by means of a dialogue between a hospital doctor and a stranger. The stranger begins by asking: 'So why do all these people challenge you?' The conversation that develops takes them over many of the arguments that have been raised in the individual chapters, and ends with the stranger making a plea for greater egalitarianism between doctors, other health care workers and patients and warning of the likely irrelevance of doctors if this does not happen. But then something occurs that calls the stranger's arguments into question.

In sum, while none of the authors in this collection predict the impending emasculation of the power of medicine as a result of the challenges surveyed, they all point to changes taking place in society that are likely to bring about a reconfiguration of professional power. These changes, which some might describe as a shift from modernity to post-modernity, are having an impact on the wider environment in which the medical profession and the health service operate. While these developments offer little support to the deprofessionalisation and proletarianisation theses, they do, at the very least, suggest the need for a re-examination and reworking of our traditional ideas about professional dominance.

ACKNOWLEDGEMENT

We should like to thank Mary Ann Elston and Mike Saks for their comments on an earlier draft of this introduction.

REFERENCES

Allsop, J. (1984) *Health Policy and the National Health Service*, Longman: London.

Annandale, E. (1989) 'The malpractice crisis and the doctor–patient relationship', *Sociology of Health and Illness*, 11: 1–23.

Armstrong, D. (1990) 'Medicine as a profession: times of change', *British Medical Journal*, 301: 691–3.

Bartlett, W. (1991) *Quasi-Markets and Contracts: A Market and Hierarchies Perspective on NHS Reform* (Studies in Decentralization and Quasi-Markets No. 3), University of Bristol: School for Advanced Urban Studies Publications.

Bauman, Z. (1991) *Intimations of Postmodernity*, London: Routledge.

Beardshaw, V. (1992) 'Prospects for nursing', in Beck, E., Lonsdale, S., Newman, S. and Patterson, D. (eds) *In the Best of Health?*, London: Chapman & Hall.

Berger, J. (1967) *A Fortunate Man*, London: Allen Lane.

Black, M. (1988) 'Self-help groups and professionals – what is the relationship?', *British Medical Journal*, 296: 1,485–6.

Bodenheimer, T.S. (1984) 'The transnational pharmaceutical industry and the health of the world's people', in McKinlay, J. (ed.) *Issues in the Political Economy of Health Care*, London: Tavistock.

Bottomore, T.B. (1979) *Political Sociology*, London: Hutchinson.

British Medical Association (Board of Science and Education) (1986) *Alternative Therapy*, London: BMA.

Brown, P. (1992) 'Popular epidemiology and toxic waste contamination: lay and professional ways of knowing', *Journal of Health and Social Behaviour*, 33: 267–81.

Brown, P. and Mikkelsen, E.J. (1990) *No Safe Place: Toxic Waste, Leukemia and Community Action*, Berkeley: University of California Press.

Bryden, P. (1992) 'The future of primary care', in Loveridge, R. and Starkey, K. (eds) *Continuity and Crisis in the NHS*, Buckingham: Open University Press.

Butland, G. (1993) 'Commissioning for quality', *British Medical Journal*, 306: 251–2.

Cox, D. (1991) 'Health service management – a sociological view: Griffiths and the non-negotiated order of the hospital', in Gabe, J., Calnan, M. and Bury, M. (eds) *The Sociology of the Health Service*, London: Routledge.

—— (1992) 'Crisis and opportunity in health service management', in Loveridge, R. and Starkey, K. (eds) *Continuity and Crisis in the NHS*, Buckingham: Open University Press.

Craddock, C. and Reid, M. (1993) 'Structure and struggle: implementing a social model of a well woman clinic in Glasgow', *Social Science and Medicine*, 36: 67–76.

Crawford, R. (1984) 'A cultural account of "health": control, release and the social body', in McKinlay, J.B. (ed.) *Issues in the Political Economy of Health Care*, New York: Tavistock Publications.

Crompton, R. (1990) 'Professions in the current context', *Work, Employment and Society*, Additional Special Issue: 147–66.

Department of Health (DH) (1989) *Working for Patients*, London: HMSO.

—— (1991) *The Patient's Charter*, London: HMSO.

—— (1992) *The Health of the Nation. A Strategy for Health in England*, London: HMSO.

Department of Health and Social Security (DHSS) (1983) *NHS Management Enquiry (Griffiths Report)*, London: HMSO.

Dingwall, R., Rafferty, A.M. and Webster, C. (1988) *An Introduction to the Social History of Nursing*, London: Routledge.

Dingwall, R., Fenn, P. and Quam, L. (1991) *Medical Negligence. A Review of the Literature*, Oxford: Centre for Socio-legal Studies, Wolfson College.

Doyal, L. (1983) 'Women, health and the sexual division of labour: a case study of the women's health movement in Britain', *International Journal of Health Services*, 13: 373–87.

Doyal, L. and Elston, M.A. (1986) 'Women, health and medicine', in Beechey, V. and Whitelegg, E. (eds) *Women in Britain Today*, Milton Keynes: Open University Press.

Elston, M.A. (1991) 'The politics of professional power: medicine in a changing health service', in Gabe, J., Calnan, M. and Bury, M. (eds) *The Sociology of the Health Service*, London: Routledge.

Fairfoot, P. (1987) 'Alternative therapies: the BMA knows best?' *Journal of Social Policy*, 16: 383–90.

Fee, E. (1983) 'Women and health care: a comparison of theories', in Fee, E. (ed.) *Women and Health: The Politics of Sex in Medicine*, Farmingdale, New York: Baywood.

Flynn, R. (1992) *Structures of Control in Health Management*, Routledge: London.

Freidson, E. (1970) *The Profession of Medicine*, New York: Dodd Mead.

Fulder, S. and Monro, R. (1981) *The Status of Complementary Medicine in the UK*, London: The Threshold Foundation.

Giddens, A. (1984) *The Constitution of Society: Outline of the Theory of Structuration*, Cambridge: Polity Press.

—— (1990) *The Consequences of Modernity*, Cambridge: Polity Press.

Greenfield, S. (1992) 'Nurse practitioners and the changing face of general practice', in Loveridge, R. and Starkey, K. (eds) *Continuity and Crisis in the NHS*, Buckingham: Open University Press.

Gussow, Z. and Tracy, G. (1976) 'The role of self-help clubs in adaptation to chronic illness and disability', *Social Science and Medicine*, 10: 407–14.

Haines, A. and Illiffe, S. (1992) 'Primary health care', in Beck, E., Lonsdale, S., Newman, S. and Patterson, D. (eds) *In the Best of Health?*, London: Chapman & Hall.

Hall, B.V. (1987) *R.G.N. Pilot Scheme Evaluation Report*, London: City of London Polytechnic.

Harrison, S. (1988) 'The workforce and the new managerialism', in Maxwell, R. (ed.) *Reshaping the NHS*, London: Policy Journals.

Harrison, S., Hunter, D. and Pollitt, C. (1990) *The Dynamics of British Health Policy*, London: Unwin Hyman.

Haug, M. (1973) 'Deprofessionalization: an alternative hypothesis for the future', *Sociological Review Monograph*, 20: 195–211.

—— (1988) 'A re-examination of the hypothesis of deprofessionalization', *Milbank Quarterly*, 66 (Suppl. 2): 48–56.

Haug, M. and Lavin, B. (1983) *Consumerism in Medicine: Challenging Physician Authority*, Beverly Hills: Sage.

Hughes, D. and Dingwall, R. (1990) 'Sir Henry Maine, Joseph Stalin and the reorganisation of the National Health Service', *Journal of Social Welfare Law*, 5: 296–309.

Hunter, D. (1991) 'Managing medicine: a response to the "crisis"', *Social Science and Medicine*, 32: 441–9.

Illich, I. (1975) *Medical Nemesis*, London: Calder & Boyars.

Jamous, H. and Peloille, B. (1970) 'Changes in the French University-Hospital System', in Jackson, J.A. (ed.) *Professions and Professionalization*, Cambridge: Cambridge University Press.

Johnson, T. (1977) 'The professions in the class structure', in Scase, R. (ed.) *Industrial Society: Class, Cleavage and Control*, London: Allen & Unwin.

Karpf, A. (1988) *Doctoring the Media*, London: Routledge.

Klein, R. (1983) *The Politics of the National Health Service*, London: Longman.

Larson, M.S. (1977) *The Rise of Professionalism*, Berkeley: University of California Press.

Light, D. and Levine, S. (1988) 'The changing character of the medical profession: a theoretical overview', *Milbank Quarterly*, 66 (Suppl. 2): 10–32.

Lund, A.B. (1992) 'Health care users as news producers', unpublished paper presented at a scientific workshop on The User Perspective in Health Services Research, Denmark, September.

McKinlay, J. and Arches, J. (1985) 'Towards the proletarianization of physicians', *International Journal of Health Services*, 15: 161–95.

McKinlay, J. and Stoeckle, J. (1988) 'Corporatization and the social transformation of doctoring', *International Journal of Health Services*, 18: 191–205.

Marcuse, H. (1969) *An Essay on Liberation*, London: Allen Lane.

Marsh, D. (1991) 'Privatization under Mrs Thatcher: a review of the literature', *Public Administration*, 69: 459–80.

Martin, J. (1993) *The Public Perception of Risk from Industrial Hazards: Case Studies of Halton, Cheshire and Halebank, Merseyside*, unpublished M.Sc. dissertation, University of Salford.

Miller, F. (1992) 'Competition law and anti-competitive professional behavior affecting health care', *Modern Law Review*, 55: 453–81.

Navarro, V. (1978) *Class Struggle, the State and Medicine*, London: Martin Robertson.

Nelkin, D. (1987) *Selling Science: How the Press Covers Science and Technology*, New York: Freeman.

Oakley, C.M. (1991) *Doctors in Management*, unpublished M.Sc. dissertation, London Guildhall University.

O'Connor, J. (1973) *The Fiscal Crisis of the State*, New York: St Martin's Press.

Oppenheimer, M. (1973) 'The proletarianization of the professional', *Sociological Review Monograph*, 20: 213–37.

Perkin, H. (1989) *The Rise of Professional Society: England Since 1880*, London: Routledge.

Popay, J., Bartley, M. and Owen, C. (1993) 'Gender inequalities in health: social position, affective disorders and minor physical morbidity', *Social Science and Medicine*, 36: 21–32.

Porter, D. and Porter, R. (1989) *Patient's Progress: Doctors and Doctoring in Eighteenth-century England*, Cambridge: Polity Press.

Robinson, D. and Henry, S. (1977) *Self-Help and Health: Mutual Aid for Modern Problems*, London: Martin Robertson.

Ruzek, S. (1986) 'Feminist visions of health: an international perspective', in Mitchell, J. and Oakley, A. (eds) *What is Feminism?*, Oxford: Basil Blackwell.

Saks, M. (ed.) (1992) *Alternative Medicine in Britain*, Oxford: Clarendon.

Salvage, J. (1988) 'Professionalization – or struggle for survival? A consideration of current proposals for the reform of nursing in the United Kingdom', *Journal of Advanced Nursing*, 13: 515–9.

Sharma, U. (1992) *Complementary Medicine Today: Practitioners and Patients*, London: Routledge.

Stacey, M. (1988) *The Sociology of Health and Healing*, London: Unwin Hyman.

Stewart, M.J. (1990) 'Professional interface with mutual aid self-help groups: a review', *Social Science and Medicine*, 31: 1,143–58.

Stocking, B. (1992) 'The introduction and costs of new technologies', in Beck, E., Lonsdale, S., Newman, S. and Patterson, D. (eds) *In the Best of Health?*, London: Chapman & Hall.

The Times (1983) 'Physician heal thyself' (editorial), 10 August: 9.

The Tomlinson Report (1992) *The Report of the Inquiry into the London Health Service, Medical Education and Research*, London: HMSO.

Trojan, A. (1989) 'Benefits of self-help groups: a survey of 232 members from 65 disease related groups', *Social Science and Medicine*, 29: 225–32.

Tudor Hart, J. (1988) *A New Kind of Doctor*, London: Merlin Press.

Turner, B.S. (1986) *Citizenship and Capitalism*, London: Allen & Unwin.

Turow, J. and Coe, L. (1985) 'Curing television's ills: the portrayal of health care', *Journal of Communication*, 35: 36–51.

Utting, D. (1991) 'Battle over the breath of life', *Guardian*, 3 July: 25.

Watkins, S. (1987) *Medicine and Labour: The Politics of a Profession*, London: Lawrence & Wishart.

White, P. (1981) *Voss*, Harmondsworth: Penguin.

Wilensky, H.L. (1964) 'The professionalization of everybody', *American Journal of Sociology*, 70: 137–58.

Williams, G.H. (1989) 'Hope for the humblest? The role of self-help in chronic illness: the case of ankylosing spondylitis', *Sociology of Health and Illness*, 11: 135–59.

—— (1991) 'Disablement and the ideological crisis in health care', *Social Science and Medicine*, 32: 517–24.

Williams, G.H. and Popay, J. (1993) 'Researching the people's health: dilemmas and opportunities for social scientists', in Popay, J. and Williams, G.H. (eds) *Social Research and Public Health* (Salford Papers in Sociology, No. 13), Department of Sociology, University of Salford.

Williams, S., Calnan, M., Cant, S. and Coyle, J. (1993) 'All change in the NHS? Implications of the NHS reforms for primary care prevention', *Sociology of Health and Illness*, 15: 43–67.

Zola, I.K. (1972) 'Medicine as an institution of social control', *The Sociological Review*, 20: 487–503.

1 From tribalism to corporatism
The managerial challenge to medical dominance

David J. Hunter

In the case of prophesising, or projecting trends into the future, due caution requires being aware of the danger of mistaking short-term, ephemeral trends for long-term trends and cyclical change for linear, progressive change.

(Freidson 1993)

THE RISE OF MANAGERIALISM

A principal feature of the evolution of management in the National Health Service (NHS) has been the struggle between doctors and managers for control of the health policy agenda and its implications for resource allocation. Successive waves of managerial reform in the NHS, beginning in 1974 and mirroring developments in other parts of the public sector, have endeavoured progressively to shift the frontier in favour of management (Hunter 1980; Harrison 1988). Numerous attempts have been made to modify the individualism, and often sectionalist tribalism, which characterises medicine (Freidson 1993) and to subject it to the corporate disciplines of management as described by Griffiths (1983). It is argued that the 1991 NHS reforms, enshrined in the 1990 NHS and Community Care Act, have further extended the management boundaries so that the bureaucratisation, or proletarianisation, of medicine and its penetration by management is virtually complete (McKinlay 1988). Doctors are being compelled to define their practices and modes of operating in ways that many believe are undermining their professional values and ability to act in accordance with such values. But there is another view, hitherto more explicitly and persuasively articulated in North America than in Britain, which challenges the notion that medical dominance is under serious or lasting threat. Rather, the managerial onslaught is causing doctors to pause and regroup around a set of countervailing practices and tactics which may be aimed at lessening, or diverting, the impact of a management-led reform agenda.

Management is a fairly recent phenomenon in health care systems and follows from a perception by policy makers that over the years health services have been over-administered and under-managed (Hunter 1980; Harrison 1988). Strengthening management, raising its profile and status, developing management skills and competencies, investing in management information systems and so on are seen as crucial to the success of policies directed towards securing value for money and improved quality of care for a given budget, while holding individuals and organisations accountable for what they do. As part of this managerial revolution in health care, it follows that doctors are expected increasingly to accept managerial responsibility (Mark 1991). It is worth noting in passing that the 'cult of managerialism' is not confined to the NHS or even to Britain. It is a feature of reforms across the public sector not only in the United Kingdom but across Europe, too. Indeed, the medicine–management interface and the changing relationship between these domains is of global significance (Hafferty and McKinlay 1993).

Drucker (1990: 218) asserts that 'management world-wide has become the new social function'. Of particular significance has been the model of management to which governments have become wedded (Hoggett 1991). It has been labelled 'new public management' (Hood 1991) and has the following distinctive features or doctrines:

1 explicit standards and measures of performance;
2 greater emphasis on outputs and results;
3 disaggregation of public bureaucracies into agencies operating on a user-pay basis;
4 greater competition through use of quasi-markets and contracting;
5 stress on private sector styles of management practice;
6 stress on performance incentives for managers;
7 stress on discipline in resource use and cost improvements;
8 emphasis on the public as customer.

Many of the changes informed by a new public management perspective may not be wholly undesirable or inappropriate in the context of health care although it is possible to see in the drive for better management an ideological commitment to curb the excesses of what Lipsky (1980) terms 'street level bureaucracy' whereby those, like doctors, who act with, and have, wide discretion over the dispensation of services and allocation of resources enjoy relative autonomy from organisational authority.

Managers are seen as the agents of central government and derive their legitimacy from the requirement on them to do the Government's bidding aided by various instruments at their disposal. In the pursuit of its ideological agenda since 1979, the Government has been able to point to, and skilfully exploit, criticisms of the NHS which charge it with being bureaucratic, paternalistic, sclerotic, insensitive, remote, and profession-led rather than user-driven (e.g. Kogan *et al.* 1978; Griffiths 1983; Strong and Robinson 1990). Many of these features are being challenged, as a result of the 1991 reforms, and a number of commentators would argue that this has been a good thing for the NHS (Klein 1993; Strong and Robinson 1990). The move to change the culture of a service that had by a wide measure of agreement become dominated by traditions of administration, hierarchy and professionalism has, these analysts argue, some positive features. While the diagnosis of the NHS's ills may invite wide support, the prescription, with its emphasis on markets and consumerism, has been greeted with a great deal of suspicion and concern over the likely outcome of what amounts to a huge social experiment.

Stewart and Walsh (1992) argue that what has to emerge if the changes being implemented in the NHS and elsewhere are to be successful is a 'new balance' as institutional traditions interact. They argue against polarising the reform agenda in ways that mislead and result in inappropriate change. For instance, they believe it is wrong to reject entirely traditional modes of public accountability in the belief that it is possible for public services to be totally responsive to individual customers when in practice this is not going to be possible if the notion of equity is to mean anything at all. Furthermore, the authors argue that there is not a generic approach to management that can be applied in all circumstances. The public sector has distinctive purposes, conditions and tasks (e.g. values of equity, justice and impartiality) which must be supported, not removed, by the latest fashion or spate of managerial reforms. As Stewart and Walsh note, although the professional culture in public service could be over-dominant, that does not mean that the professional role is unimportant.

The purpose of this chapter is to chart the management thrust of the British NHS reforms introduced in 1991 and to assess their implications for medical practice. The analysis draws upon recent studies of managers and management in the NHS and their impact on the medical profession. The chapter is organised into three sections: first, there is a brief review of the 1991 NHS reforms which traces their origins back to what happened in 1983 when general management was introduced; second, the impact of the management revolution on the medical profession is considered; and third, an attempt is made to look beyond the immediate preoccupations of doctors and managers and consider a scenario that would enable doctors to reoccupy, albeit in a different guise, territory they increasingly feel is being wrested from them. The central theme of this concluding section is that although management and managers may appear to be in the ascendency in instrumental terms, and there is some evidence to suggest that this is indeed the case, it remains possible for the overall balance of power still to operate in favour of doctors.

For all the rhetoric and claims to the contrary, it would be unwise to overestimate the extent to which doctors' influence has been seriously or irrevocably eroded or compromised by recent developments of a managerial nature. The key to an understanding of this apparent paradox is Lukes's (1974) third dimension of power to which later sections of the chapter return. According to this view, the exercise of power need not be displayed overtly or in situations of actual conflict. As Lukes (1974: 23) puts it, 'the most effective and insidious use of power is to prevent such conflict from arising in the first place'. He goes on to suggest that while A may exercise power over B by getting her or him to do what he or she does not want to do, 'he [*sic*] also exercises power over him by influencing, shaping or determining his very wants' (ibid.). This conception of power lies at the heart of the medical profession's ability to shape the health care agenda.

MANAGEMENT AND THE NHS REFORMS

The 1991 NHS reforms cannot fully be understood without going back to 1983 and the introduction of general management. This move followed a critique by the Government's health adviser, Roy Griffiths, who diagnosed the management problem in the NHS as falling into four areas: (a) management influence was low in relation to clinical professions and medicine in particular; (b) the managerial emphasis was on reacting to problems; (c) maintaining the status quo was seen as the extent of the management task; and (d) the NHS was producer rather than consumer oriented (Harrison *et al.* 1992).

Unlike previous reorganisations, the Griffiths changes were heralded as marking a significant departure from the usual practice of rejigging the structure of the NHS and the organisational boxes and charts. Rather, their novelty and significance lay in an approach to change which placed the emphasis on cultural change and on modifying the chemistry and balance of power between the key stakeholders in the NHS, notably doctors and managers. The prescription proposed by Griffiths, and accepted wholesale by the Government, centred on the introduction of general managers at all levels of the Service with a consequent diminution of the power of veto by doctors, which had been a feature of the previous consensus management arrangements. Day and Klein (1983) succinctly expressed the changed approach to managing the NHS in the following terms:

> [as a] move from a system that is based on the mobilisation of consent to one based on the management of conflict – from one that has conceded the right of groups to veto change to one that gives the managers the right to override objections.

> (Day and Klein 1983: 1813)

But, if the Griffiths management revolution in the NHS (with echoes else-where in the public sector, which was being similarly subjected to the cult of managerialism) was intended to shift the balance of power, little evidence for it could be detected during the latter half of the 1980s. A conclusion from a major study of the impact of general management was that it had not even challenged the medical domain, let alone succeeded in making significant inroads into it (Harrison *et al.* 1992). Doctors' training and career patterns remained unchanged, with the consequence that their basic beliefs and atti-tudes remained largely intact. Therefore, the management–medicine interface could not be said to have shifted to any marked degree following the intro-duction of general management, at least not during its first few years. While the *authority* of doctors may have been bruised as a consequence of general management, their *power* and *status* both within the NHS and in society more generally have remained largely intact.

A variant of this argument emerges from Pettigrew *et al.*'s study of strategic change in the NHS in selected English districts in eight regional health authorities (Pettigrew *et al.* 1992). In regard to managerial–clinical relations the researchers saw these as critical, although the pattern found was one of wide variation in their quality. The researchers reported that manager–clinician relations were easier 'where negative stereotypes had broken down, perhaps as a result of mixed roles or perceptions' (Pettigrew *et al.* 1992: 283).

The most effective managers were those who were 'semi-immersed in the world of clinicians' (ibid.) and they tended to be those general managers who had formerly been administrators. Relations were also easier to establish if clinicians themselves thought managerially and strate-gically as, indeed, a few did. But, in general, manager–clinician relations were fragile and ever-changing and were marked by 'upward and down-ward spirals' in their patterning. Moreover, 'relationships could quickly sour but were slow to build up' (ibid.).

Scarcely had the new breed of general managers settled into their posts when talk of further reform began to be heard. Sure enough, in the midst of an alleged funding crisis in the NHS in late 1987–early 1988, the Prime Minister unexpectedly announced a major review of the financing and organisation of the Service. The reform proposals subsequently announced in the 1989 White Paper *Working for Patients* are pertinent to our theme in so far as they acknowledged that the management changes ushered in following the Griffiths inquiry while laying the foundations did not go far enough. In many respects the reforms introduced in 1991 seek to address this unfinished business and are aimed at tackling the medicine–management interface more explicitly with a view to modifying medical practice. In particular, they endeavour to ensure that doctors are held accountable for their actions in a way not countenanced in previous NHS reforms.

Much of the impetus behind the 1989 reform proposals, subsequently enacted through the 1990 NHS and Community Care Act, can be seen as an attempt to secure a shift in the balance of power between doctors and managers in favour of the latter. They seek to achieve such a shift in the context of advocating improved efficiency in the use of resources and in the provision of services. Much of the management problem in the NHS has centred on the notion of undermanagement in respect of the medical side of the service. Getting a grip on the freedom enjoyed by clinicians and holding them to account for expenditure they incur is seen as the last unmanaged frontier in the NHS.

Two key aspects of the NHS reforms, which began to be implemented in April 1991, are central to the intended culture shift from a producer-led service, that is, one determined by the preferences and decisions of professionals, to a user-driven one, that is, a service shaped by the views and wishes of its customers. First, there is the purchaser–provider split, and second, there is the focus on consumerism and on listening to local voices.

The purchaser–provider split is seen as a means of liberating health authorities to develop services appropriate to the assessed needs of their resident populations unencumbered by the managerial responsibility for providing services directly. Conflating the purchaser and provider functions in a single organisation was regarded as resulting in a potential conflict of interest between the preferences of providers on the one hand and those of users on the other. The consequence, it was alleged, was a health service run rather more for the benefit of those who worked in it, especially doctors, and rather less for those who used it. By making the commissioning health authorities the 'champions of the people' the Government hoped to break the mould and create new incentives for providers to become more responsive to the needs and wishes of local people and less susceptible to provider capture.

Providing institutions, in the form of NHS trusts, were created for which health authorities have no direct responsibility. Health authorities, as purchasers, place contracts for agreed levels of service with such hospital and community health service units, but are not managerially responsible for them. The contracting system in theory allows the purchasing authority to shop around for the best deal on quality and price. The creation of a managed, or quasi-, market, wholly operated by public funds, is intended to spur providers to offer improved and more efficient services and to be more alert to their customers.

The second key theme in the reforms is the focus on consumers, neatly captured by the notion that resources should follow patients. An aim of the changes is to put the consumer in the driving seat. To do this, providers and purchasers need to invest in market research and related ways of obtaining information about needs (including hitherto unmet needs), views about services and their quality and so on. The introduction of the Patient's Charter has given an added impetus to moves to attach greater importance to consumer views. In addition, purchasing authorities are expected not merely to consult users but to involve them more actively, and in a continuing dialogue, over priorities and the development of strategies to improve health.

During the first year or so of the NHS reforms (i.e. April 1991–2) the Government was accused of ignoring the purchasing role and of giving too much attention to NHS trusts. Recent months have witnessed an attempt by ministers to remedy the situation and to set out in a number of major speeches what the purchasing/commissioning role entails (Mawhinney and Nichol 1993). The Government sees it as the engine of change in the NHS and is looking to purchasers to reshape health services, and health policy more generally, by using their powers and freedoms to think more imaginatively and creatively about meeting the needs of their local communities. Purchasers constitute what many observers regard as the most significant challenge presented by the NHS reforms. The role is a new one for which new skills and ways of working are required. Few, if any, of these are yet in place. Notions of management at a purchaser level are undergoing radical rethinking as the agendas of general managers and directors of public health overlap (Hunter 1993a). If the entire NHS reform initiative amounts to a huge social experiment, then this is especially true of the purchaser role where learning by doing is the order of the day (Hunter and Harrison 1993).

The NHS reforms have presented managers with a range of instruments and levers to challenge the medical dominance that is regarded as posing a major obstacle to achieving change in health care. There are other mechanisms available to managers. At one level, managers are now in a position to participate in the selection process for consultant and other senior clinical posts. They are also able to discuss contracts with doctors to establish with them their responsibilities and duties. Furthermore, the merit awards to which doctors are entitled to supplement their salaries now have to demonstrate management competence and not only clinical excellence. Although medical audit, which is now obligatory for all hospital doctors and GPs, is regarded primarily as an educational tool, it has major implications for the accountability of doctors and therefore their overall management, even if its purpose is currently lacking in clarity (Kerrison *et al.* 1993). In particular, there is confusion surrounding its importance for management. But this only reinforces the point that no longer are doctors wholly free agents. The micro-management of their work at the level of instrumental procedures holding them to account, such as those noted above, has served to strengthen the managerial grip on their work. These moves have been combined with others, such as encouraging the widespread introduction of clinical directorates and a more knowledge-based approach to decision-making, encouraged by the NHS R&D initiative with its focus on effectiveness and establishing health outcomes.

But analysts disagree over the extent to which the developments seem likely to hasten and complete the proletarianisation of medicine. On the one hand there are those, like Flynn (1992), who see in the 1991 NHS reforms Alford's 'corporate rationalisers' successfully confronting and conquering the 'professional monopolists' (Alford 1975). Flynn believes that the battery of management techniques introduced as a result of general management in 1983, and expanded following the 1991 reforms, will reduce clinical autonomy. Indeed, his thesis contends that 'the tendency during the last decade has been towards an erosion of professional dominance in the face of increased . . . managerial power' (Flynn 1992: 50). Other analysts, like Dent (1993), argue that while it is true that doctors are no longer the sole arbiters of health care delivery, they have not foregone their dominant position. He employs the notion of 'responsible autonomy' to describe the changed relationship between doctors and managers. What this appears to mean is that while doctors' autonomy may be limited at the level of the individual practitioner it does not follow that the collective autonomy of the profession is limited (Mechanic 1991). Doctors will continue to select and operationalise the variables in health care and interpret the data. Dent's position is akin to that of Freidson (1990), Evans (1990) and Mechanic (1991), who argue that little has in fact changed fundamentally to erode medical dominance and the ability of doctors to determine health care priorities while remaining wedded to a medical model of delivery. Interestingly, almost all these writers are of North American origin and, certainly in the USA, belong to a largely market-oriented system of health care in which the regulation of the medical profession has gone further than anything that has so far happened in the UK (Klein 1993). It may be that this experience will be of relevance in the UK as policy makers and managers develop 'managed competition' in the NHS and seek to regulate what doctors do. The final section of the chapter returns to these matters.

THE IMPACT OF THE MANAGERIAL REVOLUTION ON CLINICIANS

As the above description has sought to convey, over a period of years a more critical attitude has developed in British health care policy towards the role of doctors and their relationship not only with patients but with the organisation of which they are a key part. Indeed, a crucial, if somewhat curious, observation about the relationship between the medical profession on the one hand and the NHS on the other was made by Rowbottom (1973) some twenty years ago. It remains remarkably valid. He wrote:

> the position of doctors . . . presents a fascinating, and possibly unique, situation to any student of organisation. Never have so many highly influential figures been found in such an equivocal position – neither wholly of, nor wholly divorced from, the organisation which they effectively dominate.
>
> (Rowbottom *et al.* 1973: 73)

Up until the NHS reforms introduced in 1991 the somewhat ambivalent position in which doctors found themselves remained largely unchallenged. And even since 1991 the nature of the challenge and its implications remain unclear. Apart from any ideologically driven moves to confront and limit professional freedom in the health care sector and elsewhere in public service, the changing perception about the degree of professional freedom that was compatible with a managed service was fuelled by mounting evidence that medical practices are not always as effective as is sometimes claimed (Hunter 1993b). Wide differences are known to exist between hospital doctors in the number of patients treated, the length of time patients stay in hospital and the resources deployed in their treatment. More fundamentally, as has been pointed out, the vast majority of medical interventions are unproven in their effectiveness and in some cases may actually do more harm than good (Smith 1992).

In the light of accumulating evidence about such matters, it has been argued that what doctors do should be scrutinised more rigorously to ensure that medical care is appropriate and effective and that patients benefit from the treatment they receive (Peckham 1991). The argument that medicine can be meddlesome and the recognition that much medical practice has its basis in custom and practice rather than in scientific evidence has given added impetus to moves to stress health outcomes and effective health care procedures.

In the past year or so, reflecting these concerns, the NHS Management Executive (NHSME), itself a product of the 1991 reforms, and Department of Health have funded a number of initiatives aimed at improving our understanding of medical effectiveness and health outcomes. Some of these form part of the NHS Research and Development programme established by the NHSME and designed to improve the knowledge base of decision-making and to give health services research (HSR) a higher profile so that it does not remain overshadowed by a biomedical research bias. For the R&D initiative to succeed in its aim of changing clinical practice, managers at all levels need to be committed to it and to see real value in HSR for themselves and their work. At present the connection between R&D and management action remains weak and, for the most part, has yet to occur. Again, it forms another component of the equipping of managers, especially in purchasing authorities, with new skills and ones which hitherto have not been regarded as relevant or appropriate.

Doctors are coming to terms with the advances on their freedom in a variety of ways. Some, like a few doctors encountered in the study of general management in the NHS by Harrison *et al.* (1992), are quite simply opposed to such developments, refuse to countenance them and block them in the hope they will disappear. Others take a more pragmatic view and believe that unless they themselves address these issues others less qualified will do so for them. Typical of this group is Sir Raymond Hoffenberg, President of the Royal College of Physicians. He has argued that

> medical participation in management is imperative. By ensuring that resources are devoted optimally to serve the interests of patients, doctors will find that their own clinical freedom is maximised.
> (Hoffenberg 1987: 35)

Finally, there is a third group of clinicians who are adept at 'gaming the system'. As Caper (1988) has noted from studies conducted in America:

> As fast as regulations and review protocols are written, physicians learn to circumvent them, resenting the intrusion into their clinical autonomy.
> (Caper 1988: 1535)

Although the architects of diagnosis related groups (DRGs) – i.e. a case payment system whereby hospitals are paid a pre-established amount per case treated, with payment rates varying by type of case – assumed that managers would use them as a tool to control resource use within hospitals, this did not happen. Instead, hospital managers succeeded in limiting the effectiveness of DRG reimbursement by negotiating concessions through the political system; they exploited the opportunities offered by DRGs through documenting complications in treatment and classifying cases with imprecise diagnoses to obtain higher levels of payment; and they generally avoided challenging clinical practices. Managers were reluctant to intervene in doctors' decisions. As a consequence, efforts in the United States to control health care costs have been only partially successful. Hospitals, too, find ways of beating the system by, for example, redirecting patients to outpatient settings where cost control is virtually non-existent (Thorpe 1992).

However, both doctors *and* managers can and will find ways around efforts to control clinical behaviour and the micro-management of doctors in the USA has met with only limited success. Rising costs in the health care sector, despite numerous attempts to contain them, provide proof of the failure to manage doctors effectively even in a heavily regulated health care 'system' ('non-system' might more accurately describe arrangements in the USA).

Doctors feel a degree of ambivalence in assuming an active role in management. Griffiths may have termed them 'the natural managers' (Griffiths 1983: 19) in the NHS and sought to encourage them to accept the management responsibility that goes with clinical freedom, but doctors face a real ethical dilemma in deciding whether to accept responsibility for budgets and to participate in management. Their professional values, motivation and training all point in the direction of doing what is best for the individual patient rather than for groups of patients, which would require making explicit trade-offs between individual patients. Setting priorities between services, maintaining expenditure within agreed limits and maximising the benefit of services to the population served are all rather alien notions to doctors who, for the most part, see their role as an advocacy one on behalf of individual patients rather than as one of resource management.

Compounding the dilemma for doctors is a realisation that if they do not take action themselves to participate in management then they are likely to find external management controls over clinical activity strengthened and imposed on them.

There appear to be three broad strategies available to doctors, managers and politicians seeking to promote efficiency and effectiveness in health services (Ham and Hunter 1988). These are set out in Table 1. First, it is possible to encourage self-help among doctors to raise professional standards by medical audit, the use of standards and guidelines, and the accreditation of hospitals and other services. A second strategy is to seek to involve doctors in management by delegating budgetary responsibility to them, extending the resource management initiative (in which doctors are responsible for their budgets) throughout the NHS, and appointing doctors as managers. A third strategy is rather more assertive and interventionist and seeks to strengthen external management control of doctors by changing their contracts and encouraging managers to supervise medical work more directly.

Elements of all these strategies may be found within the NHS but attention has concentrated principally on the first two in an attempt to avoid overt confrontation and to create a culture in which doctors regard themselves as having a legitimate management role.

The extension of provider competition in the NHS following the 1991 reforms has consequences for the relationship between managers and doctors. Not least, it requires managers who negotiate to provide services for external purchasers, for example other health authorities, to negotiate in

Table 1 Strategies for managing clinical activity

(a) Raising professional standards	• Medical audit • Standards and guidelines • Accreditation
(b) Involving doctors in management	• Budgets for doctors • Resource management initiative • Doctor-managers
(c) External management controls of doctors	• Managing medical work • Changing doctors' contracts • Extending provider competition

Source: Ham and Hunter 1988: 7

turn with the consultants who work at their hospitals to deliver these services to an acceptable standard and price. To be able to do this, managers require contractual control over clinicians, financial incentives in the form of discretionary salary payments or increases in departmental budgets, or some combination of these tools. Attempts to manage doctors directly are likely to fail or result in unintended consequences unless there is both an understanding of the doctor's world and culture, and appropriate investment in developing a managerial consciousness in doctors. Securing an effective shift from tribalism to corporatism constitutes a major challenge to management.

From tribalism to corporatism

It has already been suggested that the medical profession has a rather odd relationship with the NHS, in particular the lack of a sense of belonging to a broader organisational entity. This leads one to wonder whether, despite many individual exceptions, the profession's attachment to the NHS is largely one of convenience or necessity rather than genuine commitment. The sense of attachment or belonging to an organisation could be seen as of negligible importance for the profession as a whole.

Arising from this perception of the relationship of doctors to the NHS are a number of barriers that preserve a tribalistic mode of operating rather than promote a corporate or collaborative one. The separatist nature of clinical work is reinforced by a particular interpretation of the doctor–patient relationship. The notion of 'possessive individualism' results in doctors functioning independently not only of the rest of the organisation but also of each other. This occurs despite the alleged collegiate nature of their organisation, which remains true in an overall collective sense but is less apparent at the level of inter-specialty relations. The education of doctors and the position of the Royal Colleges reinforce barriers and elitism. Postgraduate medical education continues to foster the isolation of specialties from each other. The hierarchical nature of medicine in respect of its internal stratification between consultants and junior doctors and between specialties makes it more likely that vertical relationships figure over and above horizontal ones (Hunter *et al.* 1988). There is less commitment to an integrated approach across specialties, professions and agencies as a consequence. The concept of 'interface management' between specialties is not highly valued and doctors receive little training in negotiating and team building skills (Hunter 1990). Indeed, medical education with its compartmentalised approach to modern medicine almost encourages fragmentation. It certainly institutionalises it.

There are countervailing forces at play which provide a destabilising influence as far as tribalism is concerned. A greater degree of corporatism may be the outcome. First, there is the effect of the NHS reforms. The purchaser–provider split has required providers to market their services and become more customer-oriented. Hospitals with trust status cannot assume that business will automatically fall to them if the price and quality of care are unsatisfactory. As a result, they are having to evolve a corporate culture which can only succeed if doctors are a central part of it. As the survival of the hospital may be at stake there are strong externally derived pressures on doctors and managers to sink any differences which may exist between them and to act together to ensure the long-term viability of the services being provided.

Managers are increasingly reliant on clinical directors to run services and deliver the clinicians' commitment to tighter management of their work. Clinical directorates, through which doctors play a significant role in management, are maturing, although what their long-term prognosis is in terms of involving doctors in management is not known. The evidence from studies of clinical directorates suggests that some are working more effectively than others. A great deal appears to depend on the skills, interests and personalities of the particular individuals appointed as directors. Possibly the most sensitive issue has been that clinical directors are supposed to have a management role in relation to their consultant colleagues which has not, in practice, proved easy to realise (Fitzgerald 1991). There appears on the surface to be considerable support both for the appointment of doctors as clinical directors and the development of management budgets. Hitherto, this support has come principally from non-medical general managers, i.e. the agents of government, rather than doctors themselves, with the exception of a few converts. There must be limits on how supportive non-medical general managers will continue to be when they begin to realise that by encouraging doctors to enter management they may be putting their own careers at risk or those of their successors.

As long as there exists suspicion and lack of trust between clinicians and managers it seems inconceivable that clinical directorates can function effectively. Scrivens (1988a, 1988b) found in a survey of doctors limited interest among them in management and in taking responsibility for budgets. She claims that a major effort is needed to persuade doctors of the importance of medical involvement in management. The assumption made is that it is 'a good thing' for doctors to be involved in management, as, indeed, Griffiths (1983) argued when he referred to them as the 'natural managers' in the NHS, but there is a need for clarity about both the level at which doctors are introduced to management and the purpose of their involvement.

The nub of the problem arising from the management–medicine interface is the different values upheld by those practising management and those practising medicine respectively. As Moore (1990) has put it, managerial values 'emphasise collaborative action, teamwork and collective achievement' (Moore 1990: 18). In contrast, medicine's values stress the individual, the assumption being that the doctor will work on behalf of the best interests of the individual patient. The medical profession's ideology is one of 'maximising rather than optimising . . . individually rather than collectively orientated, and behaving independently in action rather than interdependently' (ibid.).

The upshot of these developments and observations is the need for a repertoire of new skills which are principally concerned with the 'softer' side of management. These skills include an ability to listen, tolerance, keeping an open mind, a sense of humility, sharing responsibility and a preparedness to relinquish absolute professional autonomy. Perhaps more fundamentally is a need for management to establish itself as a distinct entity rather than as something which professions and politicians can in turn seek to dominate and manipulate for their own respective ends (Mark and Scott 1992). Management in the NHS is vulnerable and, somewhat paradoxically given the attention lavished upon it, susceptible to a takeover by doctors or politicians or both. The threat from the former could have particularly far-reaching consequences in terms of the future direction taken by the NHS and health policy. It is significant in this regard that whenever doctors are asked to comment on why they should participate in management, the reply is invariably along the lines of the following:

Doctors must play a bigger part in managing the health service *to protect their clinical freedom.*

(Smith *et al.* 1989: 311, emphasis added)

From a survey conducted by Parkhouse *et al.* (1988) on the views of doctors, similar responses were recorded. For example:

Doctors *must* run the NHS.

(Parkerhouse *et al.* 1988: 25)

Non-medical managers simply will not understand what health care is necessary.

(ibid.)

In short, doctors should get involved in management not to hasten or collude in the erosion of their freedom and the privileges it brings to dictate what kind of medicine is practised but to ensure that the erosion is resisted.

MEDICINE AND MANAGEMENT: A POSSIBLE SCENARIO

As the above sections have suggested, all the indications are that the involvement of doctors in management will continue to grow in keeping with the mounting pressures on governments to contain costs, to hold doctors more accountable for what they do, to investigate the causes of clinical variation and to propose solutions to them, to address issues of efficacy in respect of medical interventions to ensure that only cost-effective ones and those of proven value get adopted, and to give closer attention to the whole issue of health outcomes and the impact of health care and medicine on these.

What remains less clear is how doctors will choose to make an impact, at what level in the health care system, and with what consequences for the future shape of health services. As was noted at the outset of this chapter, the managerial challenge to medicine may be absorbed or deflected by the profession in ways which could leave it virtually intact or even strengthened. It therefore becomes necessary to examine not so much what doctors *feel* about the various influences on them but rather to assess the impact of these on practitioners' behaviour.

Evidence from the United States demonstrates that interference strategies that result in managers dominating agendas at the expense of doctors are doomed to failure (Shortell *et al.* 1990). Such strategies have had to be adapted and managerial behaviour modified to ensure that clinicians subscribed to them and that confrontation between managers and doctors was avoided. Studies such as that by Shortell and his colleagues underline the importance of developing effective interfaces and collaborative working relationships between managers and clinicians.

Moreover, there is always a risk of the 'special relationship' which doctors enjoy with the general public being invoked, thereby enabling them to sidestep or simply ignore policy/management developments of which they may disapprove. There is little evidence to substantiate the view that the social place of medicine or its intellectual dominance have been substantially or irrevocably eroded.

That medical power is reinforced by cultural factors is of great significance and sets medicine apart from other activities. The medical profession, despite its having been slightly dented by some questioning of its practices and treatments, by the increase in medical negligence claims and by the growth of alternative medicine, continues to enjoy high social status and respect – much higher, according to social surveys, than either politicians or managers.

In a survey conducted recently to find out whether members of the public would prefer doctors, managers or politicians to determine priorities in health, the majority put their faith first in hospital consultants (61 per cent), then in GPs (49 per cent) and finally in managers (22 per cent) (Heginbotham 1993).

Nor is it only members of the general public who are culturally predisposed to accept the authority of doctors. Most groups of health service workers are similarly deferential though this may be lessening, as in the case of managers imbued with the 'Local Voices' (NHSME 1992) philosophy of involving the public in decisions about which treatments should take higher priority.

Although management and managers in health care systems may be in the ascendency, it remains possible nevertheless for the balance of power still to operate in favour of doctors, regardless of whether they remain outside the management system or become managers themselves. In this respect, Lukes's (1974) analysis of power, particularly his three-dimensional model, is persuasive. The third face of power allows for consideration of the many ways in which *potential issues* are kept out of politics. The use of power in this sense can occur in the absence of actual, observable conflict.

The standard objection to Lukes's position is that since by definition the third dimension of power involves B's values and preferences being shaped by A, there remains no observable conflict of values and therefore no observable exercise of power. It becomes difficult in such circumstances to demonstrate the third dimension empirically. Lukes defends his position by arguing that it is valid for an observer to make a judgement about the 'real' ('objective') interests of actors: to reach, for instance, a conclusion that B has been manipulated into adopting preferences which are actually against B's interests. Whilst this argument is valid, it requires careful usage. A classic indicator of the presence of third-face medical power is the phrase used by non-doctors: 'Doctor knows best' (Harrison *et al.* 1992).

Lukes's conceptualisation of power is helpful in illuminating and explaining the seeming paradox of the medical profession allegedly under attack and having its freedoms curbed on the one hand while, on the other, societal views about doctors, and their status, and about the nature of medicine and health care generally reinforce the prevailing orthodoxy and serve to blunt attempts to challenge it. Empirical evidence exists to support such a view as outlined below.

Cost containment measures over the years have been modest in their aspirations. They have not sought to challenge in any fundamental way whether the medical model or medical industrial complex, which constitutes the modern health care delivery infrastructure, is worthy of the enormous investment it receives. Even the recent emphasis on, and rather modest investment in, effectiveness research largely reflects the traditional standard of scientific medicine to demonstrate the clinical value of its modalities. Nowhere in the changes affecting medicine can one find a serious challenge to the hegemony of the medical perspective (Mechanic 1991).

According to Mechanic, the evidence is slim that doctors are losing their clinical autonomy. He does not deny that such an outcome remains a possibility but so far there has been no fundamental challenge to the medical model and whether it 'is worthy of the enormous social investment it receives' (Mechanic 1991: 495). Mechanic is not alone in reaching a view that runs counter to much of the prevailing policy analysis centred on the ascendency of managerialism. As Evans (1990) notes, doctors are granted extraordinary privileges and undertake special obligations in order that they can perform in ways which best meet patient needs. He queries the commitment on the part of policy makers and managers to utilise the evidence that is currently available in respect of clinical variations in practice.

The collusive relationship with the public, referred to above, has allowed medicine's conception of health and disease to remain dominant. The NHS remains patient-, not population-, centred and it is by no means self-evident that the health strategy as set out in the *Health of the Nation* will shift this focus, although it challenges the dominant biomedical model and existing distribution of resources, and is beginning to shape the language of policy priorities (DH 1991). The Government's health strategy marks the first time in Britain that an explicit attempt has been made to set targets in selected areas by which to achieve demonstrable and measurable improvements in health. But the extent of the political commitment to such a challenge to the prevailing biomedical orthodoxy remains far from clear. Suggestions that medicine is under siege by numerous hostile forces arrayed against it in the shape of assertive managers and policy makers are almost certainly premature. The odd skirmish may afford a victory or two for the invading forces but the real issue is one of *sustainability* and the successful engineering of a new balance of power in medicine that gives managers a dominant role.

The instrument of management is double-edged and could be used to further the assault on medical power or to blunt it. It is unclear whether involving doctors in management and encouraging them to become managers represents a serious attempt to address these issues and seek movement in areas where it has been singularly lacking, or whether it is seen by doctors as a way of staving off any real threat to their privileged position. Involving doctors more centrally and pivotally in the management function could institutionalise and entrench the very forces that are likely to prevent any attempt to move from a medical model of disease to a broader, societal conception of health and illness.

The reason why many doctors get involved in management in the first place is instructive. As was pointed out earlier, research shows that it is not in order to hasten, or collude in, the erosion of their freedom but rather to ensure that the erosion is resisted or halted (Hunter 1992). Doctors as managers, then, becomes a perfectly legitimate stratagem for ensuring that no fundamental challenge is mounted to their prevailing view of the world. If colonising the strange, and somewhat alien, world of management becomes the means for securing this then so be it.

Paradoxically, having charged down the management route intent upon deploying management innovations to control or reconfigure clinical practice, the Government may have unwittingly laid the foundations for a resurgence of professional power. Far from the managerial revolution in health care successfully challenging the notion of 'provider capture', it will have unwittingly served to entrench it (Hunter 1992). If such a development occurs on a significant scale then the future status of lay, or non-medical, managers surely becomes an issue. As Mark and Scott (1992) argue, 'medical managerialism has profound implications for both present managers without clinical qualifications and future lay recruits to management in the NHS' (Mark and Scott 1992: 210).

Whatever the outcome of manoeuvrings between doctors and managers the parameters of the management agenda seem likely to remain medically defined. If a doctor is challenged to behave like his or her more efficient colleagues, the criteria of judgement are best *medical* practice and not *management* practice. In short, the new management thinking will be adopted by doctors and may lead to a re-establishing of professional power in health services which some observers, perhaps mistakenly and almost certainly prematurely, believe has been somewhat battered and bruised by the recent introduction of various management techniques designed to confront doctors and to weaken their clinical autonomy (Flynn 1992).

Doctors' trump card in this on-going struggle with policy makers is their hold over life and death. Unless managers and governments wish to become directly responsible for life and death decisions, doctors will continue to retain the upper hand in any contest with the advocates of efficiency and effectiveness. After all, they alone command public confidence in their judgement in such matters. Unless doctors lose the respect and loyalty of the public they will continue to possess considerable power to contain countervailing forces. Should public criticism of and disillusionment with medicine grow significantly, then governments and managers are likely to gain in confidence and challenge the power base of doctors. But in no health care system, including the British NHS, has this stage in the management–medicine relationship been reached. It remains unclear whether the British NHS, following what many regard as the most far-reaching reforms in its history, will provide the breakthrough. It is certainly seen as a test case to be carefully observed and systematically evaluated.

CONCLUSION

This chapter has sought to demonstrate that the proletarianisation of the medical profession as a result of the most recent management reform of the British NHS is far from complete and that doctors retain considerable influence over the allocation of resources at an operational level and over the continuing dominance of the health policy agenda. It is not denied that the position of doctors has changed and that they now have to justify and account for their actions in ways unthinkable a decade or so ago, or that the biomedical model is not under challenge as a result of a revival of the public health movement. But these forces have yet to play themselves out and it is by no means certain that doctors will have to surrender their position even if required to be more explicit about it or to share it with others in the health policy arena, or both. They could seek to maintain it.

While on the face of it developments in management and health policy can be seen to pose a major threat to medical dominance as it has traditionally been configured, the preceding analysis has sought to challenge this view by arguing that (a) the medical profession continues to enjoy high social standing, and (b) doctors may be resorting to countervailing sources of power to shape the new managerial developments to their agenda and definition of medical care. There are signs that this is already happening. For example, medical audit remains under the control of doctors despite its potential for giving managers a weapon to control ineffective doctors. It has been argued that the medical profession is more tribalistic than collegiate. An exception occurs when the profession is under threat or perceives itself to be so. Then a united front is put up as doctors combine against the common foe.

Another critical development which poses a threat to doctors lies in the R&D strategy and the new industry rapidly being built up in health services research, including outcomes research. But, for all the claims being confidently articulated in support of these developments, they could result in having a minimal impact overall on current practice if purchasing authorities in the new NHS remain weak and undeveloped or reluctant to challenge current orthodoxy and if the agenda continues to be driven by providers (Hunter and Harrison 1993). Similarly, the R&D initiative should in theory provide ammunition, in the form of empirical evidence concerning medical treatments and their effectiveness, for managers to challenge doctors. Whether it will actually function in this way depends on whether managers attach sufficient importance to R&D and whether doctors are prepared to change their practices in accordance with the research evidence. If the R&D strategy becomes captured by a biomedical perspective, as some predict, then it will most likely fail to effect real or lasting change in the NHS (Hunter 1993c).

These two examples lead this writer to be wary of claims that the proletarianisation of medicine in the British NHS is all but complete and that medical power has been successfully harnessed by the advance of managerialism. The policy landscape in health care in Britain continues to shift and remains turbulent. It is by no means certain that the tenets of the 'new public management' will continue to hold sway. Mechanic and Evans's analyses of medical dominance are more persuasive at a time of uncertainty in which the confusion over managerial and medical roles is far from being resolved. More time needs to have elapsed before we can assert with any confidence, on the basis of reliable evidence, that medical dominance has been replaced with a particular managerial ethos. This may be a perfectly respectable and reasonable position to take but it also risks ignoring the considerable political skills of doctors who are adept at redirecting or neutralising attempts by governments and managers to control them. These skills may serve them well once again as they seek to resist the corporate embrace even if part of the strategy of resistance involves adopting the trappings of corporatism.

REFERENCES

Alford, R. (1975) *Health Care Politics*, Chicago: University of Chicago Press.
Caper, P. (1988) 'Solving the medical dilemma', *New England Journal of Medicine*, 318: 1535–6.
Day, P. and Klein, R.E. (1983) 'The mobilisation of consent versus the management of conflict: decoding the Griffiths Report', *British Medical Journal*, 287: 1813–15.
Dent, M. (1993) 'Professionalism, educated labour and the State: hospital medicine and the new managerialism', *The Sociological Review*, May: 244–73.
Department of Health (DH) (1991) *The Health of the Nation*, London: HMSO.

Drucker, P. (1990) *The New Realities*, London: Mandarin.
Evans, R.G. (1990) 'The day in the night-time: medical practice variations and health policy', in Mooney, G. and Andersen, T.S. (eds) *The Challenge of Medical Practice Variations*, Basingstoke: Macmillan.
Fitzgerald, L. (1991) 'Made to measure', *Health Service Journal*, 31 October: 24–5.
Flynn, R. (1992) *Structures of Control in Health Management*, London: Routledge.
Freidson, E. (1990) 'The centrality of professionalism to health care', *Jurimetrics Journal of Law, Science and Technology*, 30: 431–45.
—— (1993) 'How dominant are the professions?', in Hafferty, F.W. and McKinlay, J.B. (eds) *The Changing Medical Profession: An International Perspective*, New York: Oxford University Press.
Griffiths, R. (1983) *NHS Management Inquiry*, Report, London: DHSS.
Hafferty, F.W. and McKinlay, J.B. (eds) (1993) *The Changing Medical Profession: An International Perspective*, New York: Oxford University Press.
Ham, C. and Hunter, D.J. (1988) *Managing Clinical Activity in the NHS*, Briefing Paper 8, London: King's Fund Institute.
Harrison, S. (1988) *Managing the National Health Service: Shifting the Frontier?*, London: Chapman & Hall.
Harrison, S., Hunter, D.J., Marnoch, G. and Pollitt, C. (1992) *Just Managing: Power and Culture in the National Health Service*, Basingstoke: Macmillan.
Heginbotham, C, (1993) *Healthcare Priority Setting: A Survey of Doctors, Managers and the General Public*, London: King's Fund College.
Hoffenberg, R. (1987) *Clinical Freedom*, London: The Nuffield Provincial Hospitals Trust.
Hoggett, P. (1991) 'A new management in the public sector', *Policy and Politics*, 19 (4): 243–56.
Hood, C. (1991) 'A public management for all seasons?', *Public Administration*, 69: 3–19.
Hunter, D.J. (1980) *Coping with Uncertainty: Policy and Politics in the National Health Service*, Chichester: Research Studies Press/Wiley & Sons.
—— (1990) 'Managing the cracks: management development for health care interfaces', *International Journal of Health Planning and Management*, 5 (1): 7–14.
—— (1992) 'Doctors as managers: poachers turned gamekeepers?', *Social Science and Medicine*, 35 (4): 557–66.
—— (1993a) 'Restructuring health care systems: a paradigm shift in policy and management', *University of Leeds Review*, 1993–4, Vol. 36.
—— (1993b) *Rationing Dilemmas in Health Care*, Research Paper No. 8, Birmingham: National Association of Health Authorities and Trusts.
—— (1993c) 'Let's hear it for R&D', *Health Service Journal*, 15 April: 17.
Hunter, D.J. and Harrison, S. (1993) *Effective Purchasing for Health Care: Proposals for First 5 Years*, Leeds: Nuffield Institute for Health.
Hunter, D.J., McKeganey, N.P. and MacPherson, I.A. (1988) *Care of the Elderly: Policy and Practice*, Aberdeen: Aberdeen University Press.
Kerrison, S., Packard, T. and Buxton, M. (1993) *Medical Audit: Taking Stock*, London: Brunel University and King's Fund Centre.
Klein, R. (1993) 'National variations on international trends', in Hafferty, F.W. and McKinlay, J.B. (eds) *The Changing Medical Profession: An International Perspective*, New York: Oxford University Press.
Kogan, M. *et al.* (1978) *The Working of the National Health Service*, Royal Commission on the NHS, Research Paper No. 1, London: HMSO.

Lipsky, M. (1980) *Street-Level Bureaucracy*, New York: Sage.

Lukes, S. (1974) *Power: A Radical View*, London: Macmillan.

McKinlay, J.B. (1988) 'Introduction', *Milbank Quarterly*, 66 (Suppl. 2): 1–9.

Mark, A. (1991) 'Where are the medical managers?' *Journal of Management in Medicine*, 5: 6–12.

Mark, A. and Scott, H. (1992) 'Management in the NHS', in Willcocks, L. and Harrow, J. (eds) *Rediscovering Public Services Management*, London: McGraw Hill.

Mawhinney, B. and Nichol, D. (1993) *Purchasing for Health*, London: NHS Management Executive.

Mechanic, D. (1991) 'Sources of countervailing power in medicine', *Journal of Health Politics, Policy and Law*, 16 (3): 485–506.

Moore, G.T. (1990) 'Doctors as managers: frustrating tensions', in Costain, D. (ed.) *The Future of Acute Services: Doctors as Managers*, London: King's Fund Centre.

NHS Management Executive (1992) *Local Voices*, London: NHSME.

Parkhouse, J., Ellin, D.J. and Parkhouse, H.F. (1988) 'The views of doctors on management and administration', *Community Medicine*, 10: 19–32.

Peckham, M. (1991) 'Research and development in the NHS', *Lancet*, 338, 10 August: 367–71.

Pettigrew, A., Ferlie, E. and McKee, L. (1992) *Shaping Strategic Change*, London: Sage.

Rowbottom, R. *et al.* (1973) *Hospital Organisation*, London: Heinemann.

Scrivens, E. (1988a) 'Doctors and managers: never the twain shall meet?' *British Medical Journal*, 296: 1,754–6.

—— (1988b) 'The management of clinicians in the NHS', *Social Policy and Administration*, 22: 22–34.

Shortell, S., Morrison, E. and Friedman, B. (1990) *Strategic Choices for America's Hospitals*, New York: Jossey Bass.

Smith, R. (1992) 'A shared future', address to NAHAT Conference, 24 June, Harrogate.

Smith, R., Grabbam, A. and Chantler, C. (1989) 'Doctors becoming managers', *British Medical Journal*, 298: 311.

Stewart, J. and Walsh, K. (1992) 'Change in the management of public services', *Public Administration*, 30: 499–518.

Strong, P. and Robinson, J. (1990) *The NHS Under New Management*, Milton Keynes: Open University Press.

Thorpe, K.E. (1992) 'Health care cost containment: results and lessons from the past 20 years', in Shortell, S.M. and Reinhardt, U.E. (eds) *Improving Health Policy and Management*, Ann Arbor, Michigan: Health Administration Press.

2 The challenge of nursing

Anne Witz

INTRODUCTION

This chapter examines the changes taking place in British nursing today and assesses the extent to which these might be seen as challenging the traditional power of medicine. Overall, I advocate a cautious stance to the challenge that nursing poses to medicine, a stance informed by an awareness of a long and chequered history of attempts by nurses to establish a distinct and autonomous sphere of competence within the health division of labour. I suggest, first, that some of the current reforms in nursing have been on the agenda for a century or more so we must contextualise these historically; second, that the constraints placed on nurses' aspirations by the medical profession have been and continue to be overstated; third, that constraints emanating from the broader environment of state-directed health policy and the hospital system of medical care have been and continue to be crucial in determining the extent to which nurses' own demands are realised; and finally, that the problem *for* nursing has been and continues to be the problem *of* gender.

I will argue that a balanced assessment of current changes in nurse education and practice will depend upon using the concept of occupational strategy rather than professionalisation, and suggest how there are historical continuities and discontinuities in nurses' occupational strategy, which I have described elsewhere (Witz 1992) as one of dual closure. This describes the double-edged occupational closure strategy of nurses, which seeks to challenge medical definitions and control over what nurses know and do (its usurpationary dimension) and to create mechanisms of occupational closure that will clearly distinguish between those who can and cannot practice as a nurse (its exclusionary dimension). Nurses traditionally sought to achieve these goals through two means: credentialist, which describes their bid to define and institutionalise a distinctive knowledge base of nursing; and legalistic, which describes their attempts to secure state support for the putting in place of occupational control mechanisms. The reform of nurse education associated with *Project 2000* represents a pulling through of a long-standing credentialist tactic, one which lay at the heart of Mrs Bedford-Fenwick's vision of nurse autonomy 100 years ago. Other elements of nurses' occupational strategy indicate a new focus on the content of nursing work, which pivots around the notion of practitioner autonomy and involves the reworking of a discourse of caring in nursing.

There are, then, two vital elements of nurses' occupational strategy today: occupational control and practitioner autonomy. As regards the challenge represented by both these developments to the traditional dominance of medicine in health care, occupational control, revolving around control of the curriculum of nursing, poses more of a challenge to the historical link between service needs and nurse education than it does to relations between nursing and medicine. It is the new focus on the content of nursing work which more directly challenges the traditional doctor-led model of health care. It does so through an increasing emphasis on a patient-centred, care-driven model of nurse practice, underpinned by a holistic model of health and elaborated by means of a discursive reworking of the centrality of caring activity as a skilled and indeterminate, theoretically informed activity at the core of the new nursing role.

An assessment of the challenge to medicine posed by changes in nurse education and practice cannot be conducted solely within the parameters of a conceptual focus on the occupational division of labour and inter-occupational relations between medicine and nursing. It is also vital to locate this within broader societal-level trends characteristic of post-industrialisation and post-Fordism, as well as in the political context of the shift in health policy that has occurred during the latter half of the 1980s and continues into the 1990s. Modes of funding, organising and delivering health care in Britain are being radically overhauled. There are three major elements of the recent National Health Service (NHS) reforms: the introduction of general management, the introduction of market principles and the increasing emphasis on health promotion and disease prevention (Williams *et al.* 1993). I shall, then, also be examining the complex relation between nursing reform, the health division of labour between nurses and doctors and the restructuring of the health service generally. I shall argue that the success of any challenge by nurses to the traditional hegemony of doctors over both nurses and patients will depend on the ability of nurses to adapt their view of the new nursing to policy makers' vision of a new health service in Britain, and that, in some respects, nurses are in a better position than doctors to respond to and capitalise upon the current process of restructuring health care in Britain. The real challenge for nurses will lie in their being proactive rather than reactive in this period of restructuring – a task rendered difficult by the lesser power and influence exercised by nurses compared to doctors in the political arena of health policy formulation and implementation (cf. Clay 1987; Rafferty 1992).

NURSE PROFESSIONALISATION PAST AND PRESENT

There would appear to be an overwhelming consensus amongst nurse leaders and commentators that the 'new nursing' (Beardshaw and Robinson 1990) is symptomatic of a 'professionalising impulse' within British nursing today. The development at a fairly abstract level of new nursing philosophies and theories and, at a more concrete level, of the nursing process methodology, the *Project 2000* reform of nurse education, and the introduction of a clinical career structure – all these may be seen as the pillars of the new nursing in Britain. Whilst some welcome these changes and are basically optimistic about the future shape of nursing (Jolley 1989; Pashley and Henry 1990; White 1988), others are critical of what they see as an outdated, sectarian and elitist 'professionalising impulse' within nursing, viewing it as out of step with both the majority view and the reality of nursing work (cf. Salvage 1985; Melia 1987; Porter 1992). However, it is necessary to dig beneath this rhetoric of 'nurse professionalisation' before it is possible to accurately assess the impact of these perceived changes on occupational relations between doctors and nurses. I want to suggest that we critically unpack the concept of 'profession' and approach current reforms in British nursing using a historically and gender sensitive concept of 'occupational strategy' rather than an ahistorical and conceptually imprecise notion of a 'professionalising impulse'.

Nurses' long-standing occupational strategy might better be termed a 'professional project', at the core of which are certain tactics for bringing about change in nursing. These we might see as legalistic, which implicates the State in support of occupational aspirations, particularly around issues such as the registration of practitioners, and credentialist, which seeks to secure a linkage between education and occupation, between theoretical knowledge and its practical application. If we accept that certain occupational strategies employ these tactical means of closure, then we might speak of 'professional projects'.

Salvage, in her more recent work, usefully argues that the rhetoric of professionalisation employed in documents proposing reform conceals what should more properly be regarded as a 'new model for occupational authority, rather than a covert bid for traditional professional status' (Salvage 1988: 519). Salvage identifies two key elements of this new model of occupational authority for nursing: first, the challenge to medical power by nurses; and second, the redefinition of nursing work through the development of 'patient centred' models of nursing. I think Salvage is absolutely correct in urging us to think more carefully about the current meaning of professionalisation in nursing. She correctly insists that:

> It is pointless simply to measure the proposals against some arbitrary check-list of professional goals. We should rather assess whether there is a coherent occupational strategy, and if so, which elements of it have persisted and which are responses to rapidly and significantly changed circumstances.
>
> (Salvage 1988: 517)

Where I would part company with Salvage is in her argument that nursing reform departs from traditional occupational strategy in nursing; rather, there *are* important continuities, as well as discontinuities. It is vital, then, to locate nurses' occupational strategy historically.

Crucial to any analysis of the relative success or failure of nurses' occupational strategy is the issue of gender. Two issues have been highlighted by feminist contributions to the sociology of nursing. First, the gendering both of the content of nursing work and of the context (both in terms of the organisation and the health division of labour) within which it is accomplished (cf. Gamarnikow 1978; Davies 1992); and second, the gendering of professional projects themselves (cf. Witz 1992). In addition, it is vital to locate both the practical accomplishment of nursing work and the strategic aspirations of nurses within the structural parameters of patriarchy, or a gender order of male dominance and female subordination, which, just as it limits and constrains the activities of women generally in society, also limits and constrains nursing's aspirations to re-evaluate the content of nursing work, renegotiate the relation between nursing and medicine, and assert the autonomy of nurses in matters of nurse education and practice. In short, any assessment of nursing progress must take on board the fact that nursing is a predominantly female occupation.

I now want to look at historical continuities and discontinuities in nursing's occupational strategy. I want to argue that there is a key historical continuity, and that this is *credentialism*, which seeks to establish a link through education and occupation by 'standardising' the providers of care and establishing practitioner *control* over the content and standards of education, over what nurses should know in order to practise and how they should acquire this knowledge. I also want to suggest that there is a new element in nurses' occupational strategy, which is the emphasis on the *content* of nursing work, and that this represents a bid to establish practitioner *autonomy* in the daily accomplishment of nursing work.

HISTORICAL CONTINUITIES IN NURSING'S OCCUPATIONAL STRATEGY

One of the major features of the 'new nursing' is the reorganisation of nurse education set in train by *Project 2000*. This represents neither a radical break with the past nor a particularly new element of nurses' occupational strategy, but was from the outset one of the key elements of what I have called elsewhere the 'female professional project' of nursing (Witz 1990, 1992). The struggle for nurse registration spearheaded by Mrs Bedford-Fenwick at the turn of the century was kick-started by her disagreement with the Hospital Association's reluctance to countenance more than twelve months' training for nurses. It was the issue of nurse training that prompted Mrs Bedford-Fenwick to create a new organisation, the British Nurses Association, in 1887 to campaign for a system of nurse registration for nurses who had gone through not less than three years' hospital training (*Nursing Record* 1892: 579). This original concern with the length of nurse training gradually expanded into a more rounded credentialism, which stood at the centre of the pro-registrationist campaign.

> The registration of nurses by Act of Parliament is the only means by which a general standard of education and a definite system of professional control can be obtained.
>
> (*British Journal of Nursing* 1904: 47)

This credentialist tactic found its ultimate expression in the demand for a single-portal system of entry into nursing, under which:

> nurses should be admitted to the Register only after (a) a three years' course of training with a definite curriculum prescribed by a Central Nursing Council, conducted in recognised hospitals and nursing schools, and (b) having passed a uniform State examination conducted by examiners appointed by, and under the supervision of, the Central Nursing Council at suitable centres throughout the Kingdom.
>
> (*British Journal of Nursing* 1916: 293)

Mrs Bedford-Fenwick advocated a single register reached by a single portal of nurse education, opposed a separate register for asylum nurses (Nolan 1993) and looked forward to the day when midwifery education and practice would be subsumed within generic nursing. Her primary objective in campaigning for a state-sponsored system of nurse registration, a Central Nursing Council run by nurses and a uniform system of nurse education and examination, was to challenge the discretionary powers then enjoyed by hospitals – particularly the voluntary hospitals with their nurse training programmes – over the length, standard and content of nurse training, as well as over the conditions of nursing labour (Witz 1990, 1992; Dingwall *et al.* 1988).

The final proposals of the United Kingdom Central Council's *Project 2000* initiative (UKCC 1987) represent the realisation, 100 years on, of many of Mrs Bedford-Fenwick's key demands. They represent a bid to create nurse control over nurse education, but pull this through more explicitly than Mrs Bedford-Fenwick ever did into the implications for nurse practice and the division of labour in nursing work. *Project 2000* represents a historical continuation of a credentialist tactic within nurses' overall occupational strategy, enabling greater *control* by nurses over what is taught, how it is taught and, crucially, where it is taught. It has introduced a single route to registration and a three-year education and training programme, comprising a common foundation followed by specialist branch programmes. This is in tune with Mrs Bedford-Fenwick's vision of a single register and a common nursing curriculum, followed by specialisation in, for example, midwifery or mental health, which assume the status of branch programmes.

None the less, midwifery has not been completely absorbed within nursing, as Mrs Bedford-Fenwick would have wished, but post-registration and direct entry programmes continue, along with the notion of separate and distinct competencies for midwives. Neither is the common nursing curriculum medically derivative, as Mrs Bedford-Fenwick tended to assume it would be (Dingwall *et al.* 1988), but derives equally from biological and social science knowledge bases. Perhaps most significantly, *Project 2000* introduces nursing control over where and how nurses are trained, by prioritising educational over service needs and effectively disentangling nurse education and training from the institutional location of the hospitals, relocating it in institutions of higher education, whilst simultaneously transforming the student nurse from a probationer on a salary into a supernumerary learner on a bursary. To dissociate nurse education and training from the service needs of hospitals, with all the discretionary power that gave to hospitals, was one of the foremost aims of Mrs Bedford-Fenwick's occupational control strategy for nursing. *Project 2000* ushers in the era of nurse, not employer, control over nurse education.

To what extent, then, does the reform of nurse education pose a challenge to medicine? The challenge is more to service needs, which have traditionally driven the organisation and content of nurse education, tying these closely to the staffing needs of the hospitals. Historically, Mrs Bedford-Fenwick was aware of the brake to practitioner control exercised by the voluntary hospitals, who proved the most powerful opponents of registration (Witz 1992). In their assessment of nurses' continued bid for professional autonomy, Dingwall *et al.* (1988) also emphasise the tension between nurse autonomy and economic, rather than medical, constraints. However, the relocation of nurse education in institutions of higher education has frequently involved the creation of departments of nursing and nursing degrees in medical faculties (in the old university sector, at least) so, paradoxically, generates the potential for increased scrutiny of nurse education by medical interests.

By analysing *Project 2000* as an element of nurses' modern occupational strategy we are thus able to move beyond the over-simplified assessment of nursing reforms in terms of an imputed goal of 'professionalisation', and begin instead to pick out key elements of a nurses' 'professional project', distinguishing between continuities (what is old) and discontinuities (what is new) in current nursing reforms. In an excellent analysis of the social history of nursing, Dingwall *et al.* (1988) also argue that nurses' occupational strategy, represented in particular by successive reforms of nurse education since the 1960s, has its roots deep in the nineteenth century and Mrs Bedford-Fenwick's aspiration to create new careers for educated women. I have suggested continuity, but there are also discontinuities. So what is new? I would suggest that, by pursuing the implications of a reformed educational programme for nurse practice, *Project 2000* also pays far more attention than has been historically the case to nurse practice, pursuing a goal of greater *autonomy* for nurses in the daily accomplishment of nursing work. This focus on practitioner autonomy is encapsulated in the delineation of the nurse of the future as a '"knowledgeable doer", able to marshall information to make an assessment of need, devise a plan of care and implement, monitor and evaluate it' (UKCC 1987: 2) and has been further enhanced by the UKCC's (1992) change in its code of practice, which places less emphasis on certification and more on general, professional competency and individual judgement in applying principles to practice. The nurse is to be actively involved in and trusted with patient care, not merely supervising its delivery on terms dictated by medicine.

THE NEW NURSING AND PRACTITIONER AUTONOMY

Underpinning the notion of the 'knowledgeable doer' and the delineation of a new specialist practitioner role is a vision of an enlarged practitioner role for nurses, which turns upon two pivotal issues: the core tasks of nursing and the degree of autonomy to be enjoyed by the nurse.

The new philosophy of nursing is encapsulated in the 'nursing process', which is, strictly speaking, a method by which a variety of nursing philosophies translate into the actual delivery of nursing care. The nursing process attempts to replace a routinised, task-oriented approach to care with a problem-solving, patient-centred one, to replace an intuitive approach to nursing with a more systematic and analytic one, which consists of four stages involved in nursing care: assessment, planning, implementation and evaluation (De La Cuesta 1983; Aggleton and Chalmers 1986). However, the challenge of nursing to medicine amounts to far more than simply introducing four steps into the delivery of nursing care. The new nursing fundamentally redefines the core tasks and responsibilities of the nurse, and has the potential to disrupt received understandings of relations between both nurse and patient, and nurse and doctor.

The 'nursing process' developed in the United States in the 1960s primarily as a teaching tool designed to encourage nurses to reflect critically upon nursing practice and, in the 1970s, rapidly transferred from the educational setting to the clinical practice setting. But it soon came to signify more than a consideration of better nursing practice. It also came to represent a strategy of nurse professionalisation. But De La Cuesta (1983) argues that, when the nursing process crossed the Atlantic to Britain in the late 1970s, it was embraced more as a method of improving job satisfaction for nurses and the quality of care for patients rather than as a strategy of nurse professionalisation. By contrast, Dickinson (1982) argues that the nursing process *has* been used by British nurses as a means of enhancing their professional status and autonomy. It provided a way forward in the light of the Royal College of Nursing's increasing concern that post-war nursing had become an extension of the doctor's diagnostic and curative role, defined more in terms of curative, medically derived technical tasks and less in terms of more traditional caring tasks, which were being delegated on to auxiliaries. This concern, taken together with initial reactions to the post-Salmon reorganisation of nursing career structures (MH/SHHD 1966), which emphasised managerial rather than clinical expertise, leads Dickinson to argue that nursing leaders needed a strategy which could 'establish the centrality of clinical nursing for qualified nurses, assert the independence of nursing from medicine and distinguish the trained nurse from the untrained auxiliary. The Nursing Process provided such a strategy' (Dickinson 1982: 62).

The proliferation of new philosophies, theories and models of nursing is part of an ongoing process of reflecting more consciously on the nursing role. The nurse is often portrayed as executing a unique function as an independent health care practitioner whose role is complementary to that of the patient, rather than subservient to that of the doctor. Nursing goals are not subsumed within a medical plan of treatment, but are legitimated in their own right. The notion of a partnership between nurses and patients is viewed as a key aspect of the new nursing (Salvage 1992), whilst the experiments with Nursing Development Units in Britain have been heralded as examples of 'the contemporary ideology of nursing in action' (Pearson 1988: 131). I shall return to consider Nursing Development Units later in this chapter, mainly in relation to reasons for their success or failure.

The new nursing embraces a people-centred rather than a task-centred approach to patients, who are treated as partners rather than receivers of care (Dickinson 1982; Salvage 1992) and the role of the nurse as patient-advocate is one way of expressing this. It creates the possibility of establishing a 'nursing veto': a sphere of competence and autonomous practice for the nurse, who makes informed judgements and decisions relating to patients' needs, as well as reclaiming primary care activities as falling within her special sphere of competence. In other words, the new nursing advocates an *enhanced* nursing role. This is sometimes seen as distinct from an *extended* nursing role, which enlarges the nurse's sphere of competence by incorporating specialist medically derived tasks, devolved on to nurses by doctors. The new nursing advocates a distinctive 'carative' route forward rather than a derivative 'curative' one. But are these two paths forward for nursing necessarily mutually exclusive? Some (cf. Orlando 1987) insist that they are; that the enhanced, 'carative' route is the independent path forward and one paved by the nursing profession itself; whilst the extended, curative route is a dependent path forward, paved for nurses by medical interests. When the enhanced nursing role is favoured over the extended role, it is seen as building on the strengths and value of nurses' traditional concerns, rather than capitalising on doctors' pragmatic concerns with escalating workloads and excessive routinisation of some medical procedures. This is the most commonly held prognosis, with the 'nursing nineties' envisaged as the decade of 'professionals of care' rather than 'handmaidens of cure' (Pashley and Henry 1990: 46).

However, these two routes forward are not seen by all as mutually exclusive (cf. White 1988). The expanded or enhanced nursing role may be seen as reflecting new developments in health care philosophy, particularly heightened perceptions of patients' needs implied in holistically driven models of health care, whilst the extended role capitalises on the search for less expensive methods of delivering health care than the doctor-controlled one and reflects new developments in health service organisation and modes of delivery. For example, some new clinical nurse specialist roles in acute care may look more like extended ones, negotiated in the context of reduced junior doctors' hours.

The 'carative' route forward is complex because it is premissed upon a number of changes: first, that a body of relatively abstract nursing knowledge, upon which judgements and explanations of patients' needs are based, is further developed; second, that nurses reclaim the core tasks of primary care as their special province; third, that nurses renegotiate those elements of their

subordination to medical authority which mitigate against practitioner autonomy in the planning, delivery and evaluation of nursing care (such as the right
to prescribe drugs); and fourth, that role boundaries between nurses and
auxiliaries are clearly renegotiated if 'knowledgeable doers' are to be distinct
from, and yet reclaim certain tasks formerly delegated to, less knowledgeable
'doers'. We may indeed see the new nursing as a dual closure strategy, which
has both exclusionary and usurpationary dimensions. Its exclusionary dimension describes how the enhanced nursing role aims to create a division of
labour in caring where diagnostic autonomy relating to care in illness and in
health becomes the privilege of the few surrounded by lesser skilled care
assistants. Its other, usurpationary, dimension describes the renegotiation of
diagnostic and decision-making responsibilities *vis-à-vis* the patient, with
certain areas of decision-making becoming the domain of nurses, whilst others
are retained by doctors.

The nursing process inevitably involves a redefinition of the nurse's role
in such a way as to have a knock-on effect on nurses' relationships with
other parties involved in patient care. The implementation of the nursing
process in clinical settings requires not only that nurses are resocialised, but
also that doctors, patients and managers alter their expectations concerning
the nursing role. The new nursing, then, is as much about demarcation and
power relations between different occupational groups in the health
division of labour – most notably doctors and nurses, but also nurses and
auxiliaries – as it is about redefining the core of nursing work. Whilst the
implementation of a nursing process methodology in practice may
routinely amount to little more than the introduction of 'care plans', which
do not radically enhance nurse autonomy, the new nursing embraces
developments that present far more radical challenges to medicine, most
notably the ideology of partnership between nurse and patient and the
translation of this in practice in experimental Nursing Development Units.

The bid for practitioner autonomy looked set to be translated into
practice in primary care as, in theory at least, World Health Organization
directives advocated a central role for community nurses in health promotion. However, the community nurse role in health promotion in Britain
seems unlikely to expand in the context of a GP-based managerial model
of primary care (Williams *et al.* 1993). The role of the nurse in health
promotion looks likely to be decided by groups other than nurses themselves, particularly the medical profession and general management (Gott
and O'Brien 1990; Williams *et al.* 1993), a prognosis which leads Gott and
O'Brien to advocate that 'urgent attention is paid to the relations of power
through which nursing work is exercised' and note how nurses have 'too
little autonomy and authority to implement programmes against the wishes
of other vested interests within their occupational environment' (Gott and

O'Brien 1990: 164). How, then, is the medical profession responding to the new nursing and how significant will this response be to the success or failure of nurses' bid for an enhanced role and practitioner autonomy in health care?

THE CHALLENGE TO MEDICINE?

Here we enter muddy waters, encountering optimistic and pessimistic assessments of the demise of medical dominance over nursing. In my view, the optimism is misplaced and comes closer to wishful thinking than a realistic assessment of the possibility of change. Are doctors really much more receptive now to innovative nursing care and is their anxiety about nurses interfering in treatment regimes diminishing as nurses simply become better at advocacy and explaining their actions, as Kershaw (1992) suggests? Or have nurses simply not paid sufficient attention to the presence of doctors, who may act as a significant brake on their bid for practitioner autonomy, as Porter (1992) suggests? Whilst it seems import- ant to identify the alternatives, it would be incautious to attempt to come down on one side or the other, or to predict how nurse–doctor relations might change, precisely because the 1990s are set to become a crucial period in changing the ways in which health care is delivered, not simply in terms of the potential re-demarcation of occupational boundaries between health care occupations, but also in terms of the broader political, economic and organisational changes currently taking place in the NHS.

It is claimed that traditional demarcations between doctors and nurses, seen as based on increasingly untenable distinctions between 'cure' and 'care', are becoming blurred and that the new nursing poses a threat to the supremacy of the medical profession within health care (Beardshaw and Robinson 1990). However, there is an element of wishful thinking about this and, indeed, Beardshaw and Robinson (1990) temper their optimism with a recognition of the continued reality of medical dominance. They see the threat to medical dominance as one of the most problematic aspects of the new nursing, largely because claims to a unique therapeutic role for nursing must necessarily involve a reassessment of patient care *relative* to cure. In Beardshaw and Robinson's view, the extent to which doctors will be willing to exchange their traditional 'handmaidens' for true clinical partners, or even substitutes, is one of the most important questions posed by the new nursing.

In the wake of the Cumberlege Report on Community Nursing (DHSS 1986) and World Health Organization directives concerning preventive health care, there appeared the very real prospect of the substitution of nurses for doctors in certain clinical areas – particularly primary care in the community, with nurses creating a central role in health promotion, screening, counselling and routine treatment work in some GP practices (Beardshaw and Robinson 1990). However, a recent evaluation of the impact of current reforms in the NHS on the role of the nurse in primary care is more pessimistic about the future shape of the community nursing role. I will return to a consideration of the role of the nurse in primary care in due course, but first want to draw attention to two ways in which the medical profession continues to play a critical role in shaping nursing futures. First, it may do so *directly* through its response to nurse-initiated changes, either opposing or supporting these, and, second, it may do so *indirectly* through its response to government-initiated changes in the organisation and funding of health care.

If the way to measure the extent of nurses' challenge to medicine is in terms of the resistance it provokes, then there certainly is evidence of medical resistance to recent developments in nursing. Doctors' response to the Cumberlege Report on neighbourhood nursing (DHSS 1986), which recommended the appointment of nurse practitioners, revealed that there were doctors who strongly resisted the idea of nurses acting autonomously (Delamothe 1988). On the other hand, the General Medical Services Committee and the Royal College of Nursing agreed that 'decisions about appropriate treatment are in practice not always made by the patient's general practitioner' and recognised that nurses working in the community are in effect prescribers of treatment (*British Medical Journal* 1988: 226). Discussions concerning the proper arrangements needed to accommodate the prescription of drugs by nurses are taking place, on the grounds that nurse prescribing raises issues relating to the legal and professional status of both the nursing and the medical professions (*British Medical Journal* 1988: 226). This suggests that renegotiations concerning the spheres of competence of doctors and nurses are on the agenda. None the less, the General Medical Council (1992) Guidelines remain ambiguous on nurse prescribing and other forms of 'delegation' of tasks under medical prerogative to nurses, stating that it has no desire to restrain delegation, but warning that doctors must be satisfied about the competence of the person to whom they are delegated, and insisting that doctors must retain ultimate responsibility for the patients, as improper delegation renders a doctor liable to disciplinary proceedings. Renegotiations around the division of responsibilities between doctors and nurses are proceeding very cautiously and to a large extent on a rather *ad hoc* basis, given the volume of letters requesting advice and clarification received from GPs by the General Medical Council.

The focus in much of the nursing literature seems to be on the challenge of the 'new' nursing to the 'old' nursing posed by nursing reform, rather than on the challenge to medicine. One doctor (Mitchell 1984) has complained in the pages of the *British Medical Journal* that doctors have not been told what the nursing process is about. Ironically, the nursing process is actually derived from the work of an American doctor, Lawrence Weed, who pioneered the 'problem-oriented record' for hospitals in 1969. This changed the way in which patient information was collected and stored by instituting one single record to which all health professionals contributed. Although the nursing process, which was part of this innovation, crossed the Atlantic to Britain, the problem-oriented record did not. Mitchell (1984) has argued that the medical profession should oppose the nursing process and give it a rough ride on the grounds that medical knowledge *must* precede nursing plans to remedy the deficencies of living activities which are, he insists, consequential upon the cause and clinical course of disease. He also accuses nurses of perpetuating a pernicious dichotomy between 'cure' and 'care', relegating the doctor to disease and elevating the nurse to the holistic care of the individual, and suspects that the nursing process is less a system of rationalising the delivery of care than a means of elevating nurses' status and securing independence from medical domination.

It is in secondary care settings that experiments with nursing beds in experimental Nursing Development Units (NDUs) have attracted overt medical opposition. In NDUs, the one-to-one relationship between the primary nurse and her patient parallels the traditional one ascribed to doctors only, and this may be read as an overt statement that there are patients who do not require the full-time attention of doctors and thus as an attempt to challenge the difference between care and cure. The Oxford NDU, which functioned between 1986 and 1989, contained sixteen nursing beds to which patients were admitted by the senior nurse. Nurses acted autonomously, admitting and discharging patients, and administering drugs, and sought to put into practice the ideology of partnership between nurse and patient, where the focus is on enhancing the patient's health knowledge and skills, maximum independence for patients, respect of individual choice, and understanding the diversity of patient needs (Salvage 1992). The Oxford NDU provides an example of how primary nursing in practice both redefines the traditional division of labour between doctors and nurses, by an exclusive nurse practitioner–patient partnership, and reworks the division of labour between nurses and auxiliaries or assistants. Because of its challenge to the traditional doctor–nurse relation-ship (and by implication, doctor–patient relationship), the unit was closed in part due to the opposition of doctors (Pembrey and Punton 1990), who declared the unit medically unsound, would not refer patients and were reluctant to provide emergency medical cover. But, as Salvage (1992) observes, the new relationship between nurses and care assistants mirrored the traditional doctor–nurse relationship. The primary nurse worked with a team of associate nurses, whilst the auxiliary was replaced by the 'care assistant', whose role combined aspects of domestic and nursing work.

NDUs would seem to demonstrate how the new nursing ideology in practice assumes the form of a successful dual closure strategy, where nurses succeed in eating into some of the prerogatives traditionally enjoyed by a dominant occupation, in this case doctors, but simultaneously create a new layer of lesser skilled care assistants by re-demarcating spheres of competence. We see here the usurpationary and exclusionary dimensions of a dual closure strategy respectively. It is perhaps not surprising that the new nursing in practice in the Oxford NDU was perceived by medical staff as a threat to their traditional roles *vis-à-vis* patients and nurses, and evoked sufficient resistance to lead to its closure.

By way of contrast, another NDU at Worthing Hospital has been welcomed rather than opposed by medical staff. This is a day ward for patients with cancer and leukaemia, where nurses administer highly toxic chemotherapy drugs and supervise the whole blood transfusion procedure, as well as operate a 'drop-in service' for patients. The crucial difference between the Oxford and Worthing NDUs, which goes some considerable way towards explaining the different responses by medical staff, would seem to be that the Oxford unit involved nurses embracing the *enhanced* nursing role, whilst the Worthing day ward involves nurses *extending* their role by taking on tasks traditionally done by doctors, particularly junior doctors. Medical opposition seems more likely to occur in response to innovations that embody the enhanced, 'carative' route of upskilling nurses, because this instates the nurse–patient partnership as an alternative to the doctor–patient relationship, and puts into practice a radical new philosophy of patient-centred work which undermines traditional, medically created distinctions between care and cure. It is, however, less likely to be encountered where nurses are extending their role by relieving doctors of more routinised medical tasks, such as administering drugs or giving blood transfusions, particularly if these tasks have been routinely performed by junior doctors.

Indeed, turning to primary care settings, the current trajectory of change in the nurse's role is much more in the direction of extending rather than enhancing her role. The growth in the number of practice nurses from 3,284 in 1983 to 17,000 in 1990, with the spurt in growth occurring in 1989 (DH 1990), points to the importance of doctors' response to changes initiated by government rather than nurses in shaping the role of the nurse in primary care. In particular, the recent introduction of GP contracts has led to a GP-centric realisation of the increasing emphasis on health promotion in British health policy, and so mitigated against the realisation of health promotion models that envisaged an enhanced, community nurse, or nurse practitioner role as the linchpin of primary care initiatives. Indeed, Williams *et al.* (1993) argue that the shift towards a GP-based managerial model of primary care is favouring the growth of practice nurses at the expense of community nurses or fully fledged nurse practitioners. In this respect, they see the crucial issue for primary care nursing of the future as 'whether the practice nurse will perform an instrumental role acting as a complement, probably a subordinate, to the general practitioner or if they will act as a substitute to the doctor becoming more fully involved in health education and counselling as a nurse practitioner' (Williams *et al.* 1993: 58). The increasing role of GPs in the management and control of resources points to the limited expansion of the nurse's role, as the practice nurse simply takes on routine tasks formerly performed by GPs, without necessarily expanding her decision-making role or forging new partnerships with patients. This raises the issue of whether the new managerialism in health impacts similarly or differently on nursing roles in the secondary care sector. I shall return to this question in the final section of the chapter, but now turn to the question of the relationship between gender, the new nursing and inter-occupational relations between nurses and doctors.

GENDER, THE NEW NURSING, AND THE CHALLENGE TO MEDICINE

Historically, the gender composition of health occupations has proved a powerful factor shaping patterns of inter-occupational dominance and subordination (cf. Gamarnikow 1978; Davies 1980; Witz 1992), so what are the chances today of nurses' bid for practitioner autonomy succeeding, given that nursing is an overwhelmingly female occupation? Any assessment of the challenge of nursing to medicine will founder on the rocks of an analysis that ignores the gender of the practitioners. There may be prescriptions of a new nursing role, there may be reforms of nurse education, but ultimately any changes in nursing will take effect at the level of practice, in the daily accomplishment of nursing work. Ultimately, the autonomous, 'knowledgeable doer' delineated in *Project 2000* proposals, the change agent who asserts her right to make decisions about patient care, has to challenge, or operate within, sets of existing power relations that have been shaped as much by gendered patterns of dominance and subordination as they have been by bodies of medical or nursing knowledge.

Nurses' occupational closure strategy is underpinned by a discursive strategy, which deploys key elements of a discourse of professionalism in the redefinition of the nurse's role. Discursive reconstructions of nurses as 'professionals of care' rather than 'handmaidens of cure' (Pashley and

Henry 1990) abound in the literature on the new nursing. The discourse of professionalism asserts the power of the practitioner and expresses this through descriptions of the practitioner in terms of 'autonomy', 'accountability', 'decision making' and so on. However, there are some abiding contradictions in the discourse of professionalism that underpins the new nursing. One is the internally contradictory nature of the bid for nurse autonomy being premised on patient-advocacy – can the nurse be both an expert decision-maker and the 'patient's friend'? Another is the embeddedness of a discourse of caring within a discourse of sexual difference/gender (e.g. Chua and Clegg 1990 and Kirkham and Loft 1993, for developing analyses of discursive constructions of professionalism, and Witz 1992). How can a discourse of professionalism that relies so heavily upon a recentring of 'caring' rather than 'medical' skills in nursing escape from the disruptive impact of a discursive equivalence between gender and caring? As Susan Reverby (1987) argues in her history of American nursing, a crucial dilemma in contemporary nursing is that it is a form of labour shaped by the obligation to care, but exists in a society that refuses to value caring. Moreover, its history and ultimately its identity cannot be understood unless the bond that has wedded it to womanhood is also unravelled and revealed. In addition, the association between nursing and gender straddles the private/public and unwaged/waged domains (Stacey 1988; Robinson 1990) and the invisibility of women's unpaid, informal caring work is paralleled to the invisibility of paid nursing work from policy analysis, health service statistics and health economics (Robinson 1990).

Ultimately, the success or otherwise of nurses' occupational strategy will be measured by the ability of nurses in possession of a body of theoretical knowledge acting on the basis of this knowledge in care settings. In other words, the 'knowledgeable doer' is faced with the problem of translating knowledge into 'doing', with all the autonomy and accountability that this implies. But the daily reality of nursing work needs to be contextualised within hierarchies of power and authority in care settings that are structured by gendered and sexualised relations of dominance and subordination. The challenge to medicine posed by nurses' bid for practitioner autonomy translates into the everyday, lived reality of women's challenge to men's authority in the delivery of health care. It is difficult to imagine a workplace situation where women are treated as autonomous, knowledgeable doers in a society that systematically constructs women as subordinate and inferior to men, and degrades work whose content is gendered by its association with women. It is difficult to imagine a successful nursing challenge to medicine around the issue of practitioner autonomy without a challenge to the systematic devaluation of women's worth and women's work in society as a whole, particularly when the vision of an enhanced or expanded nursing role pivots around people-centred and caring skills which are saturated with gender-bias and systematically undervalued precisely because they are performed by women. How can appeals to 'knowledge' rather than 'intuition' as the basis of the new nursing succeed in the face of the overwhelming pressure to construct caring tasks as something women simply 'do' rather than as skills which women, and indeed men, might need to 'acquire'?

The antithetical nature of the concepts of 'work' and 'care' is highlighted by Nicky James in her perceptive analysis of 'carework' in hospices:

> As nurses referred to it, 'care' included valued skills of attention, warmth, involvement and empathetic understanding, and techniques of assessment and intervention. . . . Nevertheless, 'care' usually remains invisible. No one knows it has been done, and it is exceedingly hard to estimate its value in quantitative terms and therefore to take adequate account of its practical effect. . . . In contrast to 'care', 'work' was much more straightforward because for the most part 'work' was visible and could be timetabled.
>
> (James 1992: 106)

The discourse of 'care' in nursing is not so much new, as Armstrong (1983) suggests, as strategic. It remains unclear whether a strategy of enhancing the scope and autonomy of the nursing role by appealing to its unique caring components will ultimately be able to transcend the discursive equivalence between caring skills and women's worth, which leads to the undervaluing of these skills in a society where women's worth is systematically denied, and where care is defined as 'non-work'.

BEYOND THE HEALTH DIVISION OF LABOUR

A sociological analysis of occupational control, the division of labour, gender and power in health occupations provides an essential, but incomplete, framework for assessing changes in the organisation of nursing and the relation between nursing and medicine. A critical factor shaping the nurse of the 1990s will be the organisational and political contexts within which nursing is located. Historically, changes deriving from an agenda set by nurses have been successful only when they have synchronised with wider organisational and governmental concerns (Rafferty 1992; Dingwall *et al.* 1988). Nursing interests have always been, and for the most part continue to be, subordinated to those of more powerful groups such as the medical profession and health service managers (Williams *et al.* 1993; Gott and O'Brien 1990). The restructuring of the health service in Britain, particularly the introduction of new managerialism following Griffiths's recommendations (DHSS 1983) and the purchaser–provider mechanism of the internal market, has profound implications for the direction of change in nursing, as well as for the future shape of authority and work relations between medicine and nursing.

Recent debates about post-Fordism and flexibility provide fruitful ways of analysing some trajectories of change (Bagguley *et al.* 1990; Piore and Sable 1984; Atkinson 1986; Aglietta 1987). Atkinson's (1986) argument, that the modern flexible firm relies increasingly on a core of functionally flexible, re-skilled workers whose jobs encompass an increasingly diverse range of tasks, surrounded by a periphery of less skilled, numerically flexible workers, would seem to capture the direction of change in the nursing workforce. Dingwall *et al.* (1988) see a continuing tension between nurse autonomy and economic constraints mainly due to the cost implications of the professionalisation of nursing in the current climate, where the economic consequences of medical autonomy are themselves subject to ever-increasing containment, as advanced societies grapple with the costs of providing national health care. However, the economic consequences of the new nurse autonomy might not be inimical to the cost-cutting goals of the new managerialism in the NHS. Robinson (1992) suggests that the traditional gap between the interests of the professionalising tendency within nursing, with its concern to create a high-status single portal of entry, and those of employers, whose concern has been to open up the entry gate in order to sustain the levels of nurses necessary to staff the service, may well be narrowing in today's climate of change in the NHS. Employers' and policy makers' worries about the potential costs of a high-status elite of 'new nurses' may be ameliorated by the prospect of a numerically flexible, cheap peripheral workforce of care assistants, created using the National Vocational Qualifications (NVQ) route (Robinson 1992). The paradoxical situation where nurses' rhetoric of professionalisation seems to be winning through in spite of a more general attack on professional monopoly, particularly that of the medical profession, may well have more to do with the cost-cutting potential of a nursing service – at the core of which are a small number of highly educated 'knowledgeable doers' surrounded by a peripheral workforce of cheaper care assistants – than with a successful renegotiation of occupational boundaries between doctors and nurses, or a significant challenge on the part of nurses to the traditional dominance of doctors over nursing and, indeed, patients.

Walby (1993) usefully locates an analysis of changes in the occupational organisation, or what she calls 'modes of governance', of both nurses and doctors within debates about the restructuring of employment relations – debates which centre around the post-Fordist thesis. She argues that in nursing there is a general move away from Fordist structures of employment in the UK, i.e. from a hierarchicalised and bureaucratised mode of work organisation, towards a post-Fordist mode of governance which enhances functional flexibility in nursing. Walby cites three trends in support of her argument: *Project 2000*, with its upgrading of nurse training; the development of primary nursing, with the shift away from task-centred division of labour towards a patient-centred form of care; and the recent UKCC change in its code of practice, which now emphasises 'principles for practice' rather than 'certificates for tasks' and embraces a holistic concept of nursing rather than one based on activities.

Walby's case for moves in the direction of post-Fordist work organisation in nursing might be further strengthened by considering the precise ways in which clinical and managerial tasks in nursing are currently being remixed, although there is considerable local variation here. As regards managerial functions in nursing (those that remain, at any rate), some of these are being devolved downwards to ward level in hospitals, whilst others, like quality assessment, are being incorporated into new nurse management roles at the level of the unit, as the increasing emphasis on patient care and 'customer satisfaction' becomes formally incorporated into the health service organisation's remit. What is interesting here is that nurses' roles in particular are being pushed more explicitly in the direction of the patient as consumer and that this is occurring as part of the general shift towards a more market-driven health service in Britain. The prospect of the nurse assuming the mantle of the model, functionally flexible worker responding closely to consumers'/patients' needs looks to be on the agenda of change in nursing. However, the question remains as to whether this reflects the spirit of development in nursing theory concerning the holistic, patient-centred model of care, or whether it dilutes or subverts the new nursing philosophy by replacing the new, functionally *specialised* nurse practitioner, who works in partnership with the patient, by a functionally *flexible* nurse practitioner, whose relationship with the patient is informed more by a rhetoric of customer satisfaction than by a philosophy of patient advocacy and partnership.

CONCLUSION

The real challenge of nursing to medicine will depend, ultimately, on the ability of nurses to harness the new nursing philosophy to the new politics of health in Britain. Some developments in health policy are conducive to the realisation of the new nursing philosophy in practice, such as the shift in the relative importance of primary and secondary care, which creates the possibility of enhanced nurse practitioner roles in the community. However, other developments mitigate against this, as we have seen in the case of new GP contracts, which give GPs the opportunity to make key decisions about what kinds of nursing services they buy in and in what ways they will use nurses in GP-led primary care. In secondary care settings, the interests of the medical profession and the new managers will be critical to the realisation of the new nursing in practice, but sometimes these may work in different directions. There has been considerable medical opposition to Nursing Development Units, which introduced nurse–patient partnerships and nursing beds, but this particular implementation of the new nursing may prove attractive to managers, especially if the costs of care using nursing beds can be kept low relative to those of doctor-led services. At the same time, it is not necessarily the case that doctors will oppose nursing beds *per se*, particularly when these are providing continuing but routinised medically derived care for patients, as we saw in the case of the day ward for the treatment of cancer patients in Worthing Hospital.

The challenge of the new nursing to medicine has yet to be won, as the trajectory of change most likely to be tolerated or welcomed by the medical profession appears to be the extension of nurses' roles through the incorporation of routinised, medically legitimated procedures into the remit of nursing practice. These procedures may well be devolved on to, rather than simply delegated to, the nurse, but this is still a long way from the vision of the new nursing with its radical recentring of caring functions and enhanced, autonomous practitioner role. However, in view of trends towards the decentralisation of health service finance and organisation, any global or collective vision of a nursing of the future is likely to be rapidly displaced by local variations in the health division of labour, within which the role of nurses will take shape, most probably in a largely pragmatic and *ad hoc* manner. It is increasingly likely, then, that the localised power of doctors and the new general managers will become more critical than in the past in shaping the possibility and direction of change in nursing, as well as the nature of work and power relations between doctors and nurses.

ACKNOWLEDGEMENTS

My thanks to those who read and provided detailed and insightful feedback on this chapter, namely Peter Nolan, Maureen Eby and the editors, to Sylvia Walby for sharing with me her thoughts on current directions in nursing, and to my colleague Gillian Hundt for egging me on towards a conclusion.

REFERENCES

Aggleton, P. and Chalmers, H. (1986) *Nursing Models and the Nursing Process*, Basingstoke: Macmillan.

Aglietta, M. (1987) *A Theory of Capitalist Regulation*, London: Verso.

Armstrong, D. (1983) 'The fabrication of nurse–patient relationships', *Social Science and Medicine*, 17 (8): 457–60.

Atkinson, J. (1986) *Changing Work Patterns: How Companies Achieve Flexibility to Meet New Needs*, London: National Economic Development Office.

Bagguley, P., Mark-Lawson, J., Shapiro, D., Urry, J., Walby, S. and Warde, A. (1990) *Restructuring: Place, Class and Gender*, London: Sage.

Beardshaw, V. and Robinson, R. (1990) *New for Old? Prospects for Nursing in the 1990s*, London: King's Fund Institute.

Chua, T. and Clegg, S. (1990) 'Professional closure: the case of British nursing', *Theory and Society*, 19 (2): 135–72.

Clay, T. (1987) *Nurses, Power and Politics*, London: Heinemann.

Davies, C. (1972) 'Professionals in organisations: observations on hospital consultants', *Sociological Review*, 20: 553–67.

—— (1980) *Rewriting Nursing History*, London: Croom Helm.

—— (1992) 'Gender, history and management style in nursing: towards a theoretical synthesis', in Savage, M. and Witz, A. (eds) *Gender and Bureaucracy*, Oxford: Blackwell/Sociological Review.

De La Cuesta, C. (1983) 'The nursing process: from development to implementation', *Journal of Advanced Nursing*, 8: 365–71.

Delamothe, T.D. (1988) 'Nursing grievances, IV: not a profession, not a career', *British Medical Journal*, 296: 271–4.

Department of Health (DH) (1990) *Health Care Parliamentary Monitor*, London: HMSO.

Department of Health and Social Security (DHSS) (1983) *NHS Management Inquiry (The Griffiths Report)*, London: DHSS.

—— (1986) *Neighbourhood Nursing: A Focus for Care*, a report of the Community Nursing Review in England (chairperson, Julia Cumberlege), London: HMSO.

Dickinson, S. (1982) 'The nursing process and the professional status of nursing', *Nursing Times*, 78: 61–4.

Dingwall, R., Rafferty, A.M. and Webster, C. (1988) *An Introduction to the Social History of Nursing*, London: Routledge.

Gamarnikow, E. (1978) 'Sexual division of labour: the case of nursing', in Kuhn, A. and Wolpe, A.M. (eds) *Feminism and Materialism*, London: Routledge & Kegan Paul.

General Medical Council (1992) *Professional Conduct and Discipline: Fitness to Practise*, London: General Medical Council.

Gott, M. and O'Brien, M. (1990) *The Role of the Nurse in Health Promotion: Policies, Perspectives and Practice*, unpublished report of a two-year research project funded by the Department of Health.

Henry, C. and Pashley, G. (1989) 'Vital links', *Nursing Times*, 82 (16): 40–1.

James, N. (1992) 'Care, work and carework: a synthesis?', in Robinson, J., Gray, A. and Elkan, R. (eds) *Policy Issues in Nursing*, Milton Keynes: Open University Press.

Jolley, M. (1989) 'The professionalization of nursing: the uncertain path', in Jolley, M. and Allen, P. (eds) *Current Issues in Nursing*, London: Chapman & Hall.

Keen, J. and Malby, R. (1992) 'Nursing power and practice in the United Kingdom National Health Service', *Journal of Advanced Nursing*, 17: 863–70.

Kenrick, K. and Simpson, A. (1992) 'The nurses' reformation: philosophy and pragmatics of Project 2000', in Soothill, K., Henry, C. and Kendrick, K. (eds) *Themes and Perspectives in Nursing*, London: Chapman & Hall.

Kershaw, B. (1992) 'Models of nursing', in Jolley, M., and Brykczynska, G. (eds) *Nursing Care: The Challenge to Change*, London: Edward Arnold.

Keyzer, D. (1988) 'Challenging the role boundaries: conceptual frameworks for understanding the conflict arising from the implementation of the nursing process in practice', in White, R. (ed.) *Political Issues in Nursing: Past, Present and Future*, vol. 3, Chichester: John Wiley.

—— (1992) 'Nursing policy, the supply and demand for nurses: towards a clinical career structure for nurses', in Robinson, J., Gray, A. and Elkan, R. (eds) *Policy Issues in Nursing*, Milton Keynes: Open University Press.

Kirkham, L.M. and Loft, A. (1993) 'Gender and the construction of the professional accountant', mimeo (forthcoming, in *Accounting, Organization and Society*).

Mackay, L. (1989) *Nursing A Problem*, Milton Keynes: Open University Press.

—— (1992) 'Nursing and doctoring: where's the difference?', in Soothill, K., Henry, C. and Kendrick, K. (eds) *Themes and Perspectives in Nursing*, London: Chapman & Hall.

Mckee, M. and Lessof, L. (1992) 'Nurse and doctor: whose task is it anyway?', in Robinson, J., Gray, A. and Elkan, R. (eds) *Policy Issues in Nursing*, Milton Keynes: Open University Press.

Melia, K. (1987) *Learning and Working: The Occupational Socialization of Nurses*, London: Tavistock.

Mitchell, J.R.A. (1984) 'Is nursing any business of doctors? A simple guide to the "nursing process"', *British Medical Journal*, 288: 216–19.

Ministry of Health and Scottish Home and Health Department (MH/SHHD) (1966) *Report of the Committee on Senior Nursing Staff Structure* (Chairperson, Brian Salmon), London: HMSO.

Nolan, P. (1993) *A History of Mental Health Nursing*, London: Chapman & Hall.

Orlando, I.J. (1987) 'Nursing in the 21st century: alternate paths', *Journal of Advanced Nursing*, 12: 405–12.

Pashley, G. and Henry, C. (1990) 'Carving out the nursing nineties', *Nursing Times*, 86: 45–6.

Pearson, A. (ed.) (1988) *Primary Nursing: Nursing in Burford and Oxford Nursing Development Units*, Beckenham: Croom Helm.

Pembrey, S. and Punton, S. (1990) 'The lessons of nursing beds', *Nursing Times*, 86: 44–5.

Piore, M. and Sable, S. (1984) *The Second Industrial Divide*, New York: Basic Books.

Porter, S. (1991) 'A participant observation study of power relations between nurses and doctors in a general hospital', *Journal of Advanced Nursing*, 16: 728–35.

—— (1992) 'The poverty of professionalisation: a critical analysis of strategies for the occupational advancement of nursing', *Journal of Advanced Nursing*, 17: 720–6.

Rafferty, A.M. (1992) 'Nursing policy and the nationalization of nursing: the representation of "crisis" and the "crisis" of representation', in Robinson, J., Gray, A. and Elkan, R. (eds) *Policy Issues in Nursing*, Milton Keynes: Open University Press.

Reverby, S. (1987) *Ordered to Care: the Dilemma of American Nursing, 1850–1945*, Cambridge, Cambridge University Press.

Robinson, J. (1990) 'Power, politics and policy analysis in nursing', in Jolley, M. and Allen, P. (eds) *Current Issues in Nursing*, London: Chapman & Hall.

—— (1991) 'Power, politics and policy analysis in nursing', in Perry, A. and Jolley, M. (eds) *Nursing: A Knowledge Base for Practice*, London: Edward Arnold.

Robinson, K. (1992) 'The nursing workforce: aspects of inequality', in Robinson, J., Gray, R. and Elkan, R. (eds) *Policy Issues in Nursing*, Milton Keynes: Open University Press.

Royal College of Nursing (1985) *The Education of Nurses: A New Dispensation*, London: RCN.

Salvage, J. (1985) *The Politics of Nursing*, Oxford: Heinemann.

—— (1988) 'Professionalization – or a struggle for survival? A consideration of current proposals for the reform of nursing in the United Kingdom', *Journal of Advanced Nursing*, 13, 515–19.

—— (1992) The new nursing: empowering patients or empowering nurses?', in Robinson, J., Gray, A. and Elkan, R. (eds) *Policy Issues in Nursing*, Milton Keynes: Open University Press.

Stacey, M. (1988) *The Sociology of Health and Healing*, London: Unwin Hyman.

United Kingdom Central Council for Nursing, Midwifery and Health Visiting (1986) *Project 2000: A New Preparation for Practice*, London: UKCC.

—— (1987) *Project 2000: The Final Proposals*, London: UKCC.

—— (1992) *The Scope of Professional Practice*, London: UKCC.

Walby, S. (1993) 'Restructuring health professions: a case of post-Fordism?', paper presented to British Sociological Association conference, Essex University, April.

Williams, S.J., Calnan, M., Cant, S.L. and Coyle, J. (1993) 'All change in the NHS? Implications of the NHS reforms for primary care prevention', *Sociology of Health and Illness*, 15: 43–67.

White, R. (1988) 'The influence of nursing on the politics of health', in White, R. (ed.) *Political Issues in Nursing: Past, Present and Future*, vol. 3, Chichester: John Wiley.

Witz, A. (1990) 'Patriarchy and professions: the gendered politics of occupational closure', *Sociology*, 24: 675–90.

—— (1992) *Professions and Patriarchy*, London: Routledge.

3 Litigation and the threat to medicine

Robert Dingwall

In 1984, Philip Strong contributed an article to *Sociology of Health and Illness* entitled 'The academic encirclement of medicine'. This continued his attack on the way sociologists had uncritically adopted the thesis of medical imperialism (Strong 1979a). The body of medicine, he argued, had come to occupy such a large space in our society that it had become a major target for entrepreneurs in other academic fields. The merest taste of its blood could satisfy the hungriest of researchers. Cumulatively, however, the medical body was beset by leeches, watching its vitality drain into the more specialised ecological niches of its parasites. Clinical researchers were losing their edge over non-clinical competitors like chemists, physiologists or pharmacologists. Community physicians saw the erosion of their advantage over Ph.D. social scientists in epidemiology, planning and economics. As a generic education, medicine no longer trained people to work at research frontiers. The most that doctors could hope to do was to learn enough to mediate between science and practice. But, Strong pointed out, this was the heart of medical jurisdiction. It was in practice, in the historic, charismatic role of the healer, that medical power found its resting place. Medicine was an occupation united by its access to this craft mystery, by experiences which no lay person could share and few would even be privileged to witness. Moreover, the role of the mediator brought its own power: medicine appropriated parts of the basic sciences around it in a process of inoculation. When looked at in this light, Strong implies, it may be difficult to tell which is the host and which the parasite. Perhaps the relationship is more symbiotic, based on mutual dependence, than a simple analysis would suggest.

The serious threats came from the other beasts in the jungle. Strong identified law as a newcomer to this competition. Ian Kennedy's (1981) Reith Lectures of 1980 staked a public claim to legal jurisdiction over large areas of health care, although, as Strong (1984: 354) comments, they 'were little more than legal imperialism in populist clothing'. This analysis reflects a common perception of the legal challenge to medicine which medical sociologists have taken over rather uncritically from the medical profession itself. In his conclusion, though, he hints at another direction when he links the challenges to medicine to changes in the forms of governmentality, the interlocking systems of values and institutions constitutive of the ordering of a society (Foucault 1979; Burchell *et al.* 1991). The threats from legal imperialism are trivial compared with the process of reconstructing the bases of authority in Anglo–American society which could only be glimpsed in 1984 and which has now run much further in its course.

It is undeniable that British doctors in the 1990s feel threatened by law. They analyse it as a constraint on clinical autonomy, something that prevents the profession from doing a variety of things that it would otherwise do. But it can be argued that this mistakes both the real character of law and the real threat which it represents to the role of medicine in social life. Law is better understood as a creative force, constitutive of social and economic orders in which medical practice occurs.

This chapter, then, will deal with the obvious challenges of law in the form of litigation and regulation mainly by way of an introduction to the shifting cultural environment created by the substitution of legalisation for medicalisation as the paramount mode of governmentality in the so-called 'contract state'. It begins with a review of the formal legal environment within which the medical profession operates and, in particular, of the profession's experience of tort litigation since 1980. It will be argued that this litigation is a problem for the medical profession rather than for the NHS and that it is part of a wider shift in the status of the professions rather than being unique to medicine. The profession's response may, then, be better understood in terms of status protest and as a symbolic expression of its discontent with other social and cultural changes.

THE LEGAL ENVIRONMENT OF MEDICAL PRACTICE

Modern medical practice is suffused by law. Doctors engage in a host of legal transactions every working day. They make contracts of employment, they lease premises and equipment, and they try to avoid committing torts. Doctors interpret and enforce laws, deciding who can get an abortion or who can get compensation from the social security system for certain industrial diseases. They collect evidence for criminal prosecutions, and authorise the detention of people with mental disorders in secure places. They are regulated by laws requiring the notification of births, deaths and specified diseases, governing the availability of organs for transplantation and restricting the right to carry out certain treatments or prescribe certain substances. Modern medicine is a profoundly socio-legal activity. But to list these entanglements is also to underline the inadequacy of a view of law, whether by doctors or medical sociologists, as a purely constraining force: doctors are also *users* of law. Every general practice relies upon the law of partnership to create the organisational forms that make this mode of professional relationship possible, for instance. The National Health Service was created by statute and is governed by a mixture of administrative legal means. All health professions are legal inventions.[1]

Nevertheless, in most medical discourse, the presence of law tends to be identified with its use to challenge individual practitioners. This perception often conflates three lines of legal development. The first is the legal form of the profession itself, the body of statutes and delegated legislation which constitute the profession as a distinctive socio-legal entity, define its membership and establish the terms of its licence and the means by which compliance will be monitored and enforced by members on each other through a governance structure. The second applies only to doctors working in the public sector or under contract with the public sector. This is the body of administrative law which provides for the redress of patient grievances through complaints to the bodies managing the service or holding the contracts.[2] The third is the general body of common law, particularly the use of the torts of negligence and battery. Of these, the first has been left relatively uncontested by the profession itself since the revolts against the governance structure of the General Medical Council in 1970–2 and the subsequent reforms (Stacey 1992: 29–44). The second has been a periodic object of scrutiny (Klein 1973; Allsop and May 1986; Mulcahy and Lloyd-Bostock 1992) but professional anxieties tend to be closely bound up with concerns about the possible interaction of the complaints system with the third type of legal intervention – tort litigation.

The tort action is the oldest means of legal redress available to dissatisfied patients. The term *tort* comes from a Norman French word meaning a wrong or a wrongdoing. Cases of this kind were recorded against practitioners of the healing arts from as early as the fourteenth century, well before any modern notion of a medical profession would be relevant (Dingwall and Fenn 1992: 2–3). Tort law rests on the theory that members of a society owe each other a duty of care, to avoid harming each other, whether the injury is to the person or to their legitimate interests. If someone fails in this duty, they should pay compensation to their victim intended to restore them to their previous condition. The risk of such a payment is an incentive for potential wrongdoers to take their duty of care seriously and to try to behave in a way that limits the possibility of harm. It is important to emphasise that there is nothing special about the position of doctors in tort law. The principles involved are exactly the same for all citizens.

There are a number of different types of tort, but only two are relevant here. The most important is the tort of *negligence*, where someone has failed to use reasonable care in the performance of a duty or obligation and has caused a material injury to another person. In the specific instance of medicine, this means that an injury has been caused to a patient by a doctor's failure to act in accordance with the profession's customary standards. Both the causal connection and the departure from practices 'accepted as proper by a responsible body of medical men skilled in that particular art' (*Bolam* v *Friern Hospital Management Committee* [1957] 2 All ER 118) must be proven for an action to succeed.

The other kind of tort which should be mentioned, although there is little actual litigation in the UK based upon it, is the tort of *battery*. This is the infliction of damage on another by the unlawful use of force. It is relevant to questions about consent to medical and especially surgical treatment. The infliction of physical injury on another person constitutes the crime of assault: the victim also has the option of recovering damages through a civil action for battery. In both instances, the allegation may be defeated by evidence of the victim's consent. A doctor who performs a surgical procedure without consent risks being sued on this ground.[3]

The profession has clearly felt under particular threat from tort litigation since 1980. Although the actual exposure to the risk of litigation varies considerably by specialty (Dingwall and Fenn 1992) most of the Royal Colleges and the BMA have had numerous conferences and working parties reviewing the situation (e.g. BMA 1983; BMA 1991; Chamberlain *et al.* 1985; Mann and Havard 1989; Royal College of Physicians 1990). These institutional concerns are paralleled by grass-roots correspondence to medical journals and coverage in the trade press. The King's Fund produced a report in 1988 (Ham *et al.* 1988) and the former Chief Medical Officer at the Department of Health, Donald Acheson, expressed his concerns in the William Power Lecture to the Royal College of Midwives in 1990. The partnership between the NHS and the medical defence organisations in managing negligence claims, which had been set up in 1954, fell apart under the pressure and was replaced by the nationalisation of responsibility for claims against NHS-employed doctors in 1990. The Labour MP Harriet Harman and the Social Democrat MP Rosie Barnes both promoted Private Members Bills seeking to reform the system, in 1990 and 1991 respectively, and the Labour Party promised changes in its 1992 election manifesto.

In fact the claims of a litigation crisis have been vastly exaggerated. There was a sharp increase in the frequency of negligence claims and their severity, the cost of settlement, during the 1980s (Ham *et al.* 1988; Fenn and Dingwall 1990). This began around 1980 and started to level off around 1987 after something like a fivefold increase in frequency and a threefold increase in severity in a 5–7 year period. Since 1986–7 the rate of increase in the frequency of claims seems to have slowed considerably. The data on severity are less directly comparable, but suggest that this has continued to increase at a rate somewhat above that of inflation but also less steeply than in the early 1980s. To put all this in perspective, however, the rate of claims in 1990–1 was 12.11 per 100,000 population compared with a US rate in excess of 30 per 100,000. Only 20–25 per cent of claims – about 1,600 a year in the whole of England – received any payment. The average closure cost was about £30,000, producing a total bill of around £50 million against the £15.426 billion operating expenditure of English health authorities in the same year (Dingwall and Fenn in press). From the perspective of a health service planner, medical negligence litigation ought to be no more than an irritant, a small cost which it would be desirable to control or reduce. At a unit level, it is at worst an occasional source of financial embarrassment if the unit is in an area with higher frequency or severity rates, or is hit by the once in a 7–10 year chance of a pay-out in excess of £$\frac{1}{4}$ million.

Clearly, there have been some real problems. The medical defence organisations were brought to the edge of bankruptcy and resorted to increases in subscription rates of 2,700 per cent between 1978 and 1988, when the system began to unravel. With hindsight, however, this looks far more explicable in terms of the undercapitalisation and lack of insurance expertise in these organisations, which left them unprepared for the sudden change in their environment. The English medical profession may also experience the pressures of litigation more acutely because of its relatively small size in relation to the population served. The intensity of litigation in 1990–1, at 10.5 new claims per 100 hospital doctors, may be closer to US rates than generally recognised.[4] Litigation is a problem for the profession in a way it is not a problem for the NHS as a whole.

However, it is not just a problem for the medical profession. One of the most striking, and neglected, findings in this area has been that almost all British professions have had a similar experience in the same period (Ham *et al.* 1988). Lawyers, accountants, architects, veterinary surgeons and engineers have all seen their liability claims increase in frequency and severity since 1980. If there is a challenge here, it is a challenge to all professions and the explanation seems likely to be found in some wider process of social or cultural change. Nevertheless, litigation against doctors has been successfully presented as a problem *sui generis*, a phenomenon peculiar to medical practice and requiring special remedies.

We may then need to think about how an alleged challenge can be used as part of a strategy of collective action. The litigation crisis might be better understood as a moral panic, where 'a condition, episode, person or group of persons emerges to become defined as a threat to . . . values and interests' (Cohen 1973: 9). The promoters, the moral entrepreneurs in Becker's (1963: 147–63) terminology, adopt a real set of behaviours as a basis for a symbolic crusade in defence of certain status interests which are under threat. These crusades commonly involve partnerships and alliances with mass media in order to generate public pressures on political actors. Their promoters are pursuing 'attempts toward cultural hegemony, to control and define the proper and expected way of life. . . . Social, economic and cultural groups struggle over the ceremonial and ritual dimensions of state action because these establish one or other modes of experiencing life as more valid and more rewarding than another' (Gusfield 1986: 209). Gusfield developed the idea of status politics as a way of understanding the response of social groups to a loss or denial of esteem to which they felt entitled:

> The self-esteem of the group member is belied by the failure of others to grant him the respect, approval, admiration and deference he feels that he justly deserves. This may occur when a segment of the society is losing status and finds that prestige-givers withhold expected deference.
>
> (Gusfield 1986: 18)

If this line of analysis can be followed, it would direct our attention on from the detailed examination of the economics of negligence to a review of the symbolic dimensions of the profession's response. What are the status politics of medical liability?

The most interesting symbolic element of the profession's response to litigation has been its dystopian depiction of the United States. The imagery of the American medical profession beset by litigation has little more validity than the account of the British experience and demonstrates a very limited understanding of the complex interactions between law, health care and insurance against personal misfortune in a country with very limited public provision for ensuring equal access to any of these institutions (Dingwall *et al.* 1991). However, as W.I. Thomas pointed out, it is what people take to be real that has real consequences. In this case, the focal assertion is that 'we (the UK medical profession) have looked at the US and seen a possible future for ourselves that we reject'. This assertion is noteworthy on two grounds.

The first ground is that it represents a marked shift from earlier, positive images of the USA as the beacon of technically advanced medicine, clinical autonomy and handsome remuneration for doctors. While there is still admiration for the technical achievements of American clinical research, even if tempered by some questions about its consideration for the quality of life produced by its interventions in terminal conditions, American doctors are now seen as beset by pressures for additional tests, documentation and practice review which have compromised their ability to act in the best interests of their patients. There is a collapse of trust between doctor and patient, a move from medical paternalism and individualised care to a regime where consumers are treated as formally identical units with certain entitlements and where the provision of the entitlement needs to be documented in order to defend the treatment against *post hoc* review. While there is some envy of the money incomes of doctors in the USA, this is also balanced by a recognition that there may be little to be gained from high earnings if a large chunk of these has to be spent on liability insurance.[5]

The second ground is that it is so much at odds with the admiration for American models of culture and social organisation which has had such an influence in the development of UK social and economic policies since the early 1980s. Rightly or wrongly, the USA has been held up as the model of a dynamic society and economy whose features should be copied by others in the hope of emulating its achievements. Given this, the privatisation of social insurance by the use of the tort system instead of reliance on social security ought to have been a cause for celebration. The profession has, instead, been urging the adoption of schemes for the public funding of liability, copied from social democratic innovations in countries like Sweden and New Zealand.

While there are other elements to the profession's response to litigation, the American motif incorporates most of the key symbolic loadings. It could, then, be plausible to argue that the litigation crisis is as much a protest against wider changes in the social and cultural environment as it is a specific reaction to a specific threat. Negligence litigation becomes a symbol of resistance to a challenge that runs far deeper than a few court appearances and the diversion of 0.2 per cent of the NHS budget. What is the problem to which the 'litigation crisis' is the answer?

MEDICINE, LAW AND SOCIAL CONTROL

Many traditional approaches to the study of medicine and law present them as conflicting institutions. Law may be invoked to counter the power of medicine, as in Kennedy's work cited above: medicine may be invoked to mitigate the harshness of law as in the arguments of writers like Barbara Wootton (1959) that delinquency might be better managed by treatment than punishment. Classically, however, sociologists have been more impressed by their complementarity. This is an insight which is particularly associated with the work of Talcott Parsons (1952: 249–325), although his treatment of the issue is clearly indebted, if unacknowledged, to Herbert Spencer.[6]

Although Spencer is easily the most important sociologist ever produced in England, his work has been largely ignored since his death in 1903. In part, as Turner (1985) suggests, this was because of his loyalty to *laissez-faire* and Social Darwinist positions in the face of the shift among English-speaking intellectuals to various forms of collectivism from the last quarter of the nineteenth century onwards. However, Turner argues, our disaffiliation from Spencer's *politics* should not blind us to the achievements of his *sociology*. This is not the place to explore these contributions in detail or to defend some of the more contentious aspects, especially the functionalist logic and the systems approach. Instead, I shall simply extract a number of themes relevant to the present discussion.

One of the features of Spencer's work is the strength of its theoretical understanding of social change. This reflects the influence of the evolutionary thinking which Spencer had developed in his earlier writings on biology. Unlike many evolutionary sociologists, however, Spencer had a clear sense of the emergence of change from the interaction between organisms and their environment. Because of the variety of environments, natural selection could not be understood as a linear process leading in a single direction. Societies developed under environmental pressures, including pressures from other societies, in different ways reacting to different conditions. Nevertheless, it should be possible to produce a theoretical model to show how different evolutionary pressures led to different forms. Spencer's model was based upon a huge corpus of descriptive studies, drawing on historical and ethnographic data, from which he tried to induce and test various elements of a theory of social organisation and social change. It is this firm grounding in empirical data that makes Spencer's model far more robust than many later works in the same tradition. He concluded that all societies needed to develop institutionalised solutions to three problems: regulation, operation and distribution. *Regulation* refers to the political integration of the whole society; *operation* to the co-ordination and control of the various units of material and cultural production; and *distribution* to the transmission of the outputs to all members. In the smallest and simplest societies, there is a low level of differentiation between these systems, but as the scale of social organisation increases, there is more and more specialisation, bringing with it new problems of co-ordination.

This is a familiar narrative in nineteenth-century sociology. However, there are two important elements which are unique to Spencer. One is his insistence on the relative autonomy of the various sub-systems that emerge. All of them confront the same problems of regulation, operation and distribution in microcosm but their local solutions do not necessarily produce societally appropriate results. This leads him to be the first sociologist to recognise the significance of professions and their arms-length relationship with the State under the conditions which had produced the societal form of industrial capitalism. This form of society derives much of its dynamism from its loose coupling, from the internal tensions between its units, which, in turn, pose considerable problems of co-ordination. The space is important for innovation and flexibility: the cost is the heightened risk of disintegration.

The other element unique to Spencer is his specific account of the evolution of medicine and law. In traditional societies, the maintenance of order and the co-ordination of activities is a rather diffuse activity. The political and the religious are often hard to distinguish. With the growth of scale, however, they become more discrete as religious ideas are elaborated into symbolic legitimations for the political order. Religion takes on two aspects as it becomes the basis of the operative system, co-ordinating the society: the 'medicine man' who drives away evil ghosts, the defender of the cultural order against external threats, and the 'priest' who invokes supernatural powers in positive support of the political order. But the religious and the political are always potentially in conflict. The role of religion as a source of legitimation gives it an independent source of power, which may be abused for sectional gain or be set against the State. As the State evolves, it is likely to create alternative bases of legitimation and to break the operative monopoly of religion. The definition of a secular realm of law is a particularly important part of this process.

The 'medicine man' is the ancestor of most professions, the specialist in the prevention of cultural disorder. Professions are the producers and orchestrators of culture or, more precisely, those elements of culture which may be of importance to the legitimation and co-ordination of the public order. Their work is both material and symbolic: the evil ghosts stand both for the forces of nature, which threaten constantly to destabilise the particular and precarious system of transactions between human beings and their environment that furnishes the physical context for any particular society, and for the anarchy which rests in the arbitrary relationship between signifier and signified. Art, music and literature are socially sanctioned arrangements of signs that bear no necessary relationship to the stream of sense-impressions that reach the human eye or ear. In their maintenance of this order, professions manage the relations between people, creating and defining a language for the sharing of experience. Culture is an operative discipline: it is *this* set of forms defining *this* set of possible relations and no other.

The loose coupling of modern societies, however, means that the definition of culture itself has areas of uncertainty. Different cultural producers are generating different possibilities for the co-ordination of the public order. At any given moment, cultural consumers can pick and choose amongst these. Shifts in consumer preferences are likely to lead to shifts in production, although there can be considerable lags in this process. Some preferences are, of course, likely to be backed by authority or material resources derived from other sub-systems so that they may have a disproportionate effect. Nevertheless, it is part of the evolutionary dynamic of these societies that such variations exist and represent a potential for change and adaptation in response to environmental shifts. This is, of course, a sketchy summary of a complex theoretical scheme. Nevertheless, it should help to establish how medicine and law co-exist as choices of operative systems of cultural management which can be used by the regulatory system as practical means of legitimation and integration.[7] What are the implications of choosing one rather than the other?

It is here that Parsons's (1952: 309–21) elaborations become more helpful. He sees two elements to the maintenance of social order. One is *insulation*, preventing alternative versions becoming the basis for self-supporting groups. The other is *isolation*, denying the possibility of any alternative having a claim to legitimacy. Law, he suggests, is primarily concerned with isolation. Criminals are excluded from society, with little prospect of reintegration, and become the basis of projections of institutionalised values. Here, Parsons is, of course, closely following Durkheim and his discussion of the functionality of crime as a means of symbolising the boundaries of the society. His original contribution comes in his discussion of insulation and the role of medicine. The sick enjoy a conditional legitimacy for their challenge to the social order and a route to reintegration through their compliance with treatment. While there are some significant differences, what the two cases have in common is their response to the problem of illegitimate gains. The criminal may violate the bodily integrity of victims as means to some pesonal gain or gratification or sequestrate the product of their labour. The sick person fails, for reasons beyond his or her control, to manage his or her body in accord with social expectations and is excluded from productive activity. Put another way, both cases are positive statements about cultural values: respect for the human body; avoidance of dependency; the spheres of nature and culture. The difference lies in the capacity ascribed to the people concerned. Criminals are volitional actors; the sick are overwhelmed by the 'evil ghosts'.

In reality, the cases may not be so pure. There is more to law than crime and more to medicine than sickness. There are complex bodies of jurisprudence around questions of intentionality in law and claims to the sick role are notoriously provisional. Nevertheless, if we want to characterise them as competing modes of social intervention, we can see that they cast their shadows in rather different ways.

MEDICAL IMPERIALISM: LEGAL COLONIALISM

The choice between medicine and law as a preferred strategy for operative co-ordination is, then, a choice between two rather different accounts of human nature, of the relationship between human beings and their material environment and of the relationships between human beings. Some part of the difference is captured by the different metaphors which are used by sociologists of medicine and of law to describe their extensions: medical *imperialism* and legal *colonialism*. Imperialism implies the incorporation of a territory and its people into the metropolitan culture and economy; colonialism the outposting of citizens to subjugate a territory and impose an economic relationship without affecting its everyday life more than necessary to achieve these objectives. It is important to note that these are both metaphors about economy and culture: the values and ideas which frame particular kinds of material relationship and which are, in turn, shaped by that material transaction.

In the twentieth century, medicine in the UK has become an increasingly collectivist enterprise. As Armstrong (1983) notes, contemporary medical discourse paints individuals in the context of their environment. To some extent, even, the environment has become more important than the individual.

> Illness, in the post-war years, began to be temporally and spatially distributed, not in a physical domain, but in a community. . . . Comprehensive health care in Britain from 1948, and the contemporary invention and importance placed on community care are simply manifestations of a new diagram of power which spreads its pervasive gaze throughout a society.
>
> (Armstrong 1983: 100)

While this might be combined with great refinements in the technology for examining individual bodies, it is a conceptual shift of considerable significance. Since 1948, British medicine has developed a social dimension to its practice. Healthy bodies can only emerge from a healthy society. While there are, clearly, still freebooting segments of the profession, its leadership, whether in the BMA, the Royal Colleges, the GMC or the Department of Health, has recognised that their constituents' interests are best served by a 'medicine of the social'. From another perspective, however, one could see this as a reflection of the political sponsorship of the social in the bipartisan collectivist politics of the same period (Armstrong 1983: 40). Social medicine has emerged in a transaction between the profession and its environment.

The argument, then, is that social medicine is an aspect of the governmentality that produced the welfare state. As such, it articulated some of the core values of that regime. These, however, marked less of a discontinuity with the past than might otherwise have been anticipated. As Strong (1979b: 183–225) has noted, the medical transactions of state medicine were essentially a nationalisation of bourgeois practice. In this respect, they were the local embodiment of the compromise between professional interests and the labour–bureaucrat coalition that shaped the NHS in 1948 (Webster 1990). The result was to perpetuate many inefficiencies and inequities and to create many opportunities for professional and corporate gain. The existing organisational cultures were also left in place (Dingwall 1979). While this removed the stigma of charity from large areas of service to the poor[8], it did not establish the service as an entitlement. It became a non-market transaction in which a benevolent and paternalist profession was funded by the State to care for those without other resources. The persistence of these elements did much to make the service acceptable to traditional conservatives who could accept the idea of a collective obligation towards the less fortunate, particularly those disadvantaged by some random natural event. It was a restatement of the values of *Gemeinschaft*, of the interdependency of human beings in local communities and of the responsibilities of the more favoured to protect those afflicted through the vulnerability of the human organism to contingent environmental occurrences. Social medicine sought to embrace these groups, to articulate values of community and to draw everyone into membership, without fundamentally changing the existing structures of social relations.

Medicalisation, then, may be better understood less as a professional project than as one aspect of the governmentality of social democracy where 'the imperfections of the market are . . . tempered by measures of social reform based on the values of an enlightened bourgeoisie' (Dingwall 1979: 17). Social democracy in practice did not elaborate a theory of citizenship to which the values of medicine and other welfare services would be subordinated. The limitations of this approach were spelled out by a number of critics in the late 1960s and 1970s, of whom the best known is probably Ivan Illich (1975, 1977). Although part of Illich's critique deals with the problems of clinical iatrogenesis, disorders resulting from unintended physical outcomes of medical intervention, his primary targets are the power of the medical profession within the social structure and the cultural effects of encouraging dependency rather than self-reliance. Medicine was merely one site for Illich's pursuit of his general critique of modern society from the perspective of a libertarian anarchist.

That society which can reduce professional intervention to the minimum will provide the best conditions for health. The greater the potential for autonomous adaptation to self, to others and to the environment, the less management of adaptation will be needed or tolerated. . . . Healthy people need no bureaucratic interference to mate, give birth, share the human condition and die. . . . Man's (*sic*) consciously lived fragility, individuality and relatedness make the experience of pain, sickness and death an integral part of his life. The ability to cope with this trio autonomously is fundamental to his health. As he becomes dependent on the management of his intimacy, he renounces his autonomy and his health *must* decline.

(Illich 1975: 169, original emphasis)

Illich's words were the harbingers of a major reappraisal of the values that had created societies in which medicalisation could progress. These calls for deprofessionalisation ushered in a very different model of human nature and social organisation, where the diffuse bonds of community gave way to the more calculating alliances of autonomous individuals. Although Illich often held out a vision of community, it was a stunted growth beside his celebration of personal autonomy. Human relations were founded on the rights of those entering into them and became specific agreements around narrow purposes. Although Illich would not necessarily have endorsed the consequence, they prepared the ground for the introduction of a mode of governmentality more congenial to the colonial aspirations of law.

Law casts human beings as self-sufficient individuals, intentional actors and guardians of their own interests. The sanctions attendant on a wrong decision, in commerce, domestic relations or interpersonal conduct, are the incentives to behave well.

The individualism embodied in modern law stresses above all that individuals are the makers of their own destiny. . . . Thus, in its purest form, it takes no account of social or cultural factors that may remove the possibility of choice from individual actors, or severely limit the choices open to them, or determine the way these choices are interpreted.

(Cotterell 1992: 119)

Law is associated with one pole of the classic sociological dichotomies within which modernity is defined: *Gemeinschaft/Gesellschaft*; community/ association; status/contract. A modern society is a society formed by law and its impersonal model of relations between people, where traditional societies rested on diffuse ties of mutual obligation and sentiment. The authors of these dichotomies thought they were witnessing a dramatic social change as traditional society gave way to the *laissez-faire* market economy of nineteenth-century Europe. But it is arguable that the contrast was overstated, or perhaps short-lived, that the rise of the welfare state in response to the failures of the market as a basis for social organisation created an environment in which the values of community could be preserved. Only at the point when economic troubles and competition from producers that had yet to test their stability against the limits of the market called the welfare state into question did the values of individualism begin to flourish again. The revolutionary agenda of neo-classical economics had been left incomplete, or betrayed, depending upon which version an author preferred. Law might be summoned as a tool to complete the programme.

As with medicine, it is important to recognise the diversity of law. Law has also discovered the social, and Armstrong's (1983) history of changes in medical thought leading eventually to the invention of a field of social sciences could be paralleled for legal thinking and socio-legal studies. The level of analysis here is symbolic and focuses on the way in which a traditional rhetoric of law has been selected to challenge the post-war language of medicine. As David Hughes and I have pointed out (Hughes and Dingwall 1990), the rhetoric of NHS reorganisation is heavily legalised but the 'contracts' and 'trusts' bear little relationship to any contemporary legal form of the same name. They are better understood as more specific signals to organisation members of the cultural changes expected than the vague formulations of Peters and Waterman (1982), the gurus of the early phases of reorganisation. These are the official values to be adopted by the 'hands-on, value-driven' manager or clinician. In their legal connotation, they emphasise the break with the past traditions of the service. They constitute signs of a change to a culture modelled on classical capitalist enterprise. This is the language within which these terms acquire their meaning.

As stressed earlier, this is not a narrow shift from a cultural form, imperialism, to an economic form, colonialism. It is, rather, a shift from a mode of governmentality which reaches out to embrace the population in a moral community, a holistic vision of a welfare society, as opposed to one which segments individuals into bundles of discrete interests pursued through specific and limited agreements.⁹ Embedded within social medicine's imperialism is a holistic vision of the patient whose life can be made better by the interventions of others. Law's colonialism does not explicitly seek to reach into the hearts and minds of individuals so much as to render them accountable for their breaches of agreements with others or to offer a framework for them to pursue those who have broken commitments. Law does not claim to prescribe the agreements that are to be made. In practice, of course, the programme does aspire to change people's values. Under the real historical conditions of colonialism, it may be possible to trade with indigenous peoples without touching their culture, although even this may be questionable if we think of the effects of introducing a cash economy to a society based on exchange or barter. In the conditions of developed societies with extensive systems of state welfare, colonialism is a challenge to the norms of the population.

In the present context, then, the rhetoric of law is being used to effect a shift in the world of health care towards a narrower conception of the responsibility of the system:

> the modern commercial contract is marked by limited commitment. Terms and conditions are specified closely, and the cost of non-performance is calculated. Furthermore, with some exceptions, the obligation is not necessarily to *fulfill* the agreement, but only to make good losses that may be incurred in case of an unjustified breach.
>
> (Selznick 1992: 479, original emphasis)

Medicine is no longer to be afforded the imperial space to deal with the 'complete physical, mental and social well-being' of the population, as the World Health Organisation charter might have it. It is, rather, to be directed towards the servicing of human bodies under a series of specific agreements between purchaser, provider and consumer, an automobile mechanic's model of medicine, in Silverman's phrase (personal communication to the author). The intervention of law becomes a way to limit the apparently infinite demand for a health care that represents a collective panacea.

THE CHALLENGE FROM LAW

To return to my earlier question: what is the problem to which the litigation crisis is the answer? This argument suggests that it could be viewed as a status protest against colonisation, the subordination of social medicine to individual law. The analysis could be further sustained if we were to consider the remedies proposed in the specific case. A no-fault response to negligence claims is a classic collectivist remedy, a paternalist provision for those in need rather than an acknowledgement of their individual rights to redress. While it deals with the economic needs of patients, it does so on a basis of social goodwill rather than entitlement. The victim of an injury would, of course, still have to satisfy the eligibility criteria: the existence of the scheme, however, would represent the beneficence of medicine and state welfare. The tort system, on the other hand, is the social insurance of a market society. But it would be a mistake to concentrate too narrowly on the specifics of the site. Although there has not been space to argue the case here, the restructuring of medicine forms part of a restructuring of all professions, including the legal profession itself.[10] The inarticulacy of the protest is symptomatic of the entanglement of the professions with the social democratic order whose legitimacy has faded. There is simply no language in which the rhetoric of the market can be engaged.[11] This lack of form, however, should not conceal the substance. The fundamental challenge to medicine is not from law but from the governmentality that favours law as its operative strategy. But we should be reluctant to round up the usual suspects too quickly. The real rise in individual claims against all professions might suggest that the shift in governmentality has followed rather than led a shift to a less deferential and more interest-oriented culture in which the individualist model of law is an obvious resource.

ACKNOWLEDGEMENTS

This paper draws heavily on research conducted over a number of years in collaboration with Paul Fenn with the assistance of Lois Quam and Dymphna Hermans. I am also grateful to Philip Strong for stimulating my interest in a number of the ideas and issues explored in this paper. None of the foregoing, however, should be held responsible for the argument advanced here.

NOTES

1 An important element of the sociology of law is the emphasis which it takes from Weber about the importance of law as a tool for thinking new social and economic forms into existence. Part of Weber's account of the rise of capitalism turns on his analysis of the conditions created by European legal and juridical thought, which is, in some respects, treated as independent of the Protestant Ethic (see Trubek 1972). Capitalism, in turn, creates the conditions for new legal forms to be invented. Much of the legal profession's work is in the role of what Cain (1983) calls *conceptive ideologists*, people who devise the cultural conditions within which actors formulate their projects.
2 It is, in fact, arguable that some aspects of administrative law may also be relevant to private institutions operating in a public fashion. However, this refinement will not be explored here.
3 The law on consent has a number of elements that are not explored here. Surgery can be performed on an unconscious person in an emergency under the defence of *necessity*, that had this person been conscious he or she would have given consent to a life-saving intervention. Equally, consent is not always a defence: fights outside a boxing ring, even by mutual agreement, can involve assault and battery, as can consensual sado-masochistic sexual relations.
4 Dewees *et al.* (1991) give a rate of 13.0 claims filed per 100 doctors in 1988 based on data published by the St Paul Fire and Marine Insurance Company, the largest commercial insurer of US physicians. Claim rates are known to have declined since then although later figures are not available in this form. It is not entirely clear that the St Paul definition of a new claim coincides exactly with ours nor how representative St Paul policy holders are of US doctors. They certainly relate to *all* doctors while our data are restricted to *hospital* doctors.
5 In fact the percentage of gross medical incomes spent on liability insurance is fairly modest: around 5–10 per cent in the late 1980s (Dingwall *et al.* 1991:

17–18), since when premium rates have actually tended to fall relative to inflation (Quam *et al.* 1990).

6   The publishing history of Spencer's work is complicated and specific citations will not be given here. However, the arguments draw mainly on material from *Principles of Sociology.*

7   At another level, of course, it should also remind us of the perils of treating either profession as homogeneous. Each profession faces the same problems of achieving a sufficient measure of unity for everyday activity to continue. This is an important *caveat* because a theoretical paper must necessarily deal with general tendencies and directions rather than specific events. It is always possible to produce contrary examples but the real question is whether the broad sweep is correct.

8   This spirit still persists in some areas, especially casualty departments dealing with vagrant or other low-status patients seeking primary care (Murray and Dingwall 1983).

9   This is not, of course, to argue that either is an entirely satisfactory social theory. See, for example, Selznick (1992) for a helpful discussion of the problems each raises.

10   The legal profession has been a particular target in the loss of its conveyancing monopoly (Administration of Justice Act, 1985; Building Societies Act, 1986) and the attempts to create a more competitive environment within the profession and between lawyers and others in the Green and White Papers of 1989 (Lord Chancellors Department 1989a, 1989b) and the consequent legislation, the Courts and Legal Services Act, 1990. One might also mention the Warne Committee's recommendations for the deregulation of architects, which have been accepted as a basis for legislation (Department of the Environment 1993).

11   As the editors have commented, this is, of course, a tendentious suggestion to throw out in a concluding paragraph. A full discussion would be the subject of another paper, if not a book. However, what is being referred to here is the collapse in the legitimacy of the traditional vocabularies of European socialism. Some of this reflects their appropriation by advocates of the market, which is cast as a more powerful engine for delivering human freedom and social justice than any interventionist state bureaucracy. Some reflects the spin-off from a generation of economic crisis, where social concern is seen as handicapping the serious challenge of economic competitiveness. Some reflects the havoc wrought on Marxism as an intellectual force by the collapse of state socialism in Eastern Europe. While it is almost certainly wrong to accept the Francis Fukuyama thesis, in *The End of History* (1992), that the class struggle is over and capitalism has won – remember Daniel Bell (1965) proclaiming *The End of Ideology* on the eve of the launch of the New Left in the 1960s – it is hard to discern any analysis of comparable power on the contemporary intellectual or political scene.

REFERENCES

Allsop, J. and May, A. (1986) *The Emperor's New Clothes: Family Practitioner Committees in the 1980s*, London: King's Fund.

Armstrong, D. (1983) *The Political Anatomy of the Body*, Cambridge: Cambridge University Press.

Becker, H.S. (1963) *Outsiders: Studies in the Sociology of Deviance*, New York: Free Press.

Bell, D. (1965) *The End of Ideology: On the Exhaustion of Political Ideas in the Fifties*, revised edn, New York: Free Press (first edn 1960).

British Medical Association (1983) *Report of the Working Party on No-Fault Compensation for Medical Injury*, London: British Medical Association.

—— (1991) *Report of the Working Party on No-Fault Compensation*, London: British Medical Association.

Burchell, G., Gordon, C. and Miller, P. (1991) *The Foucault Effect: Studies in Governmentality*, London: Harvester Wheatsheaf.

Cain, M. (1983) 'The general practice lawyer and the client: towards a radical conception', in Dingwall, R. and Lewis, P. (eds) *The Sociology of the Professions*, London: Macmillan.

Chamberlain, G.V.P., Orr, C.J.B. and Sharp, F. (eds) (1985) *Litigation in Obstetrics and Gynaecology: Proceedings of the 14th Study Group*, London: Royal College of Obstetricians and Gynaecologists.

Cohen, S. (1973) *Folk Devils and Moral Panics*, London: Paladin.

Cotterell, R. (1992) *The Sociology of Law*, second edn, London: Butterworths.

Department of the Environment (1993) *Review of the Architects (Registration) Acts 1931–1969 (Chair E.J.D. Warne)*, London: HMSO.

Dewees, D.N., Trebilcock, M.J. and Coyte, P.C. (1991) 'The medical malpractice crisis: a comparative empirical perspective', *Law and Contemporary Problems*, 54 (1): 217–51.

Dingwall, R. (1979) 'Inequality and the National Health Service', in Atkinson, P., Dingwall, R. and Murcott, A. (eds) *Prospects for the National Health*, London: Croom Helm.

Dingwall, R. and Fenn, P. (eds) (1992) *Quality and Regulation in Health Care*, London: Routledge.

—— (in press) 'Is NHS indemnity working and is there a better way?' *British Journal of Anaesthesia*.

Dingwall, R., Fenn, P. and Quam, L. (1991) *Medical Negligence: A Review and Bibliography*, Oxford: Centre for Socio-Legal Studies.

Fenn, P. and Dingwall, R. (1990) 'The problems of crown indemnity', in Gretton, J. (ed.) *Health Care UK 1989*, Birmingham: Policy Journals.

Foucault, M. (1979) *The History of Sexuality: vol. I. An Introduction*, London: Allen Lane.

Fukuyama, F. (1992) *The End of History and the Last Man*, London: Hamish Hamilton.

Gusfield, J. (1986) *Symbolic Crusade: American Politics and the Temperance Movement*, second edn, Urbana: University of Illinois Press (first published 1963).

Ham, C., Dingwall, R., Fenn, P. and Harris, D. (1988) *Medical Negligence: Compensation and Accountability*, London/Oxford: King's Fund/Centre for Socio-Legal Studies.

Hughes, D. and Dingwall, R. (1990) 'Sir Henry Maine, Joseph Stalin and the Reorganisation of the National Health Service', *Journal of Social Welfare Law*: 296–309.

Illich, I. (1975) *Medical Nemesis*, London: Calder & Boyars.

—— (1977) *The Limits to Medicine*, Harmondsworth: Penguin.

Kennedy, I. (1981) *The Unmasking of Medicine*, London: Allen & Unwin.

Klein, R. (1973) *Complaints Against Doctors*, London: Charles Knight.

Lord Chancellors Department (1989a) *The Work and Organisation of the Legal Profession* (Cm 571), London: HMSO.

—— (1989b) *Legal Services: A Framework for the Future* (Cm 740), London: HMSO.

Mann, R.D. and Havard, J. (1989) *No Fault Compensation in Medicine: The Proceedings of a Joint Meeting of the Royal Society of Medicine and the British Medical Association held at 1 Wimpole Street London W1M 8AE on 12–13 January 1989*, London: Royal Society of Medicine.

Mulcahy, L. and Lloyd-Bostock, S. (1992) 'Complaining: what's the use', in Dingwall, R. and Fenn, P. (eds) *Quality and Regulation in Health Care: International Experiences*, London: Routledge.

Murray, T. and Dingwall, R. (1983) 'Categorization in accident departments: "good" patients, "bad" patients and "children"', *Sociology of Health and Illness*, 5: 127–48.

Parsons, T. (1952) *The Social System*, London: Routledge & Kegan Paul.

Peters, T. and Waterman, R.H. (1982) *In Search of Excellence*, New York: Harper & Row.

Quam, L., Fenn, P. and Dingwall, R. (1990) 'Malpractice liability in the US: panic over?', *British Medical Journal*, 301: 949–50.

Royal College of Physicians (1990) *Compensation for Adverse Consequences of Medical Intervention*, London: Royal College of Physicians of London.

Selznick, P. (1992) *The Moral Commonwealth: Social Theory and the Promise of Community*, Berkeley: University of California Press.

Stacey, M. (1992) *Regulating British Medicine: The General Medical Council*, Chichester: John Wiley.

Strong, P.M. (1979a) 'Sociological imperialism and the profession of medicine', *Social Science and Medicine*, 13A: 199–215.

—— (1979b) *The Ceremonial Order of the Clinic*, London: Routledge & Kegan Paul.

—— (1984) 'Viewpoint: the academic encirclement of medicine', *Sociology of Health and Illness*, 6: 339–58.

Trubek, D. (1972) 'Max Weber on law and the rise of capitalism', *Wisconsin Law Journal*, 1972: 720–53.

Turner, J.H. (1985) *Herbert Spencer: A Renewed Appreciation*, Newbury Park: Sage.

Webster, C. (1990) 'Conflict and consensus: explaining the British health service', *Twentieth Century British History*, 1: 115–51.

Wootton, B. (1959) *Social Science and Social Pathology*, London: Allen & Unwin.

4 Television and medicine

Medical dominance or trial by media?

Michael Bury and Jonathan Gabe

INTRODUCTION

In the field of health and medicine there have been surprisingly few attempts to assess the importance of the media, outside of work in health education. In this latter, more applied, field there have been numerous studies of the impact (or lack of impact) of media on specific health campaigns, notably in recent years in HIV/AIDS (Wellings and McVey 1990), or in health promotion areas such as drugs, tobacco, alcohol and diet (Davies 1988; Flay and Burton 1990). However, characteristic of these studies is their lack of emphasis on the sociology of the mass media and especially of television. Though the role of the media in health campaigns is regularly assessed, the representation of health and medicine in the media is not.

Following earlier attempts to tackle some of these issues with respect to one particular area of health care, namely the controversy surrounding the use of benzodiazepine tranquillisers (Gabe and Bury 1988; Bury and Gabe 1990) we attempt, in this chapter, to begin to address the broader issue of how far the media, specifically television, currently represent a more challenging view of medicine, both in terms of the latter's knowledge base and of its professional practice. We also address the question of how health and medicine have come to play a large part in media programming.

In approaching the issue, we begin, however, with an initial sense of paradox. On the one hand there is a common view, sometimes expressed in academic circles, that medicine holds a dominant position in media coverage of health, specifically its view of disease and illness and its own self-image as a profession (McLaughlin 1975; Signorelli 1990; Turow and Coe 1985; Turow 1989). On the other hand, our work on tranquilliser dependence has often uncovered a strong sense of 'trial by media' amongst clinicians and medical scientists working in controversial areas. In order to explore these 'contours' of medicine and the media, the chapter proceeds by three main stages.

First, we outline the argument that medicine has come to dominate media coverage of health and illness. The challenges that have occurred, both to medicine's knowledge base and to its power as a profession, are seen as having been largely absorbed and therefore neutralised. The exposition we examine here is of one of the few attempts to provide a broad (and historical) analysis of medicine and the media, namely that of Anne Karpf's book *Doctoring the Media* (Karpf 1988a) (see Turow (1989) for an American analysis).

Second, we go on to outline what we regard as some of the problems with this approach. In particular, we examine the difficulties in testing, empirically, the assumptions behind the analysis offered by Karpf and the questions they raise. Third, we attempt to provide the beginning of such an empirical analysis, by taking three examples of recent British television programmes to illustrate three key formats through which television portrays medicine: the exposé format, the documentary and the drama. Through an examination of the form and content of these programmes we attempt to illustrate our argument that the medium, though falling short of putting medicine regularly on trial, now represents health and medicine in a more challenging light than it once did.

MEDICAL DOMINANCE AND THE MEDIA

Karpf's book *Doctoring the Media* (1988a) traces the links between medicine and the media in a historical context. Although somewhat polemical in tone, it draws on sociological insights to make some of its main claims. For present purposes, we should like to draw out two main strands of Karpf's analysis of media coverage of health and medicine and the changing relationship between them. First, Karpf describes in some detail the shifting interconnections between medicine and the media in Britain between two periods, the 1930s and 1940s, and the 1950s and 1960s. The latter period, she maintains, constitutes the heyday of medical dominance of the media. Second, Karpf goes on to assess the changing relationships between medicine and the media in the 1970s and 1980s which appear to contradict this picture, but which, Karpf argues, largely extend it. In the rest of this section we outline these two points in a little more detail.

Karpf begins by pointing to the very different cultural climate affecting perceptions of health in the early period of media development in Britain. During the years immediately before the Second World War, according to Karpf, a tension existed between two main preoccupations, namely austerity and poverty. In health terms, this tension could be seen in the official emphasis on an individualistic approach to staying healthy, and in the public health approach to links between poor health and poverty.

Nutrition, and maternal and infant health, were often the focus of fierce debates about these issues. Health rather than medicine therefore dominated media coverage, especially that of radio. In the main, Karpf argues, this meant an emphasis on individualistic health prevention programmes and coverage, though social issues did force themselves on to the agenda. Curative medicine was rarely touched on, partly because of its limited effectiveness and partly because the idea of broadcasting 'intimate matters' was anathema to radio and film producers.

Karpf also argues that the medical profession was reluctant to see either the media or the public meddle in what it took to be its province. Broadcasting to an 'undifferentiated audience' would only distress the frail and neurotic; hypochondria might result (Karpf 1988a: 35). The wartime 'radio doctor', Charles Hill, gave talks on such topics as how to eat and how to cook. Such advice on 'positive health' fitted in well with state control of the media's agenda and its contribution to the war effort (Karpf 1988a: 43–8).

In the 1950s and 1960s, however, a major shift in media coverage of health and medicine took place. State control of the media shifted from direct to indirect control, as institutions such as the British Broadcasting Corporation (BBC) and then Independent Television (ITV) became more influential, and as producers developed a stronger sense of the power of the media. The medical profession also altered its position, partly to meet this growing challenge, from one of reluctant involvement to one of enthusiasm and collaboration. The founding and early development of the National Health Service (NHS) had also helped in the medical profession's development of a new-found confidence, especially in the hospital sector. Technological developments and curative medicine came to occupy much greater prominence on the public policy agenda, and thence in the media. As Karpf points out, the most obvious example of this was to be found in surgery, especially transplant surgery.

Programmes such as the 'radio doctor' were soon to be seen as oldfashioned, as television opened up a whole range of possibilities to present matters medical. The expression in health terms of a language of privation and a 'collective fate' gave way to new enthusiasms for curative medicine, with an emphasis on future-oriented research. Now British television programmes, such as the BBC's *Your Life In Their Hands*, which started in 1958, provided opportunities for the scientific and technological perspective to gain ascendancy in health-related coverage. Not only that, but the medical profession's involvement also 'marked the beginning of television's infatuation with the prestigious London teaching hospitals' (Karpf 1988a: 53). The medical profession now moved centre stage to dominate the presentation of health and medicine in the media.

As leading figures within the medical profession opened up both bodies and hospitals to the public view, so television production techniques also played a part in accelerating the pace of change towards medical dominance. According to Karpf, earlier coverage had essentially been cast within the format of the illustrated lecture. Now the possibilities for drama and excitement, let alone entertainment, inherent in the hospital and medical worlds, could be explored to the full. Medical dramas, soap operas, 'hospital watch' programmes and many others proliferated.

Despite the growth of media power, the result of this interplay between a changing profession and a changing media world, Karpf maintains, brought about a period of medical dominance over the public's perceptions of both health and medicine. Earlier references to social and environmental aspects of health now almost disappeared as 'technophoria' – a strong belief in the technical role of medicine – took over. The representation of health and medicine as essentially technical issues effectively reinforced the individualistic approach to health, offering a 'dominant ideology' suggesting that health and medicine were essentially about pharmaceutical and technical progress. In drama, 'telegenic' doctors took over from the paternalistic image of the radio doctor. Under the influence of American television's preoccupation with medical dramas (Turow 1989), fictional Dr Kildare replaced the real-life Charles Hill in the public's affection.

However, Karpf's account does not end there. She notes that the dynamic unleashed in the immediate post-war decades has not simply led to a continuing story of the medical profession's open dominance of media coverage. During the last twenty years another wave of change and innovation has occurred in the media. Throughout the 1970s and 1980s a whole new set of possibilities has developed, associated with the rise of consumerism and the patient's view. In this period public attitudes towards science and technology have also become more sceptical, and the dominant position of the doctor seems to have waned.

This shift in emphasis has been marked by the appearance in media coverage of voices not usually heard in public discussions of health, those of patients or client groups themselves. Women, the disabled, and others have all made attempts, successful at times, to gain access to the media to put forward views on health which are often critical of the dominant medical approach. Consumerist programmes counteract the celebration of medical technology, and ethical issues cast doubt on the ever-expanding remit of hospital medicine. In a more pluralistic cultural environment new voices are heard and new ways of portraying medicine and health care emerge. Even the heroic and glamorous 'good doctor' image gives way to a more realistic portrayal in dramas and soap operas.

For Karpf, however, these recent changes are more apparent than real. Consumerism, though a challenge to medicine, has also meant that 'medicine has simply redrawn what it can do' (1988a: 71). Indeed, 'ideologically correct' programmes on the health promotion front seem to reinforce rather than challenge dominant ideas. The proliferation of voices does not, according to Karpf, alter fundamentally 'dominant beliefs' about medicine. Alternative medicine, for example, is much discussed, but is essentially incorporated without challenging orthodox approaches (Karpf 1988a: 179). The media, even in their most recent mode, 'not only shape the dominant beliefs about medicine, they help strengthen them' (Karpf 1988a: 132).

Because of limited feedback with audiences, programme makers are also seen to be incapable of fundamentally sustaining a critical view of medicine. Their preoccupation with the production of ideas, images and words seems to overshadow the content of which they speak. In turn, audiences come to believe that such images 'are all' (Karpf 1988a: 235). The changes in media coverage over the last twenty years are thus seen as having gone as far as they can in challenging the medical profession's power. Without a more fundamental shift in journalistic values and institutional change, Karpf argues, consumerist approaches to health actually reinforce the marginal status of many social groups and leave the medical profession largely untouched. Medicine and the media may no longer collude to tell us what to think, but they still set the health agenda.

Though a more complex picture of medicine and the media is painted by Karpf in discussing these changes, she concludes on a pessimistic note. She contends that the medical approach will 'continue to amaze and spellbind us', and that consumerism and 'look after yourself' television programmes will leave the major causes and realities of health and health disorders behind, while bringing forward ever more serried ranks of professionals, counsellors and therapists to advise us. Though medicine may feel under pressure from these changes, Karpf suggests that it need not worry: its dominance remains.

ANALYSING MEDICINE AND TELEVISION

We hope, through this brief resumé, to have conveyed the value of Karpf's historical analysis in clearing the way for a critical approach to medicine and the media. However, Karpf's argument relies, we contend, on two kinds of widely accepted and 'received' assumptions to sustain its case, especially concerning the present. In the first place, though the media are treated sympathetically at times, Karpf relies on many of the anti-media sentiments prevalent in social commentary, inside and outside academic circles, and, indeed, within media circles themselves. Most important among these is the idea that the media necessarily trivialise serious social issues and create amusement and entertainment out of personal and social tragedy. Karpf's view of the tendency of television to 'amaze and spellbind' has echoes, for example, of Neil Postman's (1986) *Amusing Ourselves to Death*, which offers a broadside against the supposed damaging effects of television on politics and public life. A more sustained critique can also be found of the limits and constraints placed on television coverage of events such as the Falklands and Gulf Wars in Eldridge (1993). Karpf's argument, in stressing the effects of the media in depoliticising and limiting the definitions of health, echoes these approaches to the media.

Second, the linked idea of the powerful, if not dominant, role of the medical profession in public life and the media draws heavily on the polemical arguments of social critics of medicine such as Illich (1975, 1977) and Kennedy (1981), and in medical sociology on the sustained case made by Eliot Freidson (1970) in *Profession of Medicine*. Freidson's exposition of the role of medical dominance over definitions of health and illness provides the basis for a critique of the power of medicine to deflect attention from the wider social causes of ill health and the alternative ways that might be fashioned to tackle them. Thus, in drawing on this approach as well as on critical views of the media, the negative aspects of both media and medical dominance reinforce one another in the analysis.

Important though this line of argument undoubtedly is, we wish to argue that a more systematic empirical check on its validity is necessary if the social and cultural changes of the last ten to fifteen years are to be adequately evaluated. Though Karpf refers to changes in current television programmes in her analysis, these tend to be slotted into her existing framework, rather than used to test it. This leaves certain questions unanswered.

For example, though Karpf argues that 'the box continues to be doctored' (1988a: 71) the question arises as to whether current television coverage actually supports a dominant medical authority or not. Following on from this, it might be asked how far the portrayal of medical treatments reflects an unchanging 'technophoria'. Furthermore, though Karpf notes the growing range and complexity of television coverage of health, the question of the impact of different programme formats remains largely unexamined. The question here is, how far do these formats provide varying opportunities to challenge medical dominance? Finally, if television coverage in general is prone to trivialise serious issues of health and medicine, do programmes within different formats really demonstrate this?

In order to examine these questions an approach needs to be developed based on an analysis of the form and content of media products and the way they are received. For, as Fiske and Hartley maintain, 'the starting point of any study of television must be with what is actually there on the screen' (1978: 21). We recognise, however, that developing a more evaluative analysis of this kind poses many difficulties, in terms of method as well as in interpretation. This is especially the case with television, which, though it now plays the major role in media coverage of health and medicine, remains notoriously difficult to assess. Yet, without such a reconsideration there is a danger that putative effects are asserted on the basis of limited evidence. We are then either left to agree with the argument that the media are 'doctored', or adopt an alternative position that the media largely reflect wider social forces (see, for example, Burns (1977) for an example of this approach).

Media sociology has, however, begun to approach the multifaceted aspects of television products and their assimilation, in a more systematic fashion. Thompson (1988, 1990), for example, has identified three dimensions to analysing mass media: the historical and institutional context within which media products are made; the construction of media messages in terms of narrative and myth; and the ways in which these messages are received and appropriated by different audiences. Here we focus on the construction process and the ways in which particular programme formats have shaped the character of what is produced on television. In so doing we shall be employing a qualitative content analysis which gives priority to a formal or discursive approach to texts in an attempt to bring out the whole range of possible meanings, including those which are 'hidden' (Thompson 1988; Larsen 1991).

We shall be focusing on three kinds of programme format which we consider central to contemporary television coverage of medicine, and which allow for a closer examination of the relationship between television and medical agenda setting. Though we select just one example of each of these formats in order to provide detail of the form and content involved, we contend that they represent a growing trend in television coverage. These are: (1) the exposé format, exemplified in our analysis by the populist ITV programme *The Cook Report*; (2) the documentary format, illustrated by a programme from a recent Channel Four series, *Operation Hospital*, dealing with the current situation in a London teaching hospital; and (3) the drama format, represented here by the popular BBC1 programme *Casualty*. We now provide an account of each of these examples.

The Cook Report

The programme from this series with which we are concerned focused on the issue of tranquilliser dependence and was transmitted in May 1988, in its weekly half-hour Tuesday evening slot, with an audience of 6 million viewers. The exposé format sets out to provide a challenge to powerful interests in an attempt to reveal alleged corruption or malpractice. Our analysis of the content of the programme on tranquilliser dependence examines how far this occurs. It provides a test case, not least because it explores a form of medical technology which has frequently been used in hospital and primary care settings in the management of anxiety and related psychological disorders.

The programme begins with a scene-setting comment from a lawyer to the effect that the ongoing litigation over benzodiazepine tranquillisers, including lorazepam (Ativan) – the product with which Cook is particularly concerned – looks like dwarfing previous cases concerning pharmaceutical products. Viewers are then confronted with pictures of Ativan being manufactured *en masse*, passing along conveyor belts, being poured through a funnel, wrapped in foil and packed in boxes, while being told that an estimated quarter of a million people in Britain are 'addicted' to the drug. Given the apparent size of the problem the question is posed, 'who is to blame'? The manufacturers, Wyeth, doctors, or both?

The programme attempts to answer this question by, in the first instance, presenting the story of one long-term Ativan user's attempt to stop taking the medication. Ada, who has been using Ativan for more than a decade, having first been prescribed it following the death of her first husband, announces to the camera that she is prepared to be videoed by her second husband undergoing withdrawal because 'I'd like everyone to know what the withdrawal symptoms are' and 'I'd like something done about it'. Edited 'highlights' of her experience over the next four days are presented, with Roger Cook providing the voice-over, interspersed on no less than seven occasions with images of tablets showering down from the top of the screen in a colourful cascade. As time goes by, revealed by a counter logging the hours at the bottom of the screen, Ada is shown experiencing mounting distress, complaining of numbness and shaking all over. The experience is underscored by the fear and apprehension she shows when asked by Roger Cook to step outside her house. On the fourth day, in a state of near panic, she starts taking the tablets again. Finally, later in the programme, she is seen as an in-patient in a London hospital, undergoing a two-week planned withdrawal programme, and facing the prospect of a further two years' struggle to rid herself of her dependence at home.

Having established the consequences of dependence for individual users Roger Cook undertakes a relentless pursuit of those who are deemed responsible. First and foremost this means the drug company Wyeth. The company provides an easy target for Cook given the pharmaceutical industry's long-standing role in contemporary society as a potent symbol of indefensible profit making. Here the argument against Wyeth is that it failed to warn doctors (and patients) about Ativan's 'addictive and serious side effects' when first marketed, despite research evidence of withdrawal symptoms when stopped abruptly, and preferred to 'put profits before patients' by continuing to sell the drug despite mounting evidence from 'respected sources' about the severe withdrawal symptoms experienced at high and low dose. Moreover, the chairman of Wyeth's refusal to grant an interview with Cook presents a perfect opportunity for him to confront the director in a public setting – in the event on a golf course – and ask him on behalf of 'sufferers like Ada' why the company continues to market a drug which is 'known to be addictive'. Footage is then shown of Cook being abused, threatened and kicked by the chairman before being struck with a golf club.

More importantly, Cook also turns the spotlight on the medical profession and its involvement in creating Ativan 'addicts'. Viewers witness Roger Cook 'doorstepping' two general practitioners (GPs) outside their surgeries on behalf of their patients. In the first case Ada's doctor is confronted by the reporter carrying a bag of the tablets, amounting to six years' supply, which Ada has hoarded having been prescribed them on a repeat basis without apparently being seen in person. The doctor, looking shaken, at first denies that she is currently prescribing Ativan to any of her patients. Then she changes tack and argues that she is 'not the only one' and that she had warned Ada 'so many times' about the risks of dependence and had tried to wean her off them. Cook retorts that according to Ada she had been prescribed the tablets continuously until her lawyer had threatened legal action, at which point her supply had been halted abruptly. Finally, to underline his point, Cook pours Ada's stash of tablets on the driveway, next to the doctor, adding for good measure that this was hardly evidence of responsible prescribing.

This theme is developed more generally by reproducing a comment from an article in the magazine *The General Practitioner* which suggests that the repeat prescribing of Ativan is 'unjustified and legally dangerous'. Moreover, the results of the programme's survey of 500 'Ativan addicts' suggests that the practice is widespread. Eighty-eight per cent of these 'addicts' indicated that they had received repeat prescriptions on a long-term basis without a consultation with their doctor.

Next, one of the respondents in this survey, Anne Broomfield, is interviewed briefly about her doctor's prescribing practices before he, too, is doorstepped outside his surgery. Again the doctor appears taken aback and tries to defend himself, claiming that he has done his best to try to help the patient withdraw. Cook replies that he should have done better and actually 'got her off' the tablets and alleges that the GP had recently advised her to accept her lot and keep taking them. As a final twist to this story Cook announces to viewers that the doctor had subsequently telephoned Anne Broomfield and threatened to stop prescribing Ativan to her unless the filmed interview was abandoned. To underline the consequences for the patient she is shown telling Cook that she is 'terrified' about being reinterviewed and that stopping the drug represents a 'real threat' to her well-being.

Like the manufacturers, Wyeth, the doctors are thus also presented as culpable. They are castigated for having failed to act responsibly or to have done their best for their patients and as willing to use their power to withdraw the supply of a prescribed drug on which their patients depended in an attempt to silence their criticisms.

What are the implications of this analysis for the argument concerning medical dominance and 'technophoria'? It seems difficult, in watching and examining such a programme, to continue to maintain that there has been no significant change in the media coverage of medicine. The exposé format clearly provides opportunities to challenge medical power which need to be acknowledged and analysed. As the representative of innocent and powerless patients, the reporter in the exposé format is bestowed with the moral authority to challenge, in this case, medical interests, identify malpractice and bring individual doctors to book. In so doing patients are brought centre-stage, challenging the doctors' version of events and participating in the construction of their account of their experiences. Moreover, by presenting a critical assessment of the risks in taking Ativan, the programme explicitly cuts across a 'technophoric' view of medical treatment.

At the same time, the analysis does provide some support for other aspects of the 'doctoring the box' position. By focusing almost exclusively on individual patients' problems withdrawing from Ativan, it could be argued that little attention is given to the social causes or context of use and to the gender imbalance amongst long-term users. As such, it could substantiate the claim that the media tend to individualise the experience of health and illness. Furthermore, by focusing on individual doctors it could be said that the exposé format highlights the existence of a few 'bad apples' without questioning the general structures that make medical dominance possible.

Operation Hospital

This series, comprising six weekly programmes, was transmitted on Channel Four in prime time on Tuesday evenings during January and February 1993, in front of an audience of approximately 1.4 million people. Here we review the first thirty-minute programme as an illustration of the documentary format. It was watched by the highest audience of the series, 1.9 million.

Documentaries treat 'particular knowledge and particular worlds – the scientific, aesthetic or political . . . in an attempt to broaden horizons of everyday culture' (Silverstone 1981: 83). They can comprise single films or, as in the current case, a series. One of the main differences between the documentary and the exposé concerns the role of the presenter. Instead of there being a clearly identified reporter such as Roger Cook, the documentary presenter takes on the role of a more 'heavyweight' journalist who is heard asking searching questions but is rarely seen. The drama and narrative element of the exposé are also played down in the documentary, in favour of a more factual report or record of social interest or concern which predominantly appeals to the intellect (Silverstone 1981: 82).

This particular documentary, dealing as it does with the portrayal of events over an extended period of time in a central London teaching hospital, King's College, offers a particularly useful opportunity to examine the relationship between the media and powerful medical interests. The documentary format of the programme also provides an opportunity to focus on current policy concerns and highlight their consequences for everyday practice. The purported tendency of the media to trivialise such issues can therefore be examined.

The first episode of *Operation Hospital* begins with pictures of night security staff on their hospital rounds on New Year's Eve 1991 with the presenter, off camera, stating that 'over the next twelve months this great hospital will be subject to a ruthless efficiency drive with everyone affected as failings are uncovered'. Examples of such failings are then catalogued briefly, ranging from dirt and decay to the unequal distribution of intensive care beds between general medicine, catering for local need, and the specialist departments with their international reputations to maintain.

As is usual in television documentaries, the opening sequence sets the scene for what is to follow. It soon becomes clear that the focus of this programme and of the series is on managers rather than doctors (or other health care workers) and, in particular, on the recently appointed Chief Executive, Derek Smith, who is introduced as the 'new man who says he will change everything'. To underline the point the caption 'Chief Executive' is then flashed on the screen before viewers are shown Smith driving to work in a suitably high-powered sports car. He is described as one of a new generation of 'hospital chiefs' who has been given 'more power by Government reforms than their predecessors ever dreamt of'. Interviewed in his office, Smith says he was attracted to King's because of its 'world-beating medicine', but on arrival was 'shocked by the hospital's physical condition' and by the 'attitude of the work force' and, in particular, by the absence of any clear objectives about the hospital as a whole.

This issue and the other problems identified in the opening sequence then become organised for the purpose of the programme under three headings: 'Management', 'Money' and 'Doctors', with a caption announcing each one in turn to viewers. For Derek Smith the management problem involves getting the right managers in the right place and performing to their maximum. To achieve this he has called in an outside management consultant to undertake an organisational audit and suggest ways of improving efficiency. It is intended that managers will be given 3,000 standards to meet and a deadline by which to meet them. Such a change is presented as moving from an oral to a written culture, with managers being required for the first time to think systematically about their work.

In the meantime the existing, informal way of doing things is presented as having its 'normal effect'. Patients are seen sitting in cramped conditions in the out-patients' department waiting for a doctor who has inexplicably failed to turn up, a fruitless search for a patient's notes is shown, and a Professor of Medicine describes the embarrassment of having to explain to patients that their notes are missing. A coronary bypass operation is shown being successfully completed despite the failure of a vital piece of equipment, and a nurse is filmed cleaning up spilt blood in a corridor because cleaners have not been trained to do so. All these problems are used to underline the argument for decisive management in the hospital.

The next segment of the programme is devoted to money matters, listing a series of possible savings in a context of difficult choices and increasing competition between King's and other hospitals to provide services for purchasing health authorities. A balance sheet is presented listing savings if fewer beds are used, if the contract for an expensive drug is renegotiated, if private telephone calls are billed and laundry jobs frozen. According to the Chief Executive, there is 'a direct linear relationship between lowering costs and increasing quality'. However, the programme suggests that these decisions also relate to spending priorities and to the outcome of King's College's bids for contracts, in the light of increasing competition from other hospitals for specialist services in the new health market. For instance, a doctor from the Accident and Emergency Department (A and E) is shown complaining about the lack of money for beds for 'the lady round the corner' while patients needing an emergency liver transplant are flown in at great expense. Likewise, the Professor and Director of Obstetrics and Gynaecology are shown criticising the publicity surrounding the launching of an alternative, 'national' foetal health centre at the rival St Thomas's Hospital.

As well as sorting out the managers and money Derek Smith is also presented as facing another, far more deep-rooted problem – the attitudes and inefficiency of doctors. In the final segment of the programme the Chief Executive's efforts to check the power of the doctors at King's is addressed. It is suggested that the task will be difficult but that the alliance he has built up with consultants who have become clinical directors should help. One of these, Dr John Costello, is said to view the particular problems in the A and E Department as 'largely the fault of doctors', many of whom are 'not interested enough in routine hospital duties' and 'too busy with other things like building their own empire'. Certainly, viewers are left in no doubt that Derek Smith means business when he states that 'where medical staff are not fulfilling their contractual commitment . . . we shall certainly be discussing with them the fact that we discontinue their contractual arrangements with us'. The final comment of the doctor from A and E that 'I'm sure everybody wishes him well', while noting the quick turnover of previous top managers and the scepticism of senior consultants who feel 'they've seen it all before', suggests that Derek Smith will face battles with the medical staff.

What implications does this account have for the medical dominance thesis? First and foremost, it is clear that medical dominance no longer underpins all television coverage of health and illness in the 1990s. The documentary format with its emphasis on 'heavyweight' reportage provides the means to portray the consequences of recent health policy developments and, in particular, the extent to which the enhanced powers of general managers provide an opportunity to challenge medical power. The fact that the programme focuses on a top manager at an elite teaching hospital and treats doctors as just one group alongside other health care workers illustrates a willingness to take this issue seriously. It certainly suggests that the media have significantly changed the way they deal with London teaching hospitals.

Second, such programmes reflect a far more critical analysis of recent developments in the organisation of health care. The focus is now on the experiences of a top manager rather than a leading consultant, on the display of managerial choices, the operation of vested interests and the effects of a market-oriented system. Third, where attention is given to high-technology medicine, this is now portrayed as being constrained by the same financial crisis as the low-status A and E Department. Fourth, the medical profession is presented as deeply divided rather than as homogeneous or dominant. Thus, an A and E specialist is given the opportunity to argue the case for more money for his department, compared with that of more expensive competitors, and critical comments are expressed about colleagues in a rival hospital making grandiose claims about a new foetal health centre which will be in competition with their own. In such a context the image of the doctor as hero, saving lives against the odds, now has to compete with a new image of the doctor as a representative of sectional interests.

Casualty

Our final example takes us from the documentary to the television drama. *Casualty* was first televised in 1986 and has recently been shown on BBC1, in prime time, on Saturday nights (and subsequently repeated later in the year on Friday nights). Watched by an audience of around 15 million it is one of the most popular programmes ever shown on British television. Here we consider the fifty-minute episode, 'Point of principle', which was first screened in December 1992 and repeated in June 1993.

The medical drama has a long history although, as Raymond Williams (1990) has pointed out, it is only in the epoch of the television serial that it has received such attention. As a television format the drama offers, in narrative form, an enacted set of fictional events, usually dominated by a main plot, with sub-plots interwoven to add interest and complexity (Kozloff 1993). Within such a format a realistic narrative develops, appealing to an audience's sense of the 'psychological realism of its characters and their individuality and to the coherence of its specific chain of events' (Fiske 1987: 129).

Underlying this first-order level of meaning, as elsewhere in television, there is a second, deeper level where characters act primarily as ideological hooks for the audience (Fiske 1987: 130). This distinction is particularly useful in analysing medical dramas, as plots and characterisation make strong appeals to the emotions and values surrounding medicine and illness. Typically, in such dramas, doctors have been seen as 'benign, trusty curers' (Karpf 1988a: 183) and medical reality has apparently been frequently trivialised.

The episode with which we are concerned here opens with a man pumping up a bicycle tyre in the back garden while arguing with his wife. It seems that he is unemployed and resents the fact that his wife is working longer hours outside the home to make ends meet. The camera then cuts to Holby City Trust Hospital and a meeting between grey-suited manager Simon Eastman and the A and E consultant, Julian Chapman, in the manager's office. The very tone of the discussion indicates the existence of a major rift between them, with Julian upset about being told that his department has been unsuccessful in its bid for a trauma unit and talking about the danger of 'transferring critically ill patients around the district', and Simon pompously dismissing his concerns as indicative of 'hurt feelings' and stressing the need to 'live in the real world'. From the word go the audience is therefore drawn into the current drama surrounding health policy and its effects. Public and private worlds are simultaneously explored.

Once the scene has been set the main story-line develops, with the consultant finding out from the charge nurse, Charlie, and the nursing sister, Duffy, that they had prior knowledge of the decision not to give Holby the trauma unit. It also becomes clear that management has presented the decision, in part, as a consequence of the consultant having not been supportive of the hospital's bid. The management's reluctance to appoint a replacement registrar is also reinterpreted as being linked with a prior knowledge of the outcome of the bid for the trauma unit.

These events provide the backdrop for the climax which, as Kozloff (1993) remarks, all television narratives require. In this case Julian confronts Simon in the corridor and accuses him of being kept in the dark about the bid, lying about his position and acting without his support. The manager retorts: 'Your support, Julian, is convenient. It is not essential.' Such a clear challenge to Julian's authority has dramatic consequences. Hearing from Charlie that the local press are outside, having got wind of a staffing crisis in A and E, Julian charges out to meet them and decides to 'go public' about the way the department is being managed. He claims that medical opinions about management decisions are being completely disregarded, patient care is deteriorating as a result of a loss of medical posts and the failure to win the bid for the trauma unit will make matters worse. In his view this state of affairs is a direct consequence of management failing to take the needs of A and E seriously, and he goes on:

I want to be a clinician. I want my department to be a centre of excellence. That is not possible when I am fighting a rearguard action against my own manager. And now I believe I am being lied to.

Asked what he is going to do about it he replies, with a final flourish, 'I intend to resign. I have no choice.'

A little later on, after things have (temporarily) calmed down, there follows a final confrontation between Julian and Simon, with the latter telling Julian that he will not be allowed to work out his three months' notice because he has made statements to the press. The consultant, outraged, replies that the manager 'can't run a department without a consultant', that 'it's the politics of this' that excites him and that he (the manager) might as well throw out the patients too for 'cluttering up the corridors' and 'pushing up the budget'. We then see Charlie, the charge nurse, unsuccessfully trying to persuade Julian to reconsider before the consultant delivers his parting shot by confirming to waiting journalists that his departure is a consequence of 'the management [being] against the NHS' rather than as a result of a personality clash. Even so, viewers are left with little doubt about the victor as the camera pans to the villainous Simon, in his upper-floor office, looking down triumphantly on Julian as he drives away in his open-topped car.

We should note here, however briefly, that alongside this dominant theme, sub-plots concerning patients' lives are interwoven. We have already mentioned the case of the unemployed man and his relationship with his wife. This comes to a head when the man has a serious accident which takes him into casualty, revealing a web of events surrounding a previous work colleague, and his wife's current employment as a poorly paid 'chat line' hostess. In addition, 'cases' of a man from a poor housing estate, involved in dog fighting, and a young woman self-injuring in order to escape from a domineering father, are also developed. These examples provide both dramatic, and to some extent stereotypical, images of hospital patients against a background of current social problems: unemployment, housing estate conditions and adolescence.

What, then, are the implications of this final example for our argument about medical dominance and health in the media? First and foremost, as in *Operation Hospital*, there is clear evidence of a major shift towards a much more challenging view of medicine and medical practice. As we have seen, the main focus is on a confrontation between the hospital manager and a consultant, with the latter winning the ethical battle but losing the war. Moreover, the fact that the nursing staff are represented as being much better informed about hospital politics than the consultant is also indicative of the shift in the portrayal of the balance of medical power. It suggests that the days of hospital drama inevitably focusing on the doctor as the dominant figure have changed significantly.

Second, the portrayal of doctors in *Casualty* only provides partial support for the argument concerning 'telegenic' doctors in medical dramas. While there is some evidence of consultant figure Julian playing the role of the glamorous, autocratic, trusty curer, he seems as much preoccupied with hospital politics as with clinical care. Brief reference is made to his love life with a staff nurse and his autocratic and unfeeling manner with female nursing staff. He is also shown using his clinical skills to save the life of one patient against the odds. At the same time he is portrayed as a member of a team of (at times divided) health care workers battling to treat an endless stream of patients under difficult circumstances. Nor is his job made any easier by a manager who seems as concerned with balancing his budget sheet as with increasing resources to provide adequate levels of care.

Third, there is much less 'technophoria' than one might have expected. The setting of an A and E department and the use of a drama format obviously lends itself to the portrayal of life-saving, heroic medicine. 'Realistic' operations feature in most episodes. However, much of the time events are portrayed in a much more mundane light. Many scenes are concerned with nurses cleaning and bandaging wounds and providing cups of tea, and with staff processing patients. This appeal to the audience's sense of realism offsets a one-sided 'technophoric' portrayal, as does the current episode's focus on the politics of health care in NHS hospitals.

Finally, though the sub-plots do tend to portray patients and the public in rather stereotypical ways, there is little evidence of a systematic divorce of individuals from their social context. If anything the reverse is now the case, with dramas such as *Casualty* seeming to go out of their way to give expression to current social problems. While this may seem to trivialise such problems, at the same time the drama format provides a powerful means for their expression and rehearsal. As with the dominant theme of managerial and medical conflict, it seems to us that the portrayal of patients and health is, today, both more serious and more critical.

CONCLUSION

This chapter has sought to examine the thesis that media coverage of health and medicine is characterised by medical dominance, that the 'box is doctored'. The evidence from recent British television coverage suggests that this thesis is difficult to sustain when exposed to empirical checks. Having said this, we fully realise we have only examined three examples of recent coverage, albeit three key examples and, moreover, ones which best illustrate our argument. It is still quite possible to find television coverage that displays clear ideological support for the medical profession and a narrow 'technophoric' view of medical practice. However, it is also clear that the media now act as carriers and amplifiers of a more challenging position.

The evidence we have presented suggests, we believe, that two broad conclusions should therefore be drawn. First, the representations of health and medicine described here reflect and reinforce the argument that major changes are under way in the 'social relations of health care' (Gabe and Bury 1991: 453). While the medical profession and the medical model of health and illness continue to hold considerable power and prestige in modern society, these are now under great pressure. A more critical view of medical knowledge and treatments, the rise of managerialism and the concomitant divisions emerging within medicine itself cut across the exercise of medical dominance.

Second, there has been a general shift in power and social influence from professional groups, including medicine, towards the media. At times this is likely to be experienced by professionals as 'trial by media', a factor which Karpf (1988b) herself has noted. The massive increase in the volume and scope of media products, including those on medicine and health, has inevitably brought about an increase in their influence on everyday life. 'Mediated experience' is no less important in health and medicine than in other areas of late modern culture (Giddens 1991). Thus the media not only reflect changes and conflicts in the social relations of health care (Gabe and Bury 1991) but also influence more powerfully agendas being set.

Future analysis of both the impact of medicine on the media and of arguments concerning medical dominance in sociology more generally need to take account of these twin developments if an adequate appraisal of medical influence in contemporary social life is to be adequately understood. At the least we would argue that the medical dominance thesis is in urgent need of revision.

ACKNOWLEDGEMENT

We should like to thank Jean Seaton for her comments on an earlier draft of this chapter.

REFERENCES

Burns, T. (1977) 'The organisation of public opinion', in Curran, J., Gurevitch, M. and Woollacott, J. (eds) *Mass Communication and Society*, London: Edward Arnold.
Bury, M. and Gabe, J. (1990) 'Hooked? Media responses to tranquillizer dependence', in Abbott, P. and Payne, G. (eds) *New Directions in the Sociology of Health*, London: Falmer Press.
Davies, J.K. (1988) 'Mass media and the prevention of illicit drug use in Scotland', *Health Education Journal*, 47: 23–5.
Eldridge, J. (ed.) (1993) *Getting the Message: News, Truth and Power*, London: Routledge.
Fiske, J. (1987) *Television Culture*, London: Routledge.
Fiske, J. and Hartley, J. (1978) *Reading Television*, London: Methuen.
Flay, B. and Burton, D. (1990) 'Effective mass communication strategies for health campaigns', in Atkin, C. and Wallack, L. (eds) *Mass Communication and Public Health*, Newbury Park: Sage.
Freidson, E. (1970) *The Profession of Medicine*, New York: Dodd Mead.
Gabe, J. and Bury, M. (1988) 'Tranquillisers as a social problem', *Sociological Review*, 36: 320–52.
—— (1991) 'Tranquillisers and health care in crisis', *Social Science and Medicine*, 32: 449–54.
Giddens, A. (1991) *Modernity and Self Identity*, Cambridge: Polity Press.
Illich, I. (1975) *Medical Nemesis*, London: Calder & Boyars.
—— (1977) *The Limits to Medicine*, Harmondsworth: Penguin.
Karpf, A. (1988a) *Doctoring the Media*, London: Routledge.
—— (1988b) 'Medicine and the media', *British Medical Journal*, 296: 1389.
Kennedy, I. (1981) *The Unmasking of Medicine*, London: Allen & Unwin.
Kozloff, S. (1993) 'Narrative theory and television', in Allen, R. (ed.) *Channels of Discourse Reassembled*, London: Routledge.
Larsen, P. (1991) 'Textual analysis of fictional media content', in Jensen, K.B. and Jankowski, N.W. (eds) *A Handbook of Qualitative Methodologies for Mass Communication Research*, London: Routledge.
McLaughlin, J. (1975) 'The doctor shows', *Journal of Communication*, 25: 182–4.
Postman, N. (1986) *Amusing Ourselves to Death: Public Discourse in the Age of Show Business*, London: Heinemann.
Signorelli, N. (1990) 'Television and health', in Atkin, C. and Wallack, L. (eds) *Mass Communication and Public Health*, Newbury Park: Sage.
Silverstone, R. (1981) *The Message of Television. Myth and Narrative in Contemporary Culture*, London: Heinemann Educational.
Thompson, J.B. (1988) 'Mass communication and modern culture: contribution to a critical theory of ideology', *Sociology*, 22: 359–83.
—— (1990) *Ideology and Modern Culture*, Cambridge: Polity Press.
Turow, J. (1989) *Playing Doctor: Television Storytelling and Medical Power*, New York: Oxford University Press.

Turow, J. and Coe, L. (1985) 'Curing television's ills: the portrayal of health care', *Journal of Communication*, 35: 36–51.

Wellings, K. and McVey, D. (1990) 'Evaluation of HEA AIDS press campaign: December 1988 to March 1989', *Health Education Journal*, 49: 108–16.

Williams, R. (1990) *Television: Technology and Cultural Form*, second edn, Routledge: London.

5   The alternatives to medicine

Mike Saks

Consideration of the position of the alternatives to medicine is of much interest not only because of its topicality, but also because it raises the question of the extent to which popular, consumer-based demand in an increasingly market-oriented society can diminish established patterns of professional dominance. The centrality of this question is highlighted by current debates in the sociology of professions about possible trends towards the proletarianisation and deprofessionalisation of the medical profession in the Anglo–American context – which focus, amongst other things, on how far the occupational control and cultural authority of the medical profession have been eroded in recent times (see, for instance, Oppenheimer 1973; Haug 1973; Starr 1982; McKinlay and Arches 1985). In exploring the fate of professional dominance in relation to the alternatives to medicine, this chapter will also address such related issues as the occupational strategies employed by the medical profession in defending its position against external competitors and the degree to which the medical response to this challenge has been imbued with the sense of public responsibility suggested by its professional ideology. In so doing, the chapter takes a neo-Weberian perspective on the professions which defines such groups as monopolistic bodies seeking to regulate market conditions in their favour in face of competition from outsiders (Saks 1983). One of the more intriguing contemporary aspects of the challenge to the orthodox medical profession comes from the external competition posed by the escalating consumer support for the alternatives to medicine, to which the discussion now turns.

GROWING CONSUMER SUPPORT FOR THE ALTERNATIVES TO MEDICINE: THE CHALLENGE TO MEDICAL ORTHODOXY

Alternative medicine in Britain has gained tremendously in popularity over the last twenty-five years – a period in which the diverse range of marginalised therapeutic approaches have come more and more into the public limelight. At first growing popular interest mainly lay in now better-known therapies such as osteopathy, homoeopathy and acupuncture. Today it is also increasingly beginning to focus on areas like crystal therapy, reflexology and aromatherapy. While this growth of interest has a significant self-help dimension, as indicated by the expansion of the over-the-counter sales of health food and herbal remedies (Bakx 1991), confirmation of the current position is most starkly highlighted by trends related to alternative therapists operating outside the orthodox profession. More specifically, recent survey evidence suggests that one in seven of the population now go to practitioners of the alternatives to medicine for treatment (Saks 1991).

This popularity has been attributed in the literature to a number of factors including, amongst others, growing awareness of the technical deficiencies of orthodox medicine, the development of a broader political culture of self-determination and the search for relationships with health practitioners in which the consumer is the engaged subject rather than simply the object of health care (Bakx 1991). There are debates about the relative weight that should be given to the various explanatory elements in this equation – as, for example, the extent to which this surge of public interest in alternative medicine is a distinctly new-age phenomenon reflecting a fundamental revolution in consciousness, as opposed merely to pragmatic patterns of discontent with the side effects and limited efficacy of orthodox medicine (Coward 1989). What, however, is not in doubt is that alternative medicine is becoming increasingly popular and that its popularity extends not only to Britain, but also to Europe and North America (Sharma 1992a; Eisenberg *et al.* 1993).

In this wider international context, popular support for alternative medicine has posed a potential threat to the biomedical principles underpinning the activities and professional standing of medical orthodoxy, in which the body tends to be viewed as a machine whose parts can be repaired on breakdown (Stacey 1988). This threat is centrally embodied in the characteristically more holistic approach of alternative practitioners operating largely outside the orthodox profession who show a greater degree of recognition of the importance of the relationship between mind and body in individual diagnosis and treatment (Saks 1992a). The ensuing conflict with the philosophy embedded in the mainstream theory and practice of the medical profession clearly challenges the power, status and wealth on which its empire is based in Britain and elsewhere, and thus raises the spectre from the viewpoint of orthodox medicine of a possible impending trend towards proletarianisation and deprofessionalisation.

PROFESSIONAL DOMINANCE AND THE MARGINALISATION OF ALTERNATIVE MEDICINE

Importantly, however, for all its force, this consumer-led challenge has not as yet fundamentally subverted the material foundations of professional dominance of British medicine, even if it has generated a greater degree of questioning of its approach. This is most clearly highlighted by the fact that the medical profession in Britain has retained the major part of its empire established following the Second World War – namely, its monopoly over National Health Service (NHS) practice on which British health care remains centrally based and from which alternative therapists without orthodox health care qualifications have been excluded as practitioners in their own right (Huggon and Trench 1992). The corollary of this is that the state-sponsored NHS has continued to be dominated by the drug treatment and surgical intervention of orthodox biomedicine, while therapies like chiropractic, healing, herbalism and osteopathy in Britain have been predominantly restricted to the private market, where the fast swelling band of non-orthodox therapists have focused their practice (Fulder 1988). Although alternative therapists in this country have the right to compete with doctors in this sector of the market within specified limits under the common law – as long as, for instance, they do not illegitimately claim to possess medical or allied health professional qualifications – access to the broad span of generally holistic therapies that they offer is obviously limited by financial barriers (Huggon and Trench 1992).

If the law in Britain places currently defined alternative practitioners in a highly disadvantageous competitive position, primarily because of their marginal status in relation to the extensive state-supported health system, this structural disadvantage is relatively new. In the eighteenth and early nineteenth centuries, before state medicine had been established and, even more importantly, before the British medical profession had gained the legislation underpinning its modern dominance, a comparatively open market existed for the wide range of therapies on offer, with many similarities to that which existed in the anti-restrictionist climate in the United States during this period (Wallis and Morley 1976). The treatments available ranged from bone-setting and healing by touch to herbal preparations and nostrums, which were offered alongside the heroic therapies of purging, sweating, vomiting and bleeding that were more strongly associated with regular practitioners in what has been termed 'the great age of quackery' (Maple 1992). At this time, all health practitioners offered their services in relatively open competition in the market place in an entrepreneurial consumerist culture, including the forerunners of the unified medical profession – the apothecaries, surgeons and physicians – who were then themselves in a minority (Porter 1989). This era, moreover, was not too alien from our own in terms of the current popular alternative health culture, in that even greater and more widespread emphasis was placed on self-help in health care and health was usually seen as the achievement of an appropriate equilibrium, involving both mind and body (Porter 1987).

However, what was to emerge from this period in Britain, following intense parliamentary debates around the mid-nineteenth century, was the 1858 Medical Registration Act which established a unified, self-regulating and exclusionary medical profession, differentiated from its irregular competitors (Waddington 1984). This legislation had the effect of underwriting the monopoly over state medical employment by doctors, and subsequently that of such allied health professions as nurses, midwives and the professions supplementary to medicine. This was to become particularly significant with the passing of the National Health Insurance Act in 1911 and then the National Health Service Act in 1946 which underlined the ascendance of the biomedical approach associated with the heightened dominance of the medical profession in the twentieth century (Saks 1987).

Conversely, the establishment of this state-underwritten medical orthodoxy also had the effect of marginalising the diverse range of therapies that did not readily fit within its frame of reference and defining them for the first time as 'alternative medicine'. In this respect, it should be stressed that the term 'alternative medicine' refers not so much to the content of these therapies – which are marked by considerable heterogeneity, for all their holistic tendencies – as to their predominant outsider status within the British health care system. This is also mirrored in their marginal position in areas such as official research funding and the orthodox health care curriculum, as witnessed by the minimal levels of spending by major funding bodies like the Medical Research Council in this field and the relative lack of official support for programmes of training in the alternative therapies (Saks 1992a). The inevitable result of this marginal standing is that the contemporary scope of availability of such alternative therapies as herbalism and naturopathy in this country is restricted, even though not as greatly as in many other states in Europe and North America where non-orthodox therapists are often completely outlawed (Gaier 1991; Salmon 1985).

The driving force behind this position of professional dominance as regards alternative therapies in Britain has come from the elite of the medical establishment, which – as in the United States (see, for example, Burrow 1963) – has for long mounted strong campaigns against its non-orthodox competitors in the medical journals, as well as in other public and professional forums. This was very evident in the Report of the British Medical Association (BMA) (1986) on alternative medicine which extolled the scientific aspects of modern biomedicine, whilst at the same time generally depicting alternative medicine as superstitious dogma. This line of attack is by no means atypical, as highlighted by the recent Report of the Royal College of Physicians on the specific area of clinical immunology and allergy, in which alternative means of treating allergies were similarly denigrated (JACM 1992). It is precisely this kind of approach that has placed alternative medicine in a double bind situation in relation to orthodox medicine – in which its proponents are criticised for not producing enough scientific evidence to support their case, at the same time as the allocation of official research funds is almost exclusively restricted to more conventional health care activities (Aldridge 1991).

THE CHANGING POSITION OF THE MEDICAL PROFESSION AND UNORTHODOX PRACTITIONERS: IMPLICATIONS FOR PATTERNS OF DOMINANCE AND MARGINALITY

This is not to say that there have been no changes of professional position in recent times. In fact, the stance generally taken by the medical elite in Britain has been increasingly at variance with developing grass-roots opinion in medicine and other orthodox health professions; while there has always been a lingering element of support in this country for alternative therapies within such professions – as represented by the small enclave of medical homoeopaths that has operated in the NHS since its foundation (Nicholls 1988) – this is now growing significantly. Within the medical profession, general practitioners have perhaps become most favourably disposed towards the alternatives to medicine, and in some cases have taken up the practice of such therapies themselves (see, *inter alia*, Reilly 1983; Wharton and Lewith 1986). The last ten years have also witnessed, amongst other things, the expanding use of acupuncture by doctors in pain clinics (Camp 1986) and the increasing application of massage and reflexology by groups like nurses and physiotherapists working under medical authority (Rankin-Box 1988). At a wider level, even the latest Report of the BMA (1993) on such therapies holds back from outright condemnation, acknowledging their popularity and avoiding direct comment on their validity. It is therefore tempting to see this budding revolution from within as pointing to a progressive erosion of professional dominance, for aside from apparently indicating that the profession is subordinating itself to expanding consumer demand, it also seems to increase the challenge that alternative therapists pose to the orthodox medical profession – not least by legitimating the operation of its competitors outside the profession, whose numbers in the United Kingdom even by the early 1980s had expanded to some 30,000 practitioners (Fulder 1988).

Ironically, though, these tendencies to incorporation in Britain – which have also been evident in the United States (Salmon 1985) – may be more plausibly seen within the neo-Weberian approach as an interest-based occupational strategy that has served to defuse the threat to orthodox medicine as a whole and maintained the privileged standing of the profession in the face of the fast-swelling ranks of the unorthodox. What is crucial in sustaining this interpretation, in which interests are defined in terms of the achievement of a positive balance between objectively determined benefits and costs (Saks 1985), is the limited manner in which incorporation has typically occurred. This can be illustrated with reference to the growing medical incorporation of acupuncture in this country, where acupuncture has primarily been employed by the medical profession for analgesic purposes, underpinned by orthodox neurophysiological explanations.

This has minimised the encouragement given to non-medically qualified acupuncturists, with their more challenging Yin–Yang theories and broader ranging applications, while at the same time opening up new territory for the profession (Saks 1992b). Such a strategy has frequently been used in successfully combating threats from without. This is highlighted historically by the way in which the medical profession in both Britain and the United States abandoned its commitment to heroic therapies in the latter half of the nineteenth century in light of the challenge to its developing power, status and wealth from the more popular and less arduous treatment by homoeopaths – even to the point of surreptitiously drawing on remedies with homoeopathic origins in smaller doses than would previously have been considered viable within the profession (Nicholls 1988; Rothstein 1972).

Paralleling these incorporationist trends, alternative practitioners have themselves frequently diluted the radicalism of their ideas in the contemporary era so that they are not always as challenging as those of their founders. The classic distinction between the purist 'straight' practitioners of non-orthodox therapies and the backsliding 'mixers' who have watered down their original oppositional philosophies and practice (Wardwell 1976) seems highly relevant in this context. In this vein, the Anglo–European College of Chiropractic in this country has recently taken the lead in fostering new generations of 'mixers' by making more restricted claims about the scope and efficacy of chiropractic and working in a more respectful relationship with biomedicine, in an attempt to gain greater academic and professional credibility (Christensen 1989). In so doing, British chiropractors have followed their Canadian counterparts, who abandoned much of their earlier radicalism and underwent partial medicalisation in order to secure licensing recognition and the inclusion of chiropractic under government health insurance (Coburn and Biggs 1986). Vincent (1992) too has argued that radical health self-help groups are readily incorporated into professional power structures and often operate to bolster orthodox health care provision, while Bakx (1991) similarly notes that even 'straight' alternative therapists can be useful to orthodoxy in filling gaps in conventional patterns of care. This may help to explain why, despite their broader social, political and economic interests, a small proportion of doctors in Britain have begun occasionally to refer patients to alternative therapists outside of the formally recognised health professions (Cant and Calnan 1991) – which they are now able to do following the lifting by the General Medical Council of ethical prohibitions on the cooperation between doctors and unorthodox practitioners in the mid-1970s (Fulder and Monro 1981).

Some alternative approaches, however, are undoubtedly less challenging to orthodox medicine than others, in part because of the differential compatibility of the epistemological, educational and therapeutic philosophies of their exponents with medical orthodoxy (Wardwell 1976). In this light, such modern trends as the selective medical incorporation of the more threatening alternative therapies and the dilution of the aims of non-orthodox health practitioners in Britain have led some commentators to suggest that the term 'alternative medicine' should now be replaced by that of 'complementary medicine' (see, for instance, Sharma 1992a). This argument is intended to reflect the increased prospects of co-operation with orthodox medicine, which have already been realised to some degree in the small-scale collaboration that has now started to take place between orthodox health professionals and non-orthodox practitioners in Britain, particularly in primary health care (see, amongst others, Budd *et al.* 1990; Reason *et al.* 1992). The suggested redefinition is also supported by the fact that a major national study has recently shown that the preponderant contemporary use of non-orthodox therapies by the public in this country is for a restricted range of problems and as a supplement, rather than an alternative, to medical orthodoxy (Thomas *et al.* 1991); this hardly suggests a major challenge to the cultural authority of the medical profession within the terms of the deprofessionalisation thesis.

None the less, although this evidence accentuates the limits of the current challenge posed to the medical profession from unorthodox practice in Britain, it should not mask the potential for conflict. In this respect, careful note should be taken of the fact that the arguments for such a reconceptualisation are often politically inspired; the non-orthodox health care organisations most willing to define their activities as 'complementary medicine' today tend to be those that have the strongest ideological interest in having their co-operative standing acknowledged by medical orthodoxy (see Haviland 1992). It would also be foolish to ignore the many practitioners who do still actively challenge medicine by operating with starkly counterposed philosophies to biomedicine – as, for example, acupuncturists who base their practice on the existence of meridians which bear little systematic relationship to the central nervous system (Macdonald 1982) and homoeopaths whose view that the more dilute a substance, the more potent its effects, does not readily fit in with the biomedical model (Kayne 1991). Nor should the existence be neglected of radical, non-hierarchical forms of health self-help groups, which are unfavourably disposed towards the involvement of professional experts – not least those centred on women's issues (Phillips and Rakusen 1989). The greatest objection to the reconceptualisation, though, is that the notion of complementary medicine plays down the institutionalised marginality of such approaches; while bodies like the renamed Institute of Complementary Medicine may wish to draw on a legitimating association with medicine, complementarity – as previously indicated – does not currently extend to anything like comparable official funding and support of the practices concerned. This does, however, prompt the question of whether alternative medicine might make a more substantial challenge to medical orthodoxy in the years ahead.

THE FUTURE CHALLENGE TO MEDICAL ORTHODOXY FROM ALTERNATIVE THERAPIES

If the alternatives to medicine are seriously to challenge the professional dominance of existing medical orthodoxy in Britain in the future – and therefore give a more meaningful ring to claims about the proletarianisation and deprofessionalisation of medicine in this area – this may well be more a result of wider socio-political forces than abstracted considerations about their biomedical integrity. In this regard, further pressure looks likely to continue to be exerted on the orthodox health professions by the continuing growth of public interest in non-orthodox therapies. It is interesting that in the debate over the professional monopoly in the health sector in the Netherlands in the 1980s, the Health Ministry gave more weight to the public demand for freedom of choice in health care than to pressure for further clinical evidence on the efficacy of the therapies concerned from the medical profession (Fulder 1988). This serves as a reminder that politicians and the State can wield a crucial influence over the outcome of events in the face of a significant level of consumer demand.

From this viewpoint, alternative therapists in Britain and the United States are now better placed than they have been for some time to challenge the dominance of orthodox medicine. In the United States this is indicated by the decisions of some individual states at least to allow groups like trained acupuncturists to practise independently of the medical profession in a primarily fee-for-service system (Chow 1985). In Britain the substantial political support now available to non-orthodox practitioners is underlined by the lobbying of the recently reformed Parliamentary Group for Alternative and Complementary Medicine which comprises a substantial number of committed all-party MPs (Saks 1992a). This has been matched by continuing pressure for greater state recognition of alternative medicine in this country from other politically influential figures, including sponsorship by members of the royal family – such as Prince Charles, who was responsible in his role as President of the BMA in the early 1980s for instigating its inquiry into alternative therapies (Saks 1991). Such support has come at a time when the Government itself has begun to put the professions under pressure as corporate groups; in the Thatcher period in particular attempts were made with varying degrees of success to change professional working practices, to reduce the powers of professional bodies and to increase the amount of direct supervision to which they were subjected – as illustrated by the 1983 Griffiths reforms in Britain which were intended to augment the power of managers in the health service at the expense of doctors and other health professionals (Burrage 1992). It was in this context that the Government began to show more substantial concern over the position of the alternative therapies in the 1980s, culminating in the creation of two junior ministerial posts with specific responsibilities for alternative medicine towards the end of the decade (Saks 1991).

However, the political process of increasing access to alternative medicine in Britain by breaching the much-prized monopoly of the medical profession within the health service is not as simple as it may at first appear. Notwithstanding claims that the American medical profession has significantly diminished in influence in recent years (see, for example, McKinlay and Stoeckle 1988), the power of the medical elite in Britain, including the Royal Colleges and the BMA, remains great, even though the medical–Ministry alliance no longer seems to be the impermeable block on the progress of alternative therapies that it was for a large part of this century (Larkin 1992). This is highlighted by the fact that, for all its interest in alternative therapies, even the current Conservative Government has not yet shown itself to be prepared to intervene directly in support of the autonomous, non-medical practice of any one of these therapies in the state sector. This is well exemplified by the case of the osteopaths who, having failed in a number of formal attempts to obtain independent registration through parliamentary means up to the mid-1980s, are now striving to establish a state register of qualified practitioners through yet another private member's bill in the wake of the much-publicised 1991 King's Fund Report on osteopathy (Sharma 1992b).

But if the osteopaths have shown recent signs of pulling together to reach a common goal after decades of internal strife (Fulder 1988), practitioners of alternative medicine in Britain have generally not helped their own case from the standpoint of pressure group politics by their manifest disunity; divisions have been particularly apparent at both the organisational and interpersonal level between practitioners with orthodox and non-orthodox qualifications, and alternative therapists wedded to differing principles of practice (Saks 1992a).

However, although such differences have by no means been absent in other societies – as amongst indigenous healers in the United States (see, for instance, Kleinman 1985) – they have been especially significant in Britain given the present view of the Government that alternative therapists should act in a more united way to put their message across (Sharma 1992b). It remains to be seen whether the current efforts of alternative practitioners to put their own house in order will be sufficient to mount a more effective challenge to orthodox medicine. There have certainly been moves in this country towards greater organisational coherence in specific fields such as acupuncture and healing which have led to the formation of the Council for Acupuncture and the Confederation of Healing Organisations respectively (Saks 1991). At a wider level too there have been similar attempts to create umbrella organisations, although these have now given rise to three overarching and potentially conflicting bodies – the Institute for Complementary Medicine, the Council for Complementary and Alternative Medicine and, most recently, the British Complementary Medical Association (Langford 1992) – which are likely to add further to the confusion.

Ultimately, though, the power of the medical profession – especially at elite level – still appears to be the major stumbling block to ending the marginalisation of alternative therapists in Britain in the future, despite the current growth in consumer interest in seeking assistance from such practitioners. Marxist authors, of course, tend to dispute the neo-Weberian professional dominance thesis in medicine on the grounds that it underplays the broader influence of financial and industrial capital in capitalist societies (see, for instance, McKinlay 1985; Navarro 1986). Indeed, it is on this basis that recent Marxist claims about the proletarianisation of the professions have been launched (Elston 1991). The marginality of alternative therapies on this perspective is typically ascribed to the power and interests of the multinational corporations dealing in pharmaceuticals and medical equipment, which are seen to be threatened by the negative impact of the growth of alternative therapies on profits from more orthodox medical products (Saks 1991). Yet, whilst it would be unwise to ignore the power of large multinationals like Ciba-Geigy and Hoffman-La Roche, which employ massive resources to promote their wares in the health sector (Saks 1987), their influence in the case of the alternatives to medicine should not be overstated; there are real dangers in ignoring, amongst other things, the diversification in product range of such corporations which gives them a stake in expanding into alternative as well as orthodox health care and the fact that governments in Britain to date have consistently managed to keep their demands under reasonable control within the NHS (Saks 1991).

The argument for the continuing dominant influence of the orthodox profession in this area in Britain is further reinforced by the fact that it is the elite of the medical profession to which the British Government still formally turns for scientifically based opinions on the safety and efficacy of alternative therapies from the viewpoint of public policy (Sharma 1992b). As such, the profession must be seen as having played a key role to date in sustaining a state-supported health care system which has not fully reflected the growth of popular interest in the alternatives to medicine. This discrepancy is highlighted by a recent MORI poll which showed that three-quarters of the population wished to have the better-known forms of alternative medicine more extensively available within the NHS (Saks 1991). Given the increasing political emphasis that has been placed on the role of the consumer in British health care – most recently epitomised by *The Patient's Charter* (1991) which makes a firm commitment to providing a health service that is responsive to the views of the public – the issue of whether the medical profession as a collectivity can be seen to have acted with a due sense of public responsibility in this area clearly needs to be addressed.

THE MEDICAL PROFESSION, ALTERNATIVE MEDICINE AND PUBLIC RESPONSIBILITY

This issue is very significant in view of the sociological debate in the Anglo-American literature on the professions over the extent to which such groups subordinate their own self-interests to the public interest. The traditionally more prominent trait and functionalist writers tend to take a more benevolent view of the translation of the altruistic ideologies of the professions into practice than those of contributors to the more critical current neo-Weberian and Marxist orthodoxy (Saks 1990). It is also not an easy issue to resolve given the complex conceptual problems involved, particularly regarding the much-contested definition of the public interest. None the less, judging the public responsibility of the medical profession in this country relativistically against the key social principles of the British liberal-democratic State – namely, securing justice, enhancing the general welfare and striving to maximise the amount of individual freedom consistent with these ends (Saks 1990) – doubts certainly arise about the integrity of the modern response of the medical profession to the challenge of the alternatives to medicine. As has been noted, its influence has not only curtailed the individual freedom of consumers, but may also be viewed as having disadvantaged the broader public in terms of justice. In this latter respect, despite the increasing, if limited, practice of various forms of alternative medicine by orthodox health personnel, access to alternative therapies within the NHS has been restricted, giving rise to both economic and geographic inequalities in the state sector – which have been exacerbated by the uneven distribution of practitioners of alternative medicine in the private sector in this country (Sharma 1992a).

However, the question of whether the medical profession has or has not acted responsibly in terms of promoting the general welfare, as well as advancing individual freedom and justice, ultimately hinges on the comparative safety, efficacy and cost-effectiveness of the alternatives to medicine.

These are difficult fields in which to make judgements, not least because the concept of alternative medicine covers a wide and heterogeneous band of therapies and therapists which can be seen to have different balances of strengths and weaknesses. In terms of safety, none the less, there are certainly dangers associated with alternative medicine from the orthodox biomedical perspective, which are usually felt to be exacerbated in the hands of the unqualified; some herbal medicines, for example, can cause haemorrhages (Eagle 1978), while hepatitis B outbreaks have followed the administration of acupuncture using non-sterilised needles (Macdonald 1982). However, problems rarely seem to be reported and the risk of their occurrence has probably been reduced by the growing number of non-orthodox practitioners who now belong to organisations that have codes of conduct and require substantial periods of training (Fulder 1988). The fact that orthodox medicine itself can also be a perilous business – as witnessed by the victims of the thalidomide and Opren disasters and the significant number of hospital admissions associated with doctor-prescribed drugs (Gould 1985) – suggests that comparative safety *per se* is not a very convincing reason for the marginalisation of the alternatives to medicine. This view is reinforced by the fact that safety is frequently cited as one of the main reasons for the rising consumer demand in this area, along with the comparative therapeutic merits of non-orthodox medicine (see, *inter alia*, Inglis 1980).

As has been seen, though, the relative effectiveness of alternative therapies has been questioned by their detractors at the apex of the medical profession, who have claimed that they are scientifically unproven – a view also reflected by the medically-inspired, 'quackbusting' Campaign Against Health Fraud, which has recently been retitled Healthwatch (Sharma 1992b). However, even within the mainstream-controlled trial methodology of the medical profession, there are a number of studies which indicate that therapies like homoeopathy may be more effective than placebos (see, amongst others, Reilly *et al.* 1986) and that some forms of alternative medicine may offer greater therapeutic benefits than orthodox procedures – as, for instance, the use of chiropractic for back problems as compared with hospital out-patient treatment (Meade *et al.* 1990). Against this, it is true that such controlled studies have only rarely been carried out on a significant scale and cannot as yet rival the weight of clinically based evidence underpinning some of the more significant achievements of orthodox medicine, which can dramatically transform the lives of patients through procedures like the replacement of faulty heart valves, the removal of cataracts and arthritic hip surgery (Gould 1985).

Nevertheless, even leaving aside the vast differential in financial support given to research into orthodox as opposed to alternative medicine that has contributed to this situation, the question of the relative efficacy of such therapies still needs to be approached with caution. In the first place, there are queries as to how far the scientific medical establishment itself lives up to its own standards. This is well illustrated by recent medical attacks on the 'gentle approach' of the Bristol Cancer Help Centre based on a study in which it was suggested that women with breast cancer who attended the Centre died sooner than those given orthodox treatment (Bagenal *et al.* 1990), despite important deficiencies in the nature of the controls employed (Stacey 1991). There are also major methodological debates about whether the randomised controlled trial is the most useful method to evaluate holistically based alternative therapies in which treatments are tailored to the individual client rather than given for a standard condition (MacEoin 1990); crucially, for most alternative practitioners, the placebo effect is to be exploited constructively in the healing relationship, rather than eliminated from consideration in pursuit of scientific rigour (Pietroni 1991). The emphasis on the mind–body relationship in alternative therapy, moreover, does seem to have produced high levels of consumer satisfaction in this country, even if this is arguably a rather blunt instrument for gauging the efficacy of such therapy (Sharma 1992a). What is perhaps more significant, though, is that the greatest apparent potential of alternative medicine lies in many of the areas where orthodox health care is at its least successful – particularly in the growing range of chronic degenerative conditions associated with the recent extension of the human life-span (Bayliss 1988).

All of this strengthens the case for extending the accessibility of certain forms of alternative medicine to a wider public within the increasingly consumer-oriented NHS. This case is enhanced further by the fact that alternative medicine is usually less expensive than orthodox biomedical techniques (Gaier 1991), as indicated by even a cursory comparison of the costs of drugs and medical equipment with, for instance, those of the remedies used in homoeopathy or the laying on of hands in healing, which is practised by the largest number of alternative therapists in Britain (Fulder 1988). This said, the average time for a consultation with an alternative therapist is up to seven times that with a general practitioner (Fulder and Monro 1981). However, in terms of cost much depends on who is delivering the alternative therapy concerned. In this respect, it should be asked whether the highly paid, biomedically educated doctor is always the most appropriately placed to practise or to have authority over diagnostic and treatment decisions associated with non-orthodox therapies, as distinct from other personnel within the broader health care division of labour. This point relates as much to competencies as to financial considerations and accentuates the potential problems posed by the continuing exclusion of well-qualified non-orthodox therapists from the NHS as practitioners in their own right.

On this basis, and subject to much-needed additional research, it seems that the restrictions that the British medical profession as a collectivity has largely imposed on both the structural location and form of alternative practice, in the face of escalating consumer demand, may at least be challenged in terms of the definition of public responsibility employed here – especially as regards the more established alternative therapies, such as acupuncture and homoeopathy. Similar queries can, of course, be raised about the operation of the medical profession in other industrial societies where orthodox medicine has been no less restrictive in its approach to outsiders – as witnessed, for example, by the longstanding attack by the American Medical Association on chiropractic, with its large public following, as an 'unscientific cult' in the United States (Caplan 1985). Interestingly, though, doctors in an international context have often moved further towards incorporating alternative medicine into their own repertoire when the legal restrictions on their external competitors have been at their strongest. Thus in France, where tight legislative regulation exists – even of the practice of alternative medicine by the professions allied to medicine – acupuncture and homoeopathy have for long been more widely employed by qualified doctors than in Britain (Bouchayer 1991). This pattern may be related to the reduced threat that outsiders have normally thereby posed to the social, political and financial interests of members of the medical profession, as compared to Britain where more open competition exists in the private sector, through the provisions of the common law (Huggon and Trench 1992).

For all this, though, the identification of a possible medically induced health crisis in the sphere of alternative medicine in Britain prompts important questions about how far the medical profession has acted altruistically and should continue to maintain the monopolistic position that underpins its current dominance in the medical market. Although the profession undoubtedly now has much more to offer from a therapeutic standpoint than when the Medical Registration Act was passed in the mid-nineteenth century – in an age before anaesthesia and antiseptic techniques were generally utilised and when hospitals were seen as 'gateways to death' (Youngson 1979) – this does not absolve it from criticism as far as the alternatives to medicine are concerned in an ever more pluralistic, consumer-based socio-political context.

CONCLUSION: MARKETS, THE MEDICAL PROFESSION AND ALTERNATIVE MEDICINE

The main conclusion of this chapter, however, is that whilst there have been important challenges posed by alternative therapies to the medical profession in Britain, these do not seem at present to have significantly reduced the latter's dominance. The upshot of this is that the proletarianisation and deprofessionalisation theses do not currently appear to fit this area very well, although they are difficult to examine empirically because they have typically been so imprecisely formulated (Elston 1991). Having said this, the authority of the British medical profession has certainly been thrown into question to some degree by the growing public demand for the alternatives to medicine. But, for the moment – assisted by its strategic incorporation of such therapies and the internal weaknesses of its non-orthodox competitors – the legitimacy of medical authority remains broadly intact, even if the use to which it has been put might be contested in terms of the wider professional altruism ideal. This view is reinforced by the fact that the medical profession in Britain has retained its powerful position within the NHS and the right to autonomous collective self-regulation, despite the limited support that alternative medicine has recently begun to win from politicians and the State. This is not, though, to deny the substantial changes that have occurred in this field over the past twenty-five years in Britain, but simply to highlight the current need to interpret their seemingly striking effects with caution.

None the less, changes in the future may cast new light on the situation. In this respect, the influence that the now much-extolled market mechanism is liable to exert over the outcome of the challenge posed to the medical profession by alternative therapies could be particularly critical. At one level, the recent creation of the internal market in the NHS following the publication of *Working for Patients* (1989) may well tilt the balance as regards the broader incorporation of alternative medicine into the health service. The extent of the changes that this reform may bring about are indicated by the confirmation given in December 1991 by Stephen Dorrell, the then Parliamentary Secretary for Health, that general practitioners are free within the new arrangements to employ alternative therapists to offer NHS treatment within their practice, either autonomously for fund holders or with the support of the Family Health Services Authority for non-fund holding practices (DH 1991). By implication, this also appears to enable hospital doctors working in the newly-formed trusts to follow a similar line. On the surface, this suggests that consumers in a competitive market may more forcefully be able to make their views on alternative medicine count in face of the dominance of the medical profession, particularly given the incentives that exist in the new system to employ therapies that are both popular and cost-effective.

How far the internal market will actually open up access to alternative therapies in the NHS at grass-roots level, however, is a moot point, especially in relation to non-orthodox practitioners. The situation is complicated by the fact that all NHS patients must still formally remain the clinical responsibility of their registered medical practitioner (DH 1991). Even if the wider interests of medical practitioners are set aside in the new environment, there may still be a reluctance on the part of individual general practitioners and others in the profession to employ exponents of such therapies as healing, homoeopathy and naturopathy without orthodox health care qualifications in light of the perceived risks involved. This raises a number of issues including, for instance, to what extent credible alternative practitioners can be recognised without a system of statutory registration and, indeed, whether alternative therapists currently in the private sector would be prepared to work in the NHS on the basis outlined (Sharma 1992a). The most likely outcome is that alternative therapies will be increasingly taken up within the NHS, but primarily in a limited manner by either doctors themselves or other subordinated health care professionals operating under their authority, which may not fully do justice to their broader potential.

But if this incorporationist scenario appears the most probable in view of the power and interests of key elements of the British medical profession, it may be reinforced by the other major new market influence in the 1990s – the creation of the Single European Market. This could constrain the possibility of widening public access to alternative therapists by imposing more restrictive legislation on such practitioners in both the public and private sectors, in line with harmonisation and mutual recognition policies in member states. If this occurs – as a result of the highly restrictive laws already surrounding alternative therapies in many other parts of Europe and the power of the European medical lobby (Huggon and Trench 1992) – it may well provide an opportunity for doctors in Britain to follow their counterparts elsewhere in expanding their own practice of the alternatives, while their competitors are more extensively shackled. There is little to indicate, therefore, that the establishment of the Single Market any more than the creation of the internal market will undermine existing patterns of professional dominance or presage substantial trends towards the proletarianisation or deprofessionalisation of medicine in this field. While access to the alternatives to medicine may be expanded, the traditional monopolistic power base of the orthodox profession still seems highly likely to dilute the scope of what is available, even at a time when the profession is coming under ever-greater challenge from the consumer in an increasingly market-based society.

REFERENCES

Aldridge, D. (1991) 'Complementary medicine in Europe: some natural perspectives', in Lewith, G. and Aldridge, D. (eds) *Complementary Medicine and the European Community*, Saffron Walden: C.W. Daniel.

Bagenal, F.S., Easton, D.F., Harris, E., Chilvers, C.E.D. and McElwain, T.J. (1990) 'Survival of patients with breast cancer attending the Bristol Cancer Help Centre', *Lancet*, 336 (2): 606–10.

Bakx, K. (1991) 'The "eclipse" of folk medicine in Western society', *Sociology of Health and Illness*, 13 (1): 20–38.

Bayliss, R.I.S. (1988) 'The National Health Service versus private and complementary medicine', *British Medical Journal*, 296: 1457–59.

Bouchayer, F. (1991) 'Alternative medicines: a general approach to the French situation', in Lewith, G. and Aldridge, D. (eds) *Complementary Medicine and the European Community*, Saffron Walden: C.W. Daniel.

British Medical Association (1986) *Report of the Board of Science and Education on Alternative Therapy*, London: BMA.

—— (1993) *Complementary Medicine: New Approaches to Good Practice*, Oxford: Oxford University Press.

Budd, C., Fisher, B., Parrinder, D. and Price, L. (1990) 'A model of cooperation between complementary and allopathic medicine in a primary care setting', *British Journal of General Practice*, 40 (338): 376–8.

Burrage, M. (1992) *Mrs Thatcher Versus the Professions: Ideology, Impact and Ironies of an Eleven Year Confrontation*, working paper, University of California: Institute of Governmental Studies.

Burrow, J.G. (1963) *AMA: Voice of American Medicine*, Baltimore: Johns Hopkins Press.

Camp, V. (1986) 'Acupuncture in the NHS', *Acupuncture in Medicine*, 3 (1): 4–5.

Cant, S. and Calnan, M. (1991) 'On the margins of the medical marketplace: an exploratory study of alternative practitioners' perceptions', *Sociology of Health and Illness*, 13 (1): 39–57.

Caplan, R. L. (1985) 'Chiropractic', in Salmon, J.W. (ed.) *Alternative Medicines: Popular and Policy Perspectives*, London: Tavistock.

Chow, E.P.Y. (1985) 'Traditional Chinese medicine: a holistic system', in Salmon, J.W. (ed.) *Alternative Medicines: Popular and Policy Perspectives*, London: Tavistock.

Christensen, A. (1989) 'Chiropractic education', *Complementary Medical Research*, 3 (3): 38–40.

Coburn, D. and Biggs, C.L. (1986) 'Limits to medical dominance: the case of chiropractic', *Social Science and Medicine*, 22 (10): 1035–46.

Coward, R. (1989) *The Whole Truth: The Myth of Alternative Health*, London: Faber & Faber.

Department of Health (DH) (1991) 'Stephen Dorrell clarifies the position on alternative and complementary therapies', press release, 3 December.

Eagle, R. (1978) *Alternative Medicine*, London: Futura.

Eisenberg, D.M., Kessler, R.C., Foster, C., Norlock, F.E., Calkins, D.R. and Delbanco, T.L. (1993) 'Unconventional medicine in the United States: pre- valence, costs, and patterns of use', *New England Journal of Medicine*, 328 (4): 246–52.

Elston, M.A. (1991) 'The politics of professional power: medicine in a changing health service', in Gabe, J., Calnan, M. and Bury, M. (eds) *The Sociology of the Health Service*, London: Routledge.

Fulder, S. (1988) *The Handbook of Complementary Medicine*, second edn, Oxford: Oxford University Press.

Fulder, S. and Monro, R. (1981) *The Status of Complementary Medicine in the UK*, London: Threshold Foundation.

Gaier, H. (1991) 'Reveille for biocentric medicine', in Lewith, G. and Aldridge, D. (eds) *Complementary Medicine and the European Community*, Saffron Walden: C.W. Daniel.

Gould, D. (1985) *The Medical Mafia*, London: Sphere.

Haug, M. (1973) 'Deprofessionalization: an alternative hypothesis for the future', in Halmos, P. (ed.) *Professionalization and Social Change*, Sociological Review Monograph 20, Keele: University of Keele.

Haviland, D. (1992) 'The differing natures of alternative and complementary medicine', *Journal of Alternative and Complementary Medicine*, 10 (11): 27–8.

Huggon, T. and Trench, A. (1992) 'Brussels post-1992: protector or persecutor?', in Saks, M. (ed.) *Alternative Medicine in Britain*, Oxford: Clarendon Press.

Inglis, B. (1980) *Natural Medicine*, Glasgow: Fontana.

JACM (1992) 'Damning RCP allergy report prompts an angry backlash', *Journal of Alternative and Complementary Medicine*, 10 (1): 9.

Kayne, S.B. (1991) 'Homoeopathy: demand and scepticism', *Pharmaceutical Journal*, 247 (6,660): 602–4.

Kleinman, A. (1985) 'Indigenous systems of healing: questions for professional, popular, and folk care', in Salmon, J.W. (ed.) *Alternative Medicines: Popular and Policy Perspectives*, London: Tavistock.

Langford, M. (1992) 'BCMA – the way forward', *Journal of Alternative and Complementary Medicine*, 10 (9): 14.

Larkin, G. (1992) 'Orthodox and osteopathic medicine in the inter-war years', in Saks, M. (ed.) *Alternative Medicine in Britain*, Oxford: Clarendon Press.

Macdonald, A. (1982) *Acupuncture: From Ancient Art to Modern Medicine*, London: Allen & Unwin.

MacEoin, D. (1990) 'The myth of clinical trials', *Journal of Alternative and Complementary Medicine*, 8 (8): 15–18.

McKinlay, J.B. (1985) 'Introduction', in McKinlay, J.B. (ed.) *Issues in the Political Economy of Health Care*, London: Tavistock.

McKinlay, J.B. and Arches, J. (1985) 'Towards the proletarianization of physicians', *International Journal of Health Services*, 15 (2): 161–95.

McKinlay, J.B. and Stoeckle, J.D. (1988) 'Corporatization and the social transformation of doctoring', *International Journal of Health Services*, 18 (2): 191–205.

Maple, E. (1992) 'The great age of quackery', in Saks, M. (ed.) *Alternative Medicine in Britain*, Oxford: Clarendon Press.

Meade, T.W., Dyer, S., Browne, W., Townsend, J. and Frank, A.O. (1990) 'Low back pain of mechanical origin: randomised comparison of chiropractic and hospital outpatient treatment', *British Medical Journal*, 300: 1431–7.

Navarro, V. (1986) *Crisis, Health and Medicine*, London: Tavistock.

Nicholls, P.A. (1988) *Homoeopathy and the Medical Profession*, London: Croom Helm.

Oppenheimer, M. (1973) 'The proletarianization of the professional', in Halmos, P. (ed.) *Professionalization and Social Change*, Sociological Review Monograph 20, Keele: University of Keele.

The Patient's Charter (1991) London: HMSO.

Phillips, A. and Rakusen, J. (eds) (1989) *Our Bodies, Ourselves*, second edn, Harmondsworth: Penguin.

Pietroni, P.C. (1991) *The Greening of Medicine*, London: Gollancz.

Porter, R. (1987) *Disease, Medicine and Society in England 1550–1860*, London: Macmillan.

—— (1989) *Health for Sale: Quackery in England 1660–1850*, Manchester: Manchester University Press.

Rankin-Box, D. (ed.) (1988) *Complementary Health Therapies: A Guide for Nurses and the Caring Professions*, London: Croom Helm.

Reason, P., Chase, H.D., Desser, A., Melhuish, C., Morrison, S., Peters, D., Wallstein, D., Webber, V. and Pietroni, P.C. (1992) 'Towards a clinical framework for collaboration between general and complementary practitioners', *Journal of the Royal Society of Medicine*, 85 (3): 161–64.

Reilly, D.T. (1983) 'Young doctors' views on alternative medicine', *British Medical Journal*, 287: 337–9.

Reilly, D.T., Taylor, M.A., McSharry, C. and Aitchison, T. (1986) 'Is homoeopathy a placebo response? Controlled trial of homoeopathic potency, with pollen in hay fever as model', *Lancet*, 333 (2): 881–5.

Rothstein, W.G. (1972) *American Physicians in the Nineteenth Century*, London: Johns Hopkins University Press.

Saks, M. (1983) 'Removing the blinkers? A critique of recent contributions to the sociology of professions', *Sociological Review*, 31 (1): 1–21.

—— (1985) 'Professions and the public interest: the response of the medical profession to acupuncture in nineteenth and twentieth century Britain', unpublished Ph.D. thesis, Department of Sociology, London School of Economics, University of London.

—— (1987) 'The politics of health care', in Robins, L. (ed.) *Politics and Policy-making in Britain*, London: Longman.

—— (1990) 'Sociology, professions and the public interest: professional ideology and public responsibility', paper presented at International Sociological Association Conference on Professions and Public Authority, Northeastern University, Boston, USA, 21–2 April.

—— (1991) 'Power, politics and alternative medicine', *Talking Politics*, 3 (2): 68–72.

—— (1992a) 'Introduction', in Saks, M. (ed.) *Alternative Medicine in Britain*, Oxford: Clarendon Press.

—— (1992b) 'The paradox of incorporation: acupuncture and the medical profession in modern Britain', in Saks, M. (ed.) *Alternative Medicine in Britain*, Oxford: Clarendon Press.

Salmon, J.W. (1985) 'Introduction', in Salmon, J.W. (ed.) *Alternative Medicines: Popular and Policy Perspectives*, London: Tavistock.

Sharma, U. (1992a) *Complementary Medicine Today: Practitioners and Patients*, London: Routledge.

—— (1992b) 'Professionalisation in complementary medicine today: an overview', paper presented at International Sociological Association Conference on Professions in Transition, University of Leicester/De Montfort University, Leicester, 21–3 April.

Stacey, M. (1988) *The Sociology of Health and Healing*, London: Unwin Hyman.

—— (1991) 'The potential of social science for complementary medicine', *Complementary Medical Research*, 5 (3): 183–6.

Starr, P. (1982) *The Social Transformation of American Medicine*, New York: Basic Books.

Thomas, K.J., Carr, J., Westlake, L. and Williams, B.T. (1991) 'Use of non-orthodox and conventional health care in Great Britain', *British Medical Journal*, 302: 207–10.

Vincent, J. (1992) 'Self-help groups and health care in contemporary Britain', in Saks, M. (ed.) *Alternative Medicine in Britain*, Oxford: Clarendon Press.

Waddington, I. (1984) *The Medical Profession in the Industrial Revolution*, London: Gill & Macmillan.

Wallis, R. and Morley, P. (1976) 'Introduction', in Wallis, R. and Morley, P. (eds) *Marginal Medicine*, London: Peter Owen.

Wardwell, W.I. (1976) 'Orthodox and unorthodox practitioners: changing relationships and the future status of chiropractors', in Wallis, R. and Morley, P. (eds) *Marginal Medicine*, London: Peter Owen.

Wharton, R. and Lewith, G. (1986) 'Complementary medicine and the general practitioner', *British Medical Journal*, 292: 1498–1500.

Working for Patients (1989), London: HMSO.

Youngson, A. (1979) *The Scientific Revolution in Victorian Medicine*, London: Croom Helm.

6 Self-help groups and their relationship to medicine

David Kelleher

INTRODUCTION

The focus of this chapter is the relationship between self-help groups for people with a medical condition and the medical profession. This will entail asking whether self-help groups are complementary to medicine and the professional health care system or part of a growing challenge, questioning medical discourse and practice.

The current attempt to control the cost of providing health care in both Britain and the USA is one aspect of a crisis that has led some to claim that the medical profession is experiencing proletarianisation as a result of medical work becoming subject to managerial control from above (Elston 1991). It will be argued here that there is another aspect to this crisis, a challenge to medicine from below, from patients who express their dissatisfaction with the limitations of medicine by turning either to other professionals working in alternative medicine (see Saks in this volume), or to each other by forming self-help groups. The proletarianising challenge from the State and the challenge from patients are not unrelated. In this chapter the theoretical perspective of Habermas (1987) will be used to suggest that the health care systems of Britain and the USA, steered in different ways by the medium of money, are distorted versions of the healing mission of Enlightenment science and that it is in this context that self-help groups have been developed for those whom medicine cannot cure, the chronically ill.

There is no doubt that self-help groups for people with chronic illness have been growing in number in recent years. In the USA it has been reported that:

> In the late seventies it was estimated that between 15 and 20 million people were involved in 500,000 self-help groups.
>
> (Arntson and Droge 1987: 149)

Vincent (1992) identifies a similar growth of health-related self-help groups in England, but also notes the difficulty of establishing just how many do exist at any one time, as not all survive beyond the interest and enthusiasm of the founder members. On mainland Europe the increase in the number of self-help groups has been equally great and sufficient to merit the attention of the World Health Organization. In the introduction to a survey of self-help groups carried out for the WHO, Kickbusch and Hatch (1983) not only support the claim that self-help groups are indeed growing in number, but also draw attention to the idea that the growth is related to the financial crisis of health care systems.

> The pace at which self-help groups and organisations have come into being over the last ten years has made self-help an issue of continuing debate in both the political and professional field, leading not only to critical assessment of the quality and efficiency of the health care system in general, but also to hopes of having found a solution to its financial crisis.
>
> (Kickbusch and Hatch 1983: 2)

Clearly, then, the self-help phenomenon is something that merits further attention in terms of what it does for individuals and what it says about the way medicine operates in contemporary society. This chapter will not attempt to provide a comprehensive account of the range of self-help groups, nor will it provide a complete list of all the activities of these groups. The intention here is to provide some description of what self-help groups do for individuals and for the wider constituency of which they are part: chronically ill people in society. This will then be used as a basis for considering what the relationship is between the groups and the medical profession, and in particular whether these groups are part of a broadly based process which is attempting to demystify and de-monopolise professional expertise in medicine. Thus, self-help groups will be considered as an aspect of high modernity where cultural values are not clearly defined and identities are at risk (Giddens 1991).

In the final section the theoretical perspective of Jurgen Habermas (1981) will be used to explore whether self-help groups are part of a new social movement, not only offering individuals a means of reconstructing their identities, but also playing a part in reinvigorating the public sphere (Habermas 1989) where communicative action can develop mutual understandings which may challenge the authority of medicine.

SELF-HELP GROUPS AND THEIR ACTIVITIES

A number of writers point to the diversity of self-help groups (Richardson and Goodman 1983; Robinson 1980) and some discuss whether the wide variation in the kind of activities that they engage in is a problem in terms of defining what is meant by self-help. A brief discussion of what self-help is will follow this description of the range of activities.

The medical conditions for which there are self-help groups are enormous in number, as can be seen from consulting a bulletin such as that collated by the National Self-help Support Centre. Some attempts have been made to organise this wide range of groups by classifying them according to what is seen to be their main function. Katz and Bender (1976), for example, suggest that groups can be classified according to whether they are 'inner-focused' or 'outer-focused'; that is, whether they are mainly concerned with providing members with an opportunity for sharing their personal problems and feelings with fellow sufferers, or whether they concentrate on acting as a pressure group representing the needs of all those with the condition to district authorities (purchasers) and professionals (providers). While this is a helpful starting point, it can be seen from the description of the three groups selected below that many groups engage in both kinds of activitity, although they may give more emphasis to one rather than the other. In the descriptions and analysis that follow, therefore, the inner/outer distinction will be employed as part of an analysis of the relationship that the groups have to the medical profession.

Most of the central features and activities can be seen by looking at three examples: groups which have been set up to help people with ankylosing spondylitis, those set up to help people who feel they are dependent on tranquillisers and those for people with diabetes.

Williams (1989) describes how the National Ankylosing Spondylitis Society was set up by doctors, physiotherapists and patients at the Royal Hospital for Rheumatic Diseases in Bath during 1976. By 1986 the Society had 4,000 members and a number of local branches. Williams notes that although, ostensibly, the Society's goals were shared by lay and professional members, there was a continuing tension between shared 'outer' concerns, such as acting as a pressure group to get better treatment facilities for patients and raising funds for research, and dealing with patients' concerns with personal experience. It appears from the description of the Society that, while there is some evidence to suggest that there is a demand for the personal sharing of experience which would be necessary if the group were to be classified as 'inner-focused', in practice the organisation is controlled by professionals who see such activity as either irrelevant or harmful. In this case, then, it appears that the professionals' control ensures that the National Society does not challenge medicine, although whether that control is able to continue operating effectively in local groups is another matter.

In the case of people who felt that they were dependent on tranquillisers Gabe (forthcoming) describes the activities of both a local group and a national organisation, TRANX. The local group was set up on a deprived housing estate by a community health worker after a survey had shown that many of the women on the estate were concerned about their drug consumption. This group met together and shared experiences in the manner of an inner-focused group, but members also developed some local initiatives as they recognised that their problems were not just personal but also part of a public issue. They made public their criticisms of the way local doctors had prescribed tranquillisers without giving them sufficient information about side effects and this led to them being invited to other community groups to discuss what further action should be taken. This local group then started as an inner-focused group but became an outer-focused one which was actively concerned in interrogating the practice of medicine.

The national self-help group for people with tranquilliser problems, TRANX, had a network of local groups and offered advice and support to individuals who telephoned, until its demise in 1990. TRANX did have an outer focus as it tried to create an awareness of the problems of long-term dependence on tranquillisers (Tattersall and Hallstrom 1992) but unlike the group described above it clearly worked with, and was guided by, the medical profession (Ettore 1986).

The third example of self-help groups, for people with diabetes, is illustrated by the work of Kelleher (1990a, 1991). He sampled the views of people with diabetes from three different populations: people with diabetes in self-help groups, those belonging to local branches of the national organisation, the British Diabetic Association (BDA), and those who have diabetes but are not members of either a self-help group or the BDA. In addition, he interviewed a small sample of consultant diabetologists (1990b).

The BDA, which was founded in 1934 and is now a national organisation with branches in most towns, seems originally to have been conceived of as a self-help group (British Diabetic Association 1980: 2). It now finances a great deal of mainly medical research and branches organise a range of activities to raise this money; they also invite health care professionals to give talks about diabetes. Branch members do engage in discussion and support which could be classified as self-help but there is no doubt that the majority of the activities are directed to either supporting medical research or to raising issues which are of general concern to all diabetic people, such as the effects that many people reported after having had their prescription changed from animal derived insulin to genetically engineered 'human' insulin. The BDA branches can, then, be classified as being like the national organisation TRANX, having mainly an outer focus and operating primarily in a way that is complementary to the medical profession.

The self-help groups with an inner focus are a recent development and arose from a letter from a diabetic person to *Balance*, the BDA patients' magazine (Cole 1987). These are local groups affiliated to the BDA but specifically not concerned with fund raising. Rather, they are groups where individuals with diabetes and their partners meet and discuss the problems they have in managing their diabetes. In this context members have the opportunity to talk about the problems of managing the dietary regimen given them by health care professionals and the issues involved in self-injecting. Often the dietary advice appeared complicated and restrictive to those in the groups, but in discussions with others who shared the experience of controlled eating they were able to voice their worries, confess their temptations to eat more and learn how others managed to go beyond eating salads and the special diabetic foods that they had been told to eat.

Discussions such as these led to people feeling less guilty about having to compromise their diet in order to fit their treatment regimen around other aspects of their lives and work. It could be argued that the opportunities to share in the exchange of such experiences and problems changed people from being worried individuals who confessed to doctors that they had 'been a bit naughty', to people who drew confidence from the group's identity, and that this psychological security is as important an aspect of managing a chronic illness as the treatment regimen is in managing the body. This kind of change in how people understand their way of managing can be described as an example of self-regulation (Conrad 1985) and taking control of one's own disorder rather than as 'naughtiness', non-compliance or deviance from the medical regimen.

In the case of groups for people with diabetes, then, the self-help groups, like the local group of women who were worried about their shared tran-quilliser problem, were inner-focused. The national organisation, the British Diabetic Association, like the National Ankylosing Spondylitis Society and TRANX, although principally an outer-focused group concerned with improving facilities for all diabetic people and closely linked with the medical profession, also contained within the local branches the opportunity for people to engage in mutual help. There is evidence too from the survey part of the diabetes study (Kelleher 1991) which suggests that there is a latent demand for more of this inner-focused, interpersonal activity. Of the sample of 271 BDA members, 60 per cent said that they found it easier to talk to another diabetic person than to a doctor or nurse, and 55 per cent also agreed with the statement that 'doctors don't encourage people to talk about their feelings'. Arntson and Droge (1987) also report that many of the people with epilepsy in the self-help groups in their study were upset that doctors were unwilling to talk about anything other than the medical aspect of their condition, asking them only about seizures, side effects and when they had last had a blood test.

The need for people to talk about their feelings and attempt to locate the illness within the context of their lives has been well documented in the literature on chronic illness. Bury (1988) writes about the way that young people with arthritis often associate the illness with old age and find it hard to accept that they have it. Williams (1989) illustrates the importance of 'narrative reconstruction' as a way of people coming to understand the place that the illness has in their lives. Arntson and Droge (1987) relate this need to construct narratives with the work which they observed to be going on in self-help groups for people with epilepsy:

> Self-help group members provide each other with the opportunities, stories and sets of behaviours in order to increase their perceived control over their physical and social conditions.
>
> (Arntson and Droge 1987: 153)

The need for this aspect of self-help group work does point to shortcomings in the care provided by doctors and other health care professionals (Lock 1986), but it is not necessarily evidence of self-help groups engaging in work which challenges the authority of medicine. Most doctors would see self-help groups where caring work is carried out or where patients 'let off steam' (Kelleher 1990b) as supportive of their own medical work. More detailed study of the activity of sharing experiences in self-help groups, however, suggests that exchanging and sharing experiences may change people's understanding of themselves and their way of managing the condition and the treatment regimen from guiltily seeing it as non-compliance to viewing it more positively. Trojan's (1989) study of sixty-five self-help groups in Germany concluded that members gained new knowledge and developed the confidence to express themselves. Gabriel (1989), in a study of long-term mental disorder in the inner city, suggests that self-help groups can help black people to discover a sense of cultural identity and self-esteem.

This confidence may lead to a person managing the condition within the parameters of the treatment regimen, in which case there is no challenge to the authority of the doctor. But when patients begin to give a higher priority to their employment, their family's needs or their social relationships than to maintaining compliance with the treatment regimen, this suggests an implicit re-evaluation of medical knowledge.

The concern of doctors is to control the disease that people have, which in the case of diabetes means controlling the level of blood glucose. This is thought to reduce the chances of a person with diabetes developing what are seen as the 'complications' of the condition; that is, damage to feet as a result of neuropathy, blindness, kidney damage and greater risk of heart disease, all of which are serious health risks. But these complications are the long-term risks of having diabetes and may not appear threatening to people in their thirties and forties. Moreover, not everyone with diabetes develops them. As Conrad (1985) shows in relation to people with epilepsy, many people have other concerns in their lives to which they may want to give priority. Diabetic people with young children, for example, may choose to put the interests of their children before considerations of their own health. Without the support of others who share such dilemmas the practice of decision-making based on their own judgement of priorities is difficult and often guilt-ridden, as it may involve deceiving the doctor at the periodic check-ups.

Providing people with the opportunity to talk about their illness is, for many, a way of coming to terms with and working out strategies for managing it. Much of what goes on in inner-focused groups is concerned with the expression of feelings about the condition and anxieties about the long-term effects. In one of the groups observed by Kelleher (1990a) a woman felt anxious because she had been told that her diabetes could no longer be controlled by diet and tablets. Apart from her fear of having to inject herself three times a day, she was concerned that her diabetes had now become more life-threatening. In responding to her anxiety other members gave her both practical and psychological support; some showed her how they injected, others talked about how they still felt anxious about pushing a needle into themselves, and yet others emphasised the greater freedom to self-regulate that injections give, as opposed to a diet-controlled regimen.

While many doctors would not be happy with their patients putting the interests of their family or work before concerns for their own health, they would no doubt broadly approve of the support given to the woman changing from a diet regimen to one based on insulin injections. They would see this kind of support as complementary to their own work. Some, though, would have reservations about patients thinking that insulin injections were a freer way of managing their diabetes than following a diet, just as some have doubts about the use of the Novopen, which allows diabetic people to give themselves small injections of insulin during the day according to what they are doing. One consultant interviewed by Kelleher (1990b) said that the Novopen encouraged people to adopt a 'bizarre' lifestyle, by which he meant varying the time they had lunch or sometimes going without lunch. The ways in which technological developments such as the Novopen could be used to liberate life as a diabetic was an important topic for discussion in the groups, as it was seen as a way for people to gain greater control and freedom to respond spontaneously to events.

As can be seen from the above examples, much of what goes on in the inner-focused self-help groups could be interpreted as complementary to medicine, as many members are clearly not overtly rejecting the medical treatment regimen prescribed for them but are simply adapting it to suit their priorities. It can also be argued though that there is, in the sharing of experiential knowledge, an acceptance that a certain level of deviation from the medical regimen is legitimate and, in the discussion of new developments such as the Novopen, an implicit challenge to medical authority which suggests a shift in power from professionals to consumers (Stewart 1990).

In a survey conducted as part of research into self-help groups for people with diabetes (Kelleher 1991), 95 per cent of BDA members and 84 per cent of diabetic people who were not BDA members thought that they could gain knowledge from other diabetics about how to control their illness, whereas only 50 per cent thought that increased awareness of the complications of diabetes would increase their compliance. Even in the outer-focused groups discussed earlier – TRANX and the BDA national organisation, both of which are medically dominated – there are examples of medical prescribing practice being interrogated on the basis of lay experience.

Having described the activities of self-help groups through these examples we can now define the common elements that run through these activities. Many of the definitions of self-help groups that are offered are little more than short descriptions of what they do. The definition set out by Katz and Bender (1976: 9), for example, starts by saying: 'Self-help groups are voluntary, small group structures for mutual aid and the accomplishment of a special purpose'. Robinson and Henry (1977: 141) offer a description of self-help group activities in terms of what self-help means to the people in the groups. They conclude that self-help groups are not a political phenomenom but 'people who are coming together to share and solve their common problems, rather than put up with the frustrations and humilations of professional services'. Some, like Wilson (1992), argue that there is clearly no evidence that self-help groups have a commitment to challenging medical practice in any fundamental way. But others like Vincent (1992: 153) argue that: 'The strength of self-help groups in health care . . . lies in their empowering of their members and the challenge they may pose to medical orthodoxy.'

The thread running through the description of self-help groups in this chapter suggests that while many of the activities of the groups can be seen as complementary to the work of the medical profession, there is nevertheless a subversive readiness to question the knowledge of doctors and to assert that experiential knowledge has value. Although Kickbusch (1989) has reservations about the relevance and soundness of lay knowledge it is argued here that, regardless of its soundness, self-help groups do give a legitimacy to experiential knowledge and support to the questioning of medical practice. The definition of self-help groups offered here, then, is that they are groups which place a value on experiential knowledge, thus implicitly challenging the authority of professional health care workers to define what it is to have a particular condition and how it should be managed.

Self-help groups and modern medicine coexist in contemporary culture and the needs of patients and their relationship with professionals is influenced by changes in the relationship between the health care system and the economy, as was suggested at the beginning of the chapter. It is in this context that the discussion of self-help groups and modern medicine is now located.

SELF-HELP GROUPS IN THE CONTEXT OF CONTEMPORARY CULTURE

Most of the contributors to the debate about the nature of contemporary society share a view of it as having become something other than the rational society of Enlightenment philosophers, where science is used to control the natural resources for the benefit of all (Foster 1985; Giddens 1991). Just what kind of society it has become is hotly debated, but there is little disagreement that it has become a confusing place to live in for many people. According to Giddens (1990), daily life is now experienced as resembling a runaway juggernaut rather than a well-controlled car. He also suggests that in a de-traditionalised society such as contemporary Britain, identities still have to be created and sustained (Giddens 1991). Bauman (1992), in describing the post-modern features of the contemporary world, sees it as a world that has been re-enchanted, instead of one where science can explain everything. It is a world in which fear has been privatised and, although it appears that people have the freedom to do anything they want, they have no guide as to what is worth doing and what is worthless. We are, he says, vagabonds wandering in the world instead of being pilgrims guided by knowledge of the truth (Bauman 1992). In such a situation it has been suggested that there is a tendency for people to become narcissistic (Lasch 1980) and concentrate on developing themselves and their relationships with intimate others, to the exclusion of contributing to public debate (Sennett 1977). Critics of self-help groups may see them as collective confessionals, as part of the fashion for confessing and revealing one's weaknesses and for self-exploration that seems to be so attractive to people who participate in radio phone-ins, or who watch television pro-grammes like the *Oprah Winfrey Show*, so popular in both the USA and Britain.

It is possible that some of the people who become members of self-help groups are influenced by these cultural trends, but the condition-specific nature of the groups makes it unlikely that this is the main reason for their growth. Another cultural trend that may have an influence on the develop-ment of groups is the high value that is placed on being healthy, a state of being which is so highly valued that it is sometimes described as 'healthism' (Glassner 1989).

In a world in which people find it difficult to feel that they have any control over the events that shape their lives, the attraction of feeling in control of one's health may be considerable. The contemporary western world is a risk-oriented world (Giddens 1991; Beck 1992) in which people are continuously warned about the dangers of overeating, drinking polluted tap water and breathing air from a polluted environment. This pursuit of fitness puts much of the responsibility for being healthy on to lay people themselves. It is an emphasis much approved of by cost-cutting governments, who see it as a cheap way of improving the health of the population that avoids confronting the social causes of ill health.

For those people who already suffer from a chronic disease such as diabetes, epilepsy or mental illness, the idea that their own faulty lifestyle may be to blame for their condition is not helpful. The chronically ill, in a period when so much emphasis is put on choosing one's own lifestyle and creating and sustaining one's identity, are subject to all the pressures to which other people are subject, but suffer an additional handicap. Some may feel stigmatised and in need of sympathetic support (Arntson and Droge 1987) and, as discussed earlier, often fail to find it within the professional health care system. Managing the stigmatisation caused by having a medically defined identity is one of the important ways in which self-help groups help their members.

This section has briefly drawn attention to the fact that self-help groups and medicine both exist in, and are influenced by, the cultural values of the western capitalist societies in which they are located. Such societies are still mainly run by expert systems. However, Bell (1973) maintains that there has been a transformation which has brought about a disjuncture between the values of the cultural system and the workings of the economic system, thus creating many uncertainties, particularly for those not well placed to participate in the market. The role of self-help groups and modern medicine in such societies will be explored more fully using the theoretical framework of Jurgen Habermas.

SELF-HELP GROUPS AS A NEW SOCIAL MOVEMENT

It is possible to apply the overall framework that Habermas (1987) develops in his *Theory of Communicative Action* to link the essential elements of self-help groups, such as the emphasis on shared understanding, the value placed on experiential knowledge and the sense of control that this may give members, with the role played by modern medicine.

Self-help groups can be seen as part of a new social movement (Habermas 1981) which is resisting the domination of the life-world by expert systems, in this case the expert system of medicine. Expert systems represent one of the differentiated mechanisms of instrumental-cognitive rationality through which a society is maintained and developed. This contrasts with the life-world, which refers to the public sphere in which people's actions are guided mainly by traditional ideas. These actions are subject to a moral-practical form of questioning, which is the basis of what Habermas calls communicative action. From this perspective medicine is one of the expert systems and self-help groups are part of the life-world.

It was revealed earlier that one of the reasons why people become members of self-help groups is because they consider that doctors and other health care professionals do not offer them the opportunity to talk about their experience of illness, the stigma and social handicap that they may feel, or their worries about incorporating their illness in their social identity; nor do doctors willingly recognise what their patients may have learned about their illness from experience. The concerns of medicine are with controlling the symptoms of disease by checking on whether patients comply with treatment regimens and by periodically testing their blood, patterns of brain activity or degree of physical movement. The argument here is not that these activities are superfluous – indeed, they may be life-saving measures – but that they define too narrowly what it is to have diabetes, epilepsy or arthritis and ignore the social psychological issues that people say are important to them in trying to live and work with these conditions.

This state of affairs has come about, it is suggested, because medicine has lost its way; it is now driven not by the needs of patients as they are defined in the life-world, but by the demands of the system with its need for measuring success by 'activity levels' and other forms of instrumental rationality. Medicine, like other expert systems in the contemporary world, is steered by the media of power and money as it concentrates more and more on expensive drug treatments (Collier 1989), screening programmes and complex surgery; it pays insufficient attention to how chronically ill people can become psychologically secure and capable of engaging fully with life.

The problem with such expert systems, Habermas (1987) suggests, is not that they involve such forms of rationality but that they have become decoupled from the life-world and its moral-practical ways of understanding human problems, thus leaving many patients with the feeling that what are to them important aspects of their condition are being neglected. This is not to say that some individual doctors, like the doctor in John Berger's (1967) story *A Fortunate Man*, do not make great efforts to understand their patients' life-world concerns, but they are working against the flow.

Habermas (1987) also suggests that not only have the system and life-world become decoupled, but that there is a tendency for the life-world to become colonised by the interests and instrumental-cognitive rationality of expert systems. This means that when medicine and the larger system of which it is a part do make an attempt to incorporate the life-world issues of patients into their gaze, as Armstrong (1984) suggests medicine does, they do so using a discourse and empiricist methods that are at odds with the real concerns of the life-world. Self-help groups are important, it is argued, because they are rooted in the life-world and offer an opportunity to discuss the experience of chronic illness within a style of discourse using a moral-practical form of reasoning. They offer people the possibility of creating an alternative way of understanding what has happened to them.

The kind of exchanges which take place in self-help groups can be seen as useful in negotiating a pathway between complete compliance with the medical regimen and its instrumental rationality and the contexted life-world concerns of individuals. In the study of self-help groups for people with diabetes referred to earlier (Kelleher 1990a, 1991) it was noticeable that while non-compliant acts were often legitimated by being recognised as a shared way of managing illness, instances of non-members ignoring their treatment regimen or complying only haphazardly were likely to be criticised too. Stories were told of people who had required amputations or who had died as a result of wild or irregular practice of the treatment regimen. It is not that such talk always produces what an outsider would consider as the best kind of answer, but that the structure of moral-practical discourse makes it possible for life-world concerns to be subjected to the tests of truthfulness in ordinary speech (Habermas 1987) rather than dismissed by professional interests.

Self-help groups, then, are part of a public sphere where life-world concerns can be discussed in the language of the life-world. In providing this kind of opportunity they can be seen as part of a social movement which is resisting change, withstanding the drive to understand human experience in ways that deny the value of knowledge constructed inter-subjectively by means of communicative action. They can be seen as part of a wide-ranging resistance to system imperatives:

> In the past decade or two, conflicts have developed in advanced Western societies that deviate in various ways from the welfare state pattern of institutionalised conflict over distribution . . . these new conflicts arise in domains of cultural reproduction, social integration and socialization . . . the new conflicts are not ignited by distribution problems but by questions having to do with the grammar of life.
>
> (Habermas 1987: 392)

CONCLUSION

What has been argued here is that self-help groups are a challenge to modern medicine because medicine has lost much of its emancipatory drive and has come to see human suffering in a technical-instrumental way. Self-help groups are complementary to medicine in that they are a way of making good one of its shortcomings, the failure to address the expressive needs of people. But, as part of a new social movement, they are important because they retain the possibility for seeing things differently, creating the opportunity for medicine to be challenged and interrogated. It is for this reason that the valuing of experiential knowledge is important. It is not that it is true, and biomedical, scientific knowledge is false. Instead, self-help groups enable a range of concerns to be kept alive, rather than being distorted by expert systems and the discourse of the market, and a form of non-coercive talk becomes possible.

REFERENCES

Armstrong, D. (1984) 'The patient's view', *Social Science and Medicine*, 18: 737–44.

Arntson, P. and Droge, D. (1987) 'Social support in self-help groups', in Albrecht, T., Adelman, M. and associates (eds) *Communicating Social Support*, Beverly Hills: Sage.

Bauman, Z. (1992) *Intimations of Postmodernity*, London: Routledge.

Beck, U. (1992) *Risk Society*, London: Sage.

Bell, D. (1973) *The Coming of Post-industrial Society*, New York: Basic Books.

Berger, J. (1967) *A Fortunate Man*, London: Allen Lane.

British Diabetic Association (1980) *In the Service of Diabetes*, London: British Diabetic Association.

Bury, M. (1988) 'Meanings at risk: the experience of arthritis', in Anderson, R. and Bury, M. (eds) *Living with Chronic Illness*, London: Unwin Hyman.

Cole, E. (1987) 'The Nottingham Experience: a self-help diabetes group', *Balance*, August/September: 60–1.

Collier, J. (1989) *The Health Conspiracy*, London: Century Hutchinson.

Conrad, P. (1985) 'The meaning of medications: another look at compliance', *Social Science and Medicine*, 20: 19–37.

Elston, M.A. (1991) 'The politics of professional power: medicine in a changing health service', in Gabe, J., Calnan, M. and Bury, M. (eds) *The Sociology of the Health Service*, London: Routledge.

Ettore, E. (1986) 'Self-help groups as an alternative to benzodiazepine use', in Gabe, J. and Williams, P. (eds) *Tranquillisers: Social, Psychological and Clinical Perspectives*, London: Tavistock Publications.

Foster, H. (1985) *Postmodern Culture*, London: Pluto Press.

Gabe, J. (forthcoming) 'Promoting benzodiazepine withdrawal', *British Journal of Addiction*.

Gabriel, S. (1989) 'Black to black', *Community Care*, 12 October: 26.

Giddens, A. (1990) *The Consequences of Modernity*, Cambridge: Polity Press.

—— (1991) *Modernity and Self-Identity*, Cambridge: Polity Press.

Glassner, B. (1989) 'Fitness and the postmodern self', *Journal of Health and Social Behavior*, 30: 180–91.

Habermas, J. (1981) 'New social movements', *Telos*, 57: 194–205.

—— (1987) *The Theory of Communicative Action*, Cambridge: Polity Press.

—— (1989) *The Structural Transformation of the Public Sphere: An Inquiry into a Category of Bourgeois Society*, Massachusetts: MIT Press.

Katz, A. and Bender, E. (1976) *The Strength in Us*, New York: New Viewpoints.

Kelleher, D. (1990a) 'Do self-help groups help?', *International Disability Studies*, 12: 66–9.

—— (1990b) 'Consultants' views of self-help groups', unpublished.

—— (1991) 'Patients learning from each other: self-help groups for people with diabetes', *Journal of the Royal Society of Medicine*, 84: 595–7.

Kickbusch, I. (1989) 'Self-care in health promotion', *Social Science and Medicine*, 29: 125–30.

Kickbusch, I. and Hatch, S. (eds) (1983) *Self-help and Health in Europe*, Copenhagen: World Health Organization.

Lasch, C. (1980) *The Culture of Narcissism*, London: Sphere Books.

Lock, S. (1986) 'Self-help groups: the fourth estate in medicine', *British Medical Journal*, 292: 1,596–9.

Richardson, A. and Goodman, M. (1983) 'Self-help and social care: mutual aid organisations in practice', *Policy Studies Institute*, Paper No. 612, London.

Robinson, D. (1980) 'The self-help component of primary care', *Social Science and Medicine*, 14a: 415–22.

Robinson, D. and Henry, S. (1977) *Self-help and Health: Mutual Aid for Modern Problems*, London: Martin Robertson.

Saks, M. (1992) *Alternative Medicine in Modern Britain*, Oxford: Clarendon Press.

Sennett, R. (1977) *The Fall of Public Man*, New York: Knopf.

Stewart, M. (1990) 'Professional interface with mutual aid self-help groups: a review', *Social Science and Medicine*, 31: 1143–58.

Tattersall, M. and Hallstrom, C. (1992) 'Self-help and benzodiazepine withdrawal', *Journal of Affective Disorders*, 24: 193–8.

Trojan, A. (1989) 'Benefits of self-help groups: a survey of 232 members from 65 disease related groups', *Social Science and Medicine*, 29: 225–32.

Vincent, J. (1992) 'Self-help groups and health', in Saks, M. (ed.) *Alternative Medicine in Modern Britain*, Oxford: Clarendon Press.

Williams, G. (1989) 'Hope for the humblest? The role of self-help in chronic illness: the case of ankylosing spondylitis', *Sociology of Health and Illness*, 11: 135–59.

Wilson, J. (1992) 'Supporting self-help groups: an action research study of the work of Nottingham self-help groups project between 1982 and 1983', unpublished M.Phil. thesis, Loughborough University.

7 Lay knowledge and the privilege of experience

Gareth Williams and Jennie Popay

> One of the main intellectual activities of our century has been the questioning, not to say the undermining, of authority.
>
> (Said 1993)

INTRODUCTION

The differences between the ways in which medicine and everyday thinking represent matters of health and illness have been well documented in recent years (Helman 1984; Calnan 1987)). Most of this work deals with 'lay beliefs' or common-sense thinking about health and illness in relation to individuals' experiences. Moreover, most studies consider the experiences of these individuals in relation to their encounters with clinical medicine, whether in primary care or hospital settings. It has now been clearly demonstrated that the ways of seeing illness and talking about it that sociologists call lay beliefs are often quite distinctive in form and content (Blaxter 1983; Williams 1986). The challenge they pose to medical knowledge and power remains largely implicit, emerging perhaps only in the high rates of non-compliance to be found in patients' responses to medical directives (Belcon *et al.* 1984) or, more dramatically and less frequently, where individual patients take grievances to court (see Dingwall in this volume). For the most part, however sophisticated and sociologically illuminating the knowledge expressed in lay beliefs may be, it remains disorganised and *ad hoc*, posing little if any direct challenge to the power of the medical profession. However much these beliefs are part of a shared culture and society, they are expressions of personal experiences which remain outside the worlds of science and politics.

Increasingly, however, some of these concerns have developed into organised protest against aspects of biomedical knowledge and its use. In relation to clinical medicine, for example, the most highly publicised recent example in Britain was that of the women of the Bristol Survey Support

Group who engaged in a battle against the medical researchers whose subjects they had been in a clinical trial (Bagenal *et al.* 1990). Not only did they take exception to the results of the trial, which had provided the evidence for serious criticisms of the Bristol Cancer Help Centre (a clinic where the women had been treated which makes use of alternative as well as orthodox therapies), the women also challenged the ethical justification and methodological rationale for the clinical trial. One of the many actions they took in their battle was the making of a television programme shown on the British independent network Channel Four in April 1992. In that programme, two of the main activists within the Support Group argued:

> We were treated as pawns. No one expected the pawns to fight back, but we did because wc didn't want this to happen to anyone in the future. And it's not just us – there are far broader issues at stake.

This is but one example of a number of situations in which the women's movement has posed an explicit challenge to medical knowledge and power. Among 'the broader issues at stake' are the relationship between the knowledge of lay people and that of biomedical and other health sciences; and the extent to which trust in the authority of experts within the arena of medicine is beginning to dissolve, as doctors and other medical experts become 'de-professionalised' (Haug and Lavin 1983). The focus principally upon the relationship between lay and expert knowledge in clinical and clinical-research settings reflects the dominant place of the hospital within modern medicine and the health services as a whole.

However, more recently within the British National Health Service (NHS), the renewed emphasis on avoidable ill health and the concept of health authorities as 'champions of the people' (Secretary of State for Health 1991), along with the development of a more central role for 'community care' (Secretary of State for Health 1989), have raised the profile of issues relating to the public health. Moreover, in so far as public health problems, by definition, transcend the problems of particular individuals, and inasmuch as public health policies can affect whole neighbourhoods, they provide an interesting and rather different case within which to consider the relationship between lay and expert biomedical knowledge. In this chapter we argue that the intervention of lay knowledge (by invitation or otherwise) into the world of public and environmental health offers the possibility of a challenge to the dominance of the medical profession. However, like self-help, anti-vivisectionism (see Kelleher and Elston in this volume) and other 'anti-modernist' developments, the relationship of this challenge to the world of expertise is an ambiguous one.

The nature of the challenge discussed in this chapter is twofold. First, lay knowledge represents a challenge to the 'objectivity' of expert knowledge. It both contests the impartiality of that knowledge *vis-à-vis* other forms of knowledge, and it raises questions about the extent to which the process of objectification – upon which the truth-claims of scientific knowledge depend – permits a proper understanding of health problems in the 'new modernity' (Beck 1992a). In this sense it provides an *epistemological* challenge to expert knowledge. Second, lay knowledge represents a challenge to the authority of professionals to determine the way in which problems are defined in the policy arena. In this sense it is a *political* challenge to the institutional power of expert knowledge in general, and medical knowledge in particular.

In the first part of this chapter we sketch out the broad contours of the epistemological challenge, reviewing some of the arguments about the nature of, and relationship between, lay knowledge and the knowledge of medical experts. In the subsequent section we present an example of the way in which the epistemological and political challenges are being played out. This draws on instances of what has come to be referred to as 'popular epidemiology' – situations in which lay people conceptualise and gather information on health problems and risks about which orthodox experts are either silent or unreliable. In these situations, we argue, lay knowledge moves beyond individual complaint to develop a public voice and provide the basis for collective action for change in policy.

In the conclusion, we argue that while lay beliefs in the clinical arena provide an implicit challenge to medical knowledge by placing it in a different interpretive context, lay knowledge in the arena of public and environmental health tests medical knowledge by exposing it to debate in the public sphere (Habermas 1989). Both represent a struggle over meaning that is perhaps the latest manifestation of a questioning and undermining of authority. Traditional epidemiology and health services research are not well-equipped to respond to this challenge. However, we maintain that a constructive response is necessary to the challenge posed by lay knowledge if experts are to find answers to the questions being asked about health in the modern world.

DIFFERENT WAYS OF KNOWING: LAY AND MEDICAL KNOWLEDGE

Medical knowledge rests upon the concept of disease; lay knowledge is rooted in the experience of illness (Helman 1984; Williams and Wood 1986). What has been lacking from this traditional 'medical model' is a means of understanding the experiences of those who have diseases; and this reflects the perceived lack of relevance of such experiences to the framing of the medical task. As medicine became more 'scientistic' and the institution of the hospital more dominant, the patient's view was excluded both because it was regarded as marginal to the practice of medicine, and because, in being subjective, it was thought to compromise that objectivity which is the *sine qua non* of medical knowledge (Jewson 1976).

Although it has been argued that medicine in the early twentieth century became increasingly interested in 'the patient's view' (Armstrong 1984), this was never seen as a form of knowledge in itself, but only as evidence of, or a window upon, pathology.

Basic biomedical research, under pressure from the human genome project and other developments in biological sciences, continues to become increasingly reductive in its frames of reference. One important consequence of this may be that the more sophisticated biological explanations for disease become (and whatever therapeutic spin-offs may ensue) the more difficult it is for the sick person to relate knowledge about the genetic configuration of disease to her or his experience of it (Comaroff and Maguire 1981). Wittgenstein argued:

> Our language can be seen as an old city: a maze of little streets and squares, of old and new houses with additions from various periods; and this surrounded by a multitude of modern sections with straight regular streets and uniform houses.

(quoted in Geertz 1983: 73)

The more bright and rectangular the language of scientific medicine becomes, the more difficult it is for those living in the little streets and squares to regard it as part of the same world.

Sociologists and anthropologists are also 'professionals', imposing perspectives of their own. However, a large body of their work has employed ideas and developed methods whose stated aim is to look at things from the point of view of the person being studied, and to become familiar with those little streets (Geertz 1983). Much of this work has attempted to rescue the views of 'patients' from what, in the context of the history of the working class, E.P. Thompson has described as 'the enormous condescension of posterity' (Thompson 1968: 13), and has provided a setting in which the views of patients and the differences between lay and professional ways of knowing could be articulated.

Sociologists have focused for the most part on the experiences of individuals *qua* individuals, and on clinical interactions in institutional settings (Brown 1992). This research has uncovered the informal knowledge about health and illness held by lay people and analysed the role it plays in their dealings with experts. There have also been occasional attempts to develop a more *gemeinschaftlich* sense of a locality's own understanding of health and illness (Cornwell 1984). In contrast to the clinical focus on disease, this work has emphasised the importance of understanding the meaning of illness and health for the individual by focusing on the *consequences* of illness for ordinary, everyday life, the *significance* of symptoms and experiences for the person who has them (Bury 1991), and the linkages between biography and knowledge (Williams 1984).

One important effect of this work has been a growing understanding of the complexity of lay perspectives on health and illness. From the traditional medical perception lay beliefs are at best unreliable and at worst irrational (Gillick 1985), useful only in so far as they cast light on the causes of 'non-compliance' (Conrad 1985). Sociological and anthropological work, in contrast, has explored their coherence and validity in terms of the purposes they fulfil for the person who holds them (Blaxter 1983; Helman 1984). Lay knowledge may incorporate expert knowledge but it has to be reinterpreted in terms of the experience of everyday life (Davison *et al.* 1991).

It would not be possible to summarise all this work here, but at least four key themes have emerged. First, lay beliefs about illness are many and varied. They do not simply mimic the supposedly more sophisticated understandings of medical science. Second, lay perspectives on illness are logically consistent and coherent, even where the empirical contents of lay knowledge are at variance with what is accepted within medical science. Lay perspectives have been shown to hold together different aspects of the person's experience of the onset, course and effects of his or her illness, in an attempt to makes sense of this in causal terms (Blaxter 1983). Third, lay perspectives are biographical. They are narrative reconstructions of the relationship between the illness and the person's life conceived as a whole (Cornwell 1984; Williams 1984; Kelly 1986). Fourth, lay concepts of illness are culturally framed within certain systems of belief and action (Helman 1984). Although many studies of lay beliefs are based on groups of individuals who are 'unrepresentative' in a statistical sense, in an equally important sense lay knowledge is 'representative' of the discourses upon which it draws. In formulating their perspectives, individuals draw upon ideas that are general. Lay knowledge is both personal and social knowledge in the sense that shared knowledge informs the private understanding of illness (Williams 1993).

Lay knowledge incorporates different notions of cause to those found in the biomedical model. The medical model attempts to make sense of the causes of disease. Lay perspectives, in contrast, attempt to make sense of the causes of disease in relation to the experience of its impact. They are concerned with more than the question, What has caused this disease? They have additional questions which are not addressed, or not addressed adequately, within the framework of the biomedical model. For example, for someone afflicted with a serious illness or disability the questions that arise are: Why has this happened to me? Why has this happened now? Doctors are often unable to provide credible answers to these questions addressing, as they do, the meaning of an individual life. While someone with illness may share with his or her doctor an interest in understanding the cause of disease as an abstract process, he or she will also be interested in relating this knowledge to experience through narrative and biography, and to his or her locality – the concrete knowledge about the features of the world the person inhabits. Reflecting on these aspects of lay knowledge, the challenge to medicine becomes apparent, because it means taking subjectivity seriously rather than seeing it as an impediment to understanding.

This perspective on lay knowledge has certain methodological implications. Lay knowledge could not be examined in the way it has been without using certain kinds of research methods. Understanding the nature of lay knowledge requires an approach to data collection that is, in a sense, egalitarian, and most certainly phenomenologically open. Methods like unstructured interviews have been used, therefore, which allow a story to emerge. Not only does lay knowledge pose problems for medicine because it represents a different form of knowledge, it also challenges the methods with which medical science is most comfortable because it remains inaccessible to them.

In lying outside the conventions of positivism lay knowledge challenges the search for abstract facts understood as things that exist independently of our interpretation of them. Lay knowledge, in being open to variation, difference, and local significance, has always been post-modern. The vogue of post-modernism, with its emphasis on 'the contextuality of truth-claims' (Giddens 1990), provides a neat legitimation for lay resistance to expert systems of knowledge, and a useful theoretical justification for the empirical work by sociologists and others in this area. Lay knowledge about health and illness thus provides an epistemological challenge to medicine. It offers a view of illness that is subjective and often highly coherent. Once the narrative structure is recognised, the beliefs it carries cannot be easily dismissed as irrational, and non-compliance may be better understood as a subversion of medical dominance and a critique of objectification. However, in so far as such knowledge about illness remains private, expressed only in the clinic, the home, or in casual encounters with others, it offers no direct political challenge to the power of medicine.

The defiant nature of lay knowledge becomes more explicit in relation to problems of public and environmental health. In these situations we can see the way in which the role of lay knowledge in public debate about issues relating to expert knowledge is politically unsettling for those who hold power in society, and for those who are accustomed to being able to have their truth claims vindicated by reference to a body of technical knowledge.

POPULAR EPIDEMIOLOGY AND PUBLIC HEALTH

Although ecological critiques of the effects of industrialism and capitalism on the environment and health are not new (R. Williams 1989), environmental problems are increasingly prominent in contemporary debate, both globally and locally (British Medical Journal 1991; Finnegan 1991; Lancet 1992; Pithers 1992). In addition to the concerns about large-scale ecological degradation relating to ozone depletion and global warming, waste disposal (Walker 1991), the safety of drinking water (Walker 1992), air pollution (Godlee 1991) and the state of bathing beaches (Philipp *et al.* 1993) are sources of anxiety at the present time. In addition, disasters and smaller accidents have given rise to public concern about the way in which potentially dangerous plant and machinery is managed (Martin 1993). From lay perspectives, however, 'environmental problems' are not only those high-profile spillages and emissions which hit the newspaper headlines. For people living in urban areas, busy roads, litter, dogs, vandalism, noise, derelict properties and poor street-lighting constitute the hazardous reality of everyday life (Percy-Smith and Sanderson 1992).

The World Health Organization's (WHO) *Health for All* strategy asserted:

> It is a basic tenet of the health for all philosophy that people must be given the knowledge and influence to ensure that health developments in communities are made not only for, but also with and by the people.
>
> (WHO 1985: 11)

Stimulated by this, and by the various developments taking place in relation to the 'new public health' (Ashton and Seymour 1988), a more social and participative vision of public health entered the mainstream in Britain with the publication of the report *Public Health in England*, which defined public health as: 'The science and art of preventing disease, prolonging life and promoting health through the organized efforts of society' (Secretary of State for Social Services 1988). In the wake of these developments fundamental changes are taking place in the way in which we view public health in Britain (Lancet 1991). Although many of the key issues recall the nineteenth century (Acheson 1990; Porter and Porter 1990), the 'new public health' emphasises the structural causes of ill-health, environmental concerns, health promotion, intersectoral collaboration and the importance of working 'with the people'. Working with the people means participation, and participation by lay people means taking lay knowledge seriously.

In recent years in Britain there have been cases of communities using the courts to fight industries perceived to be polluting the environment (Utting 1991, 1992); and at a less dramatic level community groups have mounted protests against urban hazards such as unsafe housing, congested roads, and public parks littered with excrement, broken glass and discarded syringes. In these situations there is often both a simple political protest against something unpleasant and dangerous, and an attempt to change the way in which risks are defined and the way in which priorities for action are decided (Watt 1987).

Popular epidemiology in Massachusetts

A focus on these sorts of issues is a key feature of much of the 'citizen action for environmental health' in the USA (Freudenberg 1984), and many examples of 'popular epidemiology' (Brown 1987) arise from community responses to problems such as toxic waste (Masterson-Allen and Brown 1990). Popular epidemiology is a synthesis of political activism and lay knowledge, and a form of public participation in the pursuit of scientific knowledge and political change. As Brown, a prominent American writer in this field, notes, it is:

> the process whereby laypersons gather scientific data and other information, and also direct and marshall the resources of experts in order to understand the epidemiology of disease.
>
> (Brown 1992: 269)

In the USA, where it has been most prominent, popular epidemiology is an extension of the community based protest and activism which is characteristic of political culture in the USA; a culture which has often exhibited a robust disdain for the claims of experts of any kind (Walzer 1983), including politicians and experts on public health and environmental issues (Harris 1984). The empirical work from which Brown's own ideas emerged was much more than a battle between lay people and medical or scientific experts.

In the mid-1970s, the residents of Woburn, a working-class and lower-middle-class town in Massachusetts, about twelve miles north of Boston, began to worry that their children were contracting leukaemia with considerable frequency – four times higher than would normally be expected. For decades, moreover, residents had complained about the smell and taste of their drinking water. The first detection efforts were begun by one woman, Ann Anderson, whose son, Jimmy, had been diagnosed with acute lymphocytic leukaemia in 1972:

Anderson put together information during 1973–1974 about other cases by meetings with other Woburn victims in town and at the hospital where Jimmy spent much time. Anderson hypothesised that the alarming leukaemia incidence was caused by a water-borne agent. In 1975 she asked state officials to test the water but was told that testing could not be done at an individual's initiative.

(Brown 1992: 270)

What is interesting from the point of view of our analysis here is that the community response included a refusal to accept the conclusions of the 'independent' experts sent in by the Centers for Disease Control in collaboration with the Massachusetts Department of Public Health. The official report concluded that the cases of childhood leukaemia were more than twice as high as expected. However, because the case-control method failed to find characteristics that differentiated victims from non-victims, and because there were no environmental water exposure data going back before 1979, the report argued that it was not possible to conclude that the increased incidence was related to the water supply.

The long story which was eventually told illuminated the parts played by business, government, environmental watch-dogs, and governmentally employed scientists – none of whom come out of it very clean. Brown's study went on to show how the local community, in the form of a pressure group, 'For a Cleaner Environment', enlisted the help of its own experts from the Harvard School of Public Health. By jointly collecting and analysing more data, they managed to get their case heard in the courts and to challenge the results of the official researchers. Brown's study, therefore, reveals the conflict between legal and medical experts over the nature of evidence and the understanding of 'cause' and 'effect' (Brown and Mikkelsen 1990), as well as the crucial role of the media in publicising people's stories and providing a place where alternative accounts of information and events can be published.

In view of the public context within which it works, popular epidemiology is very rarely a simple bilateral struggle between lay and expert scientific knowledge. There may well be a number of different lay perspectives on the situation in a given case, and also a number of different expert viewpoints. For example, there may be differences of opinion between those working in a factory and those living near it (Brown and Mikkelsen 1990; Phillimore and Moffatt in press), and there may be disagreements between the experts called in to assess the situation. In any given case there will be a multitude of voices and a plurality of perspectives (Williams and Popay 1993). Moreover, in addition to the conflict between diverse groups with different interests, where there is a direct governmental interest in the nature of the knowledge that emerges about a situation, the State may become more directly involved.

Something that might be described as an example of popular epidemiology has appeared more recently in Britain (Phillimore and Moffatt in press; Rice *et al.* in press). In order to illustrate in more detail the epistemological and political challenges posed by these situations to medical and other expertise, we want to examine the events that surrounded a water contamination incident in England in 1988, and the response of the local community to it.

THE CASE OF THE CAMELFORD POISONING

On 6 July 1988, a lorry driver accidentally tipped 20 tonnes of aluminium sulphate solution into the treated water reservoir of the Lowermoor Water Treatment Works supplying the residents of Camelford and the surrounding area in north Cornwall. In addition to the close historical relationship between public health and the water supply (Johnson 1986), this incident was especially noticeable in view of its having taken place very soon after the Thatcher Government's privatisation of the water authorities of England and Wales. The Camelford episode has been the subject of two government-backed reports by an expert group, the second under a Department of Health imprint, chaired by Dame Barbara Clayton, a well-respected chemical pathologist (CISDHA 1989; Department of Health 1991). This group, the Lowermoor Incident Health Advisory Group (the Clayton Committee), was set up in January 1989 at the instigation of the Parliamentary Under Secretary of State for Health to provide 'independent expert advice' (CISDHA 1989: 1) to the Cornwall and Isles of Scilly District Health Authority.

The appointment of this expert group was the Governmental response to considerable pressure from residents and people who had been on holiday at the time, who attributed a variety of symptoms to water contamination, and had not been convinced by locally generated expert advice. In addition to Barbara Clayton herself, the Committee consisted of a number of different experts: a neurochemical pathologist, the Chief Scientist of the Water Research Centre, and a Professor of Epidemiology and Population Sciences. The pressure from the locality came from residents who organised themselves very quickly to express their concerns. They formed both a general support group, the Lowermoor Support Group, and what was called the Camelford Scientific Advisory Panel (CSAP), a local group which included individuals who themselves had considerable expertise in particular areas relevant to the incident. They monitored the incident and its effects from the outset.

In the wake of the first Clayton report, published exactly a year after the incident, there was little disagreement between Clayton and the local residents over the immediate health effects. According to Clayton, these included: 'nausea, vomiting, diarrhoea, headaches, fatigue, itching skin, rashes, sore eyes, and mouth ulcers'. The report goes on to register that some people felt 'generally unwell' while others complained of 'aches and pains'. CSAP produced its own questionnaire which was completed by 432 respondents between mid-July and mid-August 1988. The most commonly reported complaints were similar to those which the official group had identified.

In its first report, therefore, the Clayton Committee noted that 'many of the early symptoms reported to CSAP and at our meeting in Camelford can be attributed to the incident' (CISDHA 1989: 3). However, it pointed out that 'general practitioners' consulting patterns did not show any overall increase in the number of patients seen by doctors in the month following the incident' (ibid.). The Committee also argued that detailed analysis of the CSAP information was not appropriate because 'it cannot be assumed that those who responded are representative of the local population; the questionnaires were left at strategic points for collection and returned by anyone who wished to participate, so introducing an element of self selection' (ibid.).

These methodological caveats appear to have provided the basis for the dispute that followed between the Clayton Committee and the local community. The disagreement centred on the validity of claims and counterclaims about the 'delayed or persistent effects' of the incident. The first Report (1989) notes that the Health Authority had compiled a register of people complaining about symptoms occurring or persisting long after the incident. At the time the report was written in July 1989 there were 280 people on the register. These chronic symptoms fell into four broad categories:

1 Joint pains, exacerbation of arthritis, and non-specific aches and pains;
2 Memory loss, poor concentration, speech problems, depression and behavioural disorders in children;
3 Rashes and mouth ulcers;
4 Gastrointestinal disorder.

The Clayton Committee examined existing research evidence regarding the detrimental health effects of a variety of contaminants in the Lowermoor water using European Community standards. For lead, zinc, copper and sulphate, they concluded that the amounts likely to have been absorbed, even on worst-case assumptions ('drinking up to two litres of the most heavily contaminated water per day' (CISDHA 1989: 4)), would have no long-lasting effects on the health of the population. In relation to aluminium, the major pollutant, and in view of the complaints of memory loss and the recent attention given to the possibility of a link between aluminium and Alzheimer's disease, the report presents its summary of the evidence regarding the dietary sources, metabolism and toxicology of aluminium. On the basis of this it concluded that any ill-health caused by the aluminium was temporary:

> All the known toxic effects of aluminium are associated with chronically elevated exposure and we have concluded therefore that delayed or persistent effects following such brief exposures are unlikely.
>
> (CISDHA 1989: 14)

Although the Clayton Committee claimed to refute the link between the contamination and long-term health effects, as the quote illustrates, it clearly felt obliged to offer some explanation for the health problems being reported by local residents:

> In our view it is not possible to attribute the very real current health complaints to the toxic effects of the incident, except inasmuch as they are the consequence of the sustained anxiety naturally felt by many people.
>
> (ibid.)

In its criticism of the evidence produced by local residents and the local District Health Authority in support of their claims about long-term effects, the Clayton Committee commented on 'the difficulties in both carrying out and interpreting environmental epidemiological studies of acute incidents' (CISDHA 1989: 11). The Committee also targeted the local and national media for particular criticism for their role in relation to the incident:

> Some of the reporting of the incident has been inaccurate and without scientific foundation. . . . Some statements have . . . in our opinion caused unnecessary anxiety and suffering.
>
> (CISDHA 1989: 12)

The response to the Clayton report

The press and other media played a major role in publicising the Camelford incident, and in discussing points of view opposed to the conclusions and recommendations of the Advisory Group. After the publication of the first report, local people continued to complain of symptoms of malaise, and, in particular, problems with memory and other aspects of cognitive functioning. In view of the continuing commotion, a special conference was convened by the Cornwall and Isles of Scilly Health Authority in February 1990, which gave rise to a special report (CISDHA 1990). Three papers presented at the conference fuelled the debate: a clinical biochemist found high concentrations of aluminium in blood samples one year after the incident; a neuropsychologist reported evidence 'consistent with the effects of minor brain injury'; and a clinical psychologist discovered significant memory defects. The fact that the conference report did not get published until the findings were leaked to the press, almost six months after the conference met, led some local people and journalists to feel that something was being hidden.

Throughout the period since July 1988 to now, organised opposition to the official view has been articulated by local people through the Lowermoor Support Group and the Camelford Scientific Advisory Panel. The latter, according to one report, is 'an *ad hoc* group of people living in the area who have academic or campaigning skills. It includes Liz Sigmund, a veteran of the campaign against chemical weapons, Dr Newman (a local GP who has himself experienced problems with memory), and Doug Cross, an environmental consultant' (Kennedy 1990).

The Department of Health reacted strongly to the accusations by local residents and the media which had given them a platform. The then Junior Health Minister, Stephen Dorrell, in a letter to the *Guardian*, criticised the newspaper for:

> grossly misrepresent[ing] the properly cautious conclusions of the [Clayton] report, based as it was on a detailed and thorough assessment of the scientific data available. No more and no less would be expected from a group of truly independent and distinguished scientists, who are acknowledged experts in the relevant fields.
>
> (Dorrell 1990)

In a parliamentary reply in July, according to a report by the *Guardian*'s columnist Melanie Phillips, Stephen Dorrell characterised the local critics of the Clayton Report as 'malicious people, down there stirring things up, and worrying people for their own short-term gains' (Phillips 1990).

In addition to underlining the highly political nature of anything to do with water at the very time that the national water companies were in the process of being privatised, there is an irony in the fact that, also at the same time, the then Secretary of State for the Department of the Environment (Chris Patten) was publishing a White Paper urging precisely such active citizenship in relation to our 'common inheritance' (Department of the Environment 1990).

Continuing pressure from local people, both through individual legal action and collective protest, forced the Government to decide that the Clayton Committee should be reconvened. Its terms of reference were: '"To assess reports which have become available since July 1989 of persistent symptoms and clinicopathological findings amongst people who were resident in the Camelford area at the time of the Lowermoor incident;

and to advise the Department of Health and the Cornwall and Isles of Scilly District Health Authority on the implications of these findings"' (Department of Health 1991: 1).

The fact that the Committee was to have the same membership, with the addition of a clinical psychologist to interpret psychometric data, was greeted with dismay by local residents and their supporters. Liz Sigmund of CSAP was quoted in the newspapers as saying: 'One whitewash will be followed by another, unless they are all prepared to admit they were wrong, which seems highly unlikely' (16 October 1990). Another leading member of the local residents wrote mockingly: 'What wonderful news for those of us labelled by the [Clayton] committee as victims of mass hysteria and what an extraordinary opportunity for the committee to examine the effects of this mass hysteria' (Burgess 1990). The fact that the second Clayton report includes a six-page appendix listing 'people who have provided medical, scientific and technical advice' (Department of Health 1991: 40) suggests that the Committee may have anticipated the reaction. For whatever reasons, this list does not seem to include anyone, other than local general practitioners, who could have been said to have been selected to represent the views of local people. In an editorial devoted to the issue, the *Guardian* itself commented:

> There are two purposes in setting up Committees of Inquiry: to seek out the truth and to reassure the public. Clayton is perceived in Cornwall to have failed with the first; and demonstrably been unsuccessful in the second. Reconstituting the committee now to the reassess the evidence will put members under intense pressure to look for facts which will justify their original conclusions, rather than objectively reviewing the new evidence to see if they were wrong.
>
> (The *Guardian* 1990)

As it turned out the second report of the Lowermoor Incident Health Advisory Group (Department of Health 1991) reiterated the conclusions of the first report: 'The research reported to us does not provide convincing evidence that harmful accumulation of aluminium has occurred, nor that there is greater prevalence of ill-health due to toxic effects of the water in the exposed population' (Department of Health 1991: 1). Although denying that the first Report had intended to imply that symptoms in the population had been caused by 'hysteria', the second report nevertheless maintained that 'The physical problems associated with all the worry and concern and the psychological harm could last a long time for some people. Such a situation is well recognised following major accidents' (Department of Health 1991: 2). In response to the continuing protests, the Chief Medical Officer insisted that Clayton and her colleagues 'have again carried out a difficult task with sensitivity and integrity' (Calman 1991).

The implications of Camelford

It would be possible to regard what happened after the spillage at Camelford as idiosyncratic. Although there were a number of unusual aspects to the community response at Camelford – as there would be in any case study – they clearly fit the description of the movement against toxic waste which:

> can be seen as part of a larger social trend toward increased public demand for a role in scientific and technological decision-making which challenges scientific criteria for assessing risk and experts' claims to technical knowledge.
>
> (Masterson-Allen and Brown 1990)

The disagreements to which the Camelford incident and the various inquiries gave rise were partly to do with the nature of different kinds and sources of evidence: the carefully collated evidence of local people's own experiences, on the one hand, and the highly technical toxicological and clinical measurements of the Committee and its expert witnesses. The hope of the official bodies involved was that the disagreements would be resolved once the evidence had been appraised by the experts in a sober and dispassionate manner. This did not happen and what we have described in Camelford is a profound disjuncture between the local people's and the experts' perspectives on the evidence and the way it was handled. This could be seen as a difference between 'subjectivity' and 'objectivity', or between opinion and science, and this is what the Clayton Committee seems to imply in both the first and the second report. The Committee's use of the community diagnosis of 'sustained anxiety' (CISDHA 1989: 14) to explain the local community's beliefs was a way of indicating its unreliability and, therefore, its distance from the standards of scientific discourse.

What happened at Camelford was not just a matter of the local community insisting that its own evidence was as reliable as that of the scientists, although this was primarily the level at which the debate was conducted. Local people were issuing a political challenge to biomedical knowledge in so far as they were refusing to permit the authority of scientists to be used to disempower them. And they were issuing an epistemological challenge in two ways: first by refusing to accept that the Clayton Committee's knowledge was impartial simply by virtue of having been produced by scientists, and second, by insisting that local knowledge based on shared biographical experiences cannot be invalidated by reference to some standard of objectivity derived from abstract scientific knowledge.

As was the case in Brown's study of Woburn, the role of the media was important in these challenges. From the point of view of the Clayton Committee, the role of the media was unhelpful, serving to amplify the anxieties that were already being experienced by the local community, and therefore preventing the imposition of a rational judgement (Renn *et al.* 1992).

From the perspective of the local residents, however, the media could be seen as playing a role similar to that of the coffee-house in previous centuries (Sennett 1993): providing a setting within civil society in which personal troubles can be debated and taken forward into political action over public issues.

CONCLUSION

Within clinical medicine, non-compliant actions and the beliefs surrounding them are often seen as the product of ignorance and irrationality. However, work on the nature of lay beliefs has indicated that although they may suggest lack of knowledge of anatomy and physiology, and although they may be based upon strong emotions, they can be coherent and logical, and provide narrative reconstructions of the relationship between illness and the individual's perception of her or his place in the world. There are many reasons for continuing attempts to define lay knowledge as something more than an interesting but infuriating curiosity. One is the continuing inadequacy of traditional medical explanations for a range of chronic and terminal diseases which provide the ill person with little that helps him or her make sense of what is going on. Another reason is the fact that explanation within medical science is becoming so reductive that it excludes virtually all matters of significance from the person's own point of view. A person who has cancer may have some interest in the behaviour of her or his cells and the impact of chemotherapy upon them. However, she or he also needs to make sense of a predicament in terms of the narrative of her or his own life. Finally, at the level of practice there has been the manifest failure of high-tech, top-down interventions – in both curative and preventive medicine – to develop adequate solutions to the health problems people face.

In a world in which science takes itself off to ever more distant shores, and religion often does little to help people deal with metaphysical concerns in a way that makes sense to them, narratives woven out of a variety of threads provide a meaningful texture. While these views may not challenge medicine directly, and usually do not seek to do so, they provide an alternative way of seeing and talking about illness in everyday life which, to some extent, may feed the deprofessionalisation process.

In relation to public and environmental health, challenges to experts are often dismissed by the experts themselves in a similar fashion: as capricious, unpredictable and irrational; an irritating reflection of general scientific illiteracy (Cvetkovich and Earle 1992). Popular epidemiology, both in its latest ecological form, and in the form in which the community health movement used it to fight against poor housing conditions and other unhealthy aspects of local environments, is also, in essence, a struggle over meaning. It is a struggle over the meaning of health, of the good life, of acceptable risk, and of hazard. It is a struggle not just over the landscape but over the 'lifescape' (Eyles *et al.* 1993). However, in defining as public dangers what might otherwise be perceived as private risks (Scott *et al.* 1992), popular epidemiology poses a direct threat to those who have conventionally been invested with the authority to pronounce on the meaning and significance of public and environmental health problems. This kind of mobilisation of lay knowledge expresses a critique of the manner in which health risks are conceptualised and measured, a profound mistrust of the experts given responsibility for doing the defining (Hayes 1992), and a rejection of existing public health policies (Vaughan and Seifert 1992).

Part of what is needed to overcome these problems is greater pluralism involving more openness to lay or popular participation; a commitment to grasping lay perspectives (Kelly 1990). Such participation would need to go beyond lay discussion of the results of research to include an active role in the conceptualisation and specification of the nature of the problem, and the design and conduct of the research. This process would involve widening the portfolio of methods considered legitimate within research, and acknowledging the important input lay knowledge can make to the design of conventional research measures. The dogmatic division of knowledge into 'science' and 'non-science' will make this difficult, but as Brown argues in relation to his study of the citizens of Woburn: 'Popular epidemiology is not antiscientific. Rather, it has a different concept of what science is, whom it should serve, and who should control it' (Brown 1987: 83).

Once the struggle over meaning becomes public in this way, the question arises as to how science can be both technical and democratic at the same time (Fiorino 1989). As one enlightened epidemiologist has argued: 'Epidemiology is a human science, inevitably entangled with society . . . unthinking neutrality is a stance that can have even greater political implications than open commitment' (Susser 1989: 487). Once this is recognised, the epidemiologist and any other expert needs to do something other than dismiss the statements of critics as 'unscientific' or 'politically motivated'.

Epidemiology cannot resolve the public health problems of everyday life by retiring into the epistemology of medicine. The changing relationship between experts and the public means that the experts can no longer refuse to listen to people on the grounds that they are engaged in the pursuit of truth (Harris 1984). The loss of trust in expert systems (Giddens 1990) and the collapse of the 'grand narratives' within which the legitimacy of 'science' resides (Lyotard 1984) have made such deference to the authority of experts less automatic. In our own time, it is no longer possible to say that science is something separate from politics and that knowledge has nothing to do with power.

One of the consequences of the 'scientisation of politics' is that issues to do with the environment and public health have tended to be reduced to abstract technical calculations. However, in a society in which technological risks have become endemic, discussions of public and environmental health cannot be confined to expert seminars. They need to be located within an 'ecological extension of democracy', which means:

> playing off the concert of voices and powers, the development of the independence of politics, law, the public sphere and daily life against the dangerous and false security of a 'society from the drawing board. . . .' The public sphere, in co-operation with a kind of 'public science' would be charged as a second centre of the 'discursive checking' of scientific laboratory results in the crossfire of opinions.
>
> (Beck 1992b: 119)

It is important to understand that such a development would inevitably involve more than just getting the public involved in 'science'. It would mean thinking about science quite differently. Lay knowledge is a proclamation of 'the privilege of experience' (Adorno 1973: 40). Once biomedical and other scientific knowledge becomes caught in the crossfire of opinions it inevitably involves dealing with questions like: 'How do we wish to live?', or 'Why do we feel ill all the time?'. It means taking account of these questions and being prepared to discuss them in the formulation of environmental and health policies. The lay challenge to medical knowledge is not a complaint about the aesthetics of discourse, it is a political challenge to the status of scientific knowledge and the power of those whom we are encouraged to trust with such knowledge. What we have described in this chapter, therefore, in terms of a challenge to medicine is also an important characteristic of the unfolding debate on the nature of the modern world.

REFERENCES

Acheson, E.D. (1990) 'Edwin Chadwick and the world we live in', *Lancet*, 336: 1,482–5.

Adorno, T.W. (1973) *Negative Dialectics*, London: Routledge.

Armstrong, D. (1984) 'The patient's view', *Social Science and Medicine*, 18: 737–44.

Ashton, J. and Seymour, H. (1988) *The New Public Health*, Milton Keynes: Open University Press.

Bagenal, F.S., Easton, D.F., Harris, E., Chilvers, C.E.D. and McElwain, T.J. (1990) 'Survival of patients with breast cancer attending Bristol Cancer Help Centre', *Lancet*, 336: 606–10.

Beck, U. (1992a) *Risk Society: Towards a New Modernity*, London: Sage.

—— (1992b) 'From industrial society to risk society: questions of survival, social structure and ecological enlightenment', *Theory, Culture, and Society*, 9: 97–123.

Belcon, M., Haynes, B. and Tugwell, P. (1984) 'A critical review of compliance studies in rheumatoid arthritis', *Arthritis and Rheumatism*, 27: 1227–33.

Blaxter, M. (1983) 'The causes of disease: women talking', *Social Science and Medicine*, 17: 59–69.

British Medical Journal (1991) 'Lessons of Chernobyl', editorial, *British Medical Journal*, 303: 1,347–8.

Brown, P. (1987) 'Popular epidemiology: community response to toxic-waste induced disease in Woburn, Massachusetts', *Science, Technology, and Human Values*, 12: 78–85.

—— (1992) 'Popular epidemiology and toxic waste contamination', *Journal of Health and Social Behaviour*, 33: 267–81.

Brown, P. and Mikkelsen, E.J. (1990) *No Safe Place: Toxic Waste, Leukemia, and Community Action*, Berkeley: University of California Press.

Burgess, M. (1990) 'Cautious welcome for reconvened inquiry into water poisoning', letter, *Guardian*, 17 October.

Bury, M. (1991) 'The sociology of chronic illness: a review of research and prospects', *Sociology of Health and Illness*, 13: 451–68.

Calman, K. (1991) 'Camelford Report's clear lines of inquiry', letter, *Guardian*, 12 November.

Calnan, M. (1987) *Health and Illness: The Lay Perspective*, London: Tavistock.

Comaroff, J. and Maguire, P. (1981) 'Ambiguity and the search for meaning: childhood leukaemia in the modern clinical context', *Social Science and Medicine*, 15B: 115–23.

Conrad, P. (1985) 'The meaning of medications: another look at compliance', *Social Science and Medicine*, 20: 29–37.

Cornwall and Isles of Scilly District Heatlh Authority (CISDHA) (1989) *Water Pollution at Lowermoor North Cornwall: Report of the Lowermoor Incident Health Advisory Group* (chairperson: Professor Dame Barbara Clayton), Truro: Cornwall and Isles of Scilly District Health Authority.

—— (1990) *Lowermoor Water Incident* (conference proceedings), Truro: Cornwall and Isles of Scilly District Health Authority.

Cornwell, J. (1984) *Hard-Earned Lives: Accounts of Health and Illness from East London*, London: Tavistock.

Cvetkovich, G. and Earle, T.C. (1992) 'Environmental hazards and the public', *Journal of Social Issues*, 48: 1–20.

Davison, C., Davey-Smith, G. and Frankel, S. (1991) 'Lay epidemiology and the prevention paradox: the implications of coronary candidacy for health promotion', *Sociology of Health and Illness*, 13: 2–19.

Department of the Environment (1990) *This Common Inheritance*, Government White Paper, London: HMSO.

Department of Health (1991) *Water Pollution at Lowermoor North Cornwall: Second Report of the Lowermoor Incident Health Advisory Group* (chairperson: Professor Dame Barbara Clayton), London: HMSO.

Dorrell, S. (1990) 'Government concern over the suffering in Camelford', letter, *Guardian*, 27 July.

Eyles, J., Taylor, M., Johnson, N. and Baxter, J. (1993) 'Worrying about waste: living close to solid waste disposal facilities in southern Ontario', *Social Science and Medicine*, 37: 805–12.

Finnegan, M. (1991) 'Secret of toxic tip', *Manchester Evening News*, 5 September (front page 'exclusive').

Fiorino, D.J. (1989) 'Technical and democratic values in risk analysis', *Risk Analysis*, 9: 293–9.

Freudenberg, N. (1984) 'Citizen action for environmental health: report on a survey of community organizations', *American Journal of Public Health*, 74: 444–8.

Geertz, C. (1983) *Local Knowledge: Further Essays in Interpretive Anthropology*, New York: Basic Books.

Giddens, A. (1990) *The Consequences of Modernity*, Oxford: Polity Press.

Gillick, M.R. (1985) 'Common-sense models of health and disease', *New England Journal of Medicine*, 313: 700–2.

Godlee, F. (1991) 'Strategy for a healthy environment', *British Medical Journal*, 303: 836–8.

Guardian (1990) 'Muddy waters', editorial, *Guardian*, 17 October.

Habermas, J. (1989) *The Structural Transformation of the Public Sphere: An Enquiry into a Category of Bourgeois Society*, Cambridge, MA: MIT Press.

Harris, D. (1984) 'Health department: enemy or champion of the people?', *American Journal of Public Health*, 74: 428–30.

Hayes, M.V. (1992) 'On the epistemology of risk: language, logic and social science', *Social Science and Medicine*, 35: 401–7.

Helman, C. (1984) *Culture, Health and Illness*, Bristol: John Wright.

Haug, M. and Lavin B. (1983) *Consumerism in Medicine: Challenging Physician Authority*, Beverly Hills: Sage.

Jewson, N. (1976) 'The disappearance of the sick man from medical cosmology: 1770–1870', *Sociology*, 10: 225–44.

Johnson, W. (1986) 'The privatization of public health', *Radical Community Medicine*, 25: 4–11.

Kelly, M.P. (1986) 'The subjective experience of chronic disease: some implications for the management of ulcerative colitis', *Journal of Chronic Diseases*, 39: 653–66.

—— (1990) 'The role of research in the new public health', *Critical Public Health*, 3: 4–9.

Kennedy, M. (1990) 'Water blunder turned the good life sour', *Guardian*, 11 June: 4.

Lancet (1991) 'What's new in public health?', editorial, *Lancet*, 337: 1381–2.

—— (1992) 'Environmental pollution: it kills trees, but does it kill people', editorial, *Lancet*, 340: 821–2.

Lyotard J.-F. (1984) *The Post-Modern Condition: A Report on Knowledge*, Manchester: Manchester University Press.

Martin, J. (1993) *The Public Perception of Risk from Industrial Hazards: Case Studies of Halton, Cheshire and Halebank, Merseyside*, unpublished M.Sc. dissertation, University of Salford.

Masterson-Allen, S. and Brown, P. (1990) 'Public reaction to toxic waste contamination: analysis of a social movement', *International Journal of Health Services*, 20: 485–500.

Percy-Smith, J. and Sanderson, I. (1992) *Understanding Local Needs*, London: Institute for Public Policy Research.

Phillimore, P. and Moffatt, S. (in press) 'Discounted knowledge: local experience, environmental pollution and health', in Popay, J. and Williams, G. (eds) *Researching the People's Health*, London: Routledge.

Philipp, R., Pond, K. and Rees, G. (1993) 'Litter and medical waste on bathing beaches in England and Wales', *British Medical Journal*, 306: 1042.

Phillips, M. (1990) 'The seeping sickness of Camelford', *Guardian*, 26 October: 19.

Pithers, M. (1992) 'Two die in blast at chemical works', *Independent*, 22 September.

Porter, D. and Porter, R. (1990) 'The ghost of Edwin Chadwick', *British Medical Journal*, 301: 252.

Renn, O., Burns W.J., Kasperson, J.X., Kasperson, R.E. and Slovic, P. (1992) 'The social amplification of risk: theoretical foundations and empirical applications', *Journal of Social Issues*, 48: 137–60.

Rice, C., Roberts, H., Smith, S.J. and Bryce, C. (in press) '"It's like teaching your child to swim in a pool full of alligators": lay voices and professional research on child accidents', in Popay, J. and Williams G. (eds) *Researching the People's Health*, London: Routledge.

Said, E. (1993) 'Speaking truth to power' (The Reith Lectures), *Independent*, 22 July: 12.

Scott, S., Williams, G., Platt, S. and Thomas, H. (eds) (1992) *Private Risks and Public Dangers*, Aldershot: Avebury.

Secretary of State for Health (1989) *Caring for People: Community Care in the Next Decade and Beyond*, London: HMSO.

—— (1991) *The Health of the Nation: A Consultative Document for Health in England*, London: HMSO.

Secretary of State for Social Services (1988) *Public Health in England: The Report of the Committee of Inquiry into the Future Development of the Public Health Function* (chairperson, Sir Donald Acheson), London: HMSO.

Sennett, R. (1993) *The Fall of Public Man*, London: Faber.

Susser, M. (1989) 'Epidemiology today: 'a thought-tormented world', *International Journal of Epidemiology*, 18: 481–9.

Thompson, E.P. (1968) *The Making of the English Working Class*, Harmondsworth: Penguin.

Utting, D. (1991) 'Battle over the breath of life', *Guardian*, 3 July.

—— (1992) 'The burden of proof', *Guardian*, 22 July.

Vaughan, E. and Seifert, M. (1992) 'Variability in framing risk issues', *Journal of Social Issues*, 48: 119–35.

Walker, A. (1991) 'Waste disposal: fresh looks at a rotting problem', *British Medical Journal*, 303: 1391–4.

—— (1992) 'Drinking water: doubts about quality', *British Medical Journal*, 304: 175–8.

Walzer, M. (1983) *Spheres of Justice: A Defence of Pluralism and Equality*, Oxford: Basil Blackwell.

Watt, A. (1987) 'Room for movement? The community response to medical dominance', *Radical Community Medicine*, 29: 40–5.

Williams, G.H. (1984) 'The genesis of chronic illness: narrative reconstruction', *Sociology of Health and Illness*, 6: 175–200.

—— (1986) 'Lay beliefs about the causes of rheumatoid arthritis: their implications for rehabilitation', *International Rehabilitation Medicine*, 8: 65–8.

—— (1993) 'Chronic illness and the pursuit of virtue in everyday life', in Radley, A. (ed.) *Worlds of Illness: Biographical and Cultural Perspectives on Health and Disease*, London: Routledge.

Williams, G.H. and Popay, J. (1993) 'Researching the people's health: dilemmas and opportunities for social scientists', in Popay, J. and Williams, G.H. (eds) *Social Research and Public Health*, Salford Papers in Sociology No. 13, Department of Sociology, University of Salford.

Williams, G.H. and Wood, P.H.N. (1986) 'Common-sense beliefs about illness: a mediating role for the doctor', *Lancet*, II: 1435–7.

Williams, R. (1989) *Resources of Hope: Culture, Democracy, and Socialism*, London: Verso.

World Health Organization (1985) *Targets for Health for All*, Copenhagen: World Health Organization Regional Office for Europe.

8 Changing medicine?

Gender and the politics of health care

Lesley Doyal

INTRODUCTION

In the late 1960s women began to document male bias in medicine, not just in Britain but all over the developed world (Ruzek 1978; Boston Women's Health Book Collective 1971; Doyal 1983; Phillips and Rakusen 1978; Zimmerman 1987). During the 1970s these observations were combined with a number of other strands to form a substantial critique of both the theory and the practice of modern medicine (Ehrenreich 1978). The insights deriving from feminist analysis were among the most analytically sophisticated and deeply rooted of these new challenges to medicine but, despite their initial vitality, they have had relatively little impact on the way British doctors practise medicine. Many women have altered their own perceptions of health and healing, but it is less obvious that the majority of doctors have done the same (Elston 1981).

There have been few attempts to measure the impact of feminism on medicine – or on any other sectors of British society. However, doctors do appear to have had considerable success in resisting – or at least ignoring – many of women's demands for reform. The obstacles to change in medical care are complex and need further research, but it is clear that the institutional power of the profession itself has played a significant part in maintaining male dominance in the National Health Service (NHS).

The NHS has undoubtedly been of major value in providing universal care free of charge. Women in particular benefited from its introduction, since many had previously been denied access to treatment (Doyal 1985). However, they were offered these services on doctors' terms and attempts to make their voices heard have been consistently silenced by the centralised and bureaucratic nature of the system (Doyal 1983; Stacey 1985). The NHS has never had effective mechanisms of accountability for users and few can afford to purchase treatment from the private sector. As a result women have had little opportunity to exert pressure on doctors to change their practice. Paradoxically, perhaps, more market-oriented systems such as that in the USA have offered an incentive for some providers to offer more women-friendly services – but only for those who can afford to pay (Stacey 1985).

As other contributors in this book have demonstrated, the British medical profession has recently come under sustained attack. The most powerful of these challenges have come from politicians, civil servants and senior managers who have succeeded in imposing many of their demands on a protesting profession. However, women's issues have not had a high priority in these developments and the Department of Health has exerted little pressure on the medical care system to meet women's needs more effectively. In Australia, by contrast, the Federal Government invested considerable resources in a National Women's Health Policy launched by the Prime Minister in 1989 (Commonwealth Department of Community Services and Health 1989).

In the United States, too, women's health needs have received particular attention. The National Institutes of Health have recently published a sophisticated analysis of current research priorities for women's health (US Public Health Service 1992). A new Office of Research on Women's Health was set up within the office of the Director of the National Institutes of Health, and a fourteen-year, $625 million study of the health problems of 15,000 women was initiated (US Public Health Service 1992). While this will not have an immediate effect on services, it will put some of the key issues in women's health firmly on the political agenda.

The reasons for these national differences are complex but they reflect in part the responsiveness of the individual governments to pressure groups in general and to women in particular. In the United States and Australia women appear to be taken more seriously both as voters and as actors in the wider social arena. In the UK, on the other hand, the relative invisibility of women and their lack of political influence have contributed to the current situation where the major changes going on in the NHS have not included any attempt to address gender issues in health and health care.

IS THERE A FEMINIST CRITIQUE OF MEDICINE?

The basic elements of feminist critiques of medicine have been similar in Britain, the United States and Australia. However, both writing and campaigning on women's health issues appear to have declined in the UK in recent years. This stems in part from a broader concern about current changes in the NHS and an understandable reluctance to challenge existing practice (Doyal 1983). However, it also reflects a shift of direction within feminism itself, away from campaigning issues towards a concern with theory, emphasising the social construction of gender discrimination rather than its empirical documentation. In the United States and Australia, on the other hand, a more activist women's health movement continues to flourish, offering important lessons for British women and their doctors (Health Sharing Women 1990; Kerby-Eaton and Davies 1985; Ruzek 1986).

These developments in the wider feminist agenda have involved not only a more theoretical orientation but also a process of differentiation and deconstruction (Lovell 1990; Humm 1992). As a result, it is now difficult to identify a single feminist critique of medicine. Instead, a variety of feminist approaches to health and health care have emerged. Black women, for instance, have focused on the racism often inherent in their experiences of health care as well as the eugenic assumptions implicit in many fertility control policies (White 1990; Larbie 1985; Douglas 1992). They have contrasted their own experiences of pressure to accept abortion or sterilisation with those of many white women concerned only about lack of access to fertility control. Similarly, lesbian women have pointed to the heterosexist assumptions inherent in many of their experiences of medical care (Health Care for Women International 1992).

There have also been major debates about particular aspects of medical practice between women who would all identify themselves as feminists. In the area of new reproductive technologies, for instance, some women have campaigned to end the use of techniques such as IVF, seeing them as potentially genocidal and of no value to women (Arditti *et al.* 1984; Corea 1985; Spallone 1989). Others have taken a rather different approach, acknowledging potential problems but calling for greater female control over the technologies and wider access for those who could benefit (Stanworth 1985; Stacey 1992). Any attempt to understand how women are challenging medicine must therefore take account of the growing diversity of feminist theory and practice.

To add still further to this complexity, a number of the most sustained criticisms of medicine have come from women who would not describe themselves as feminists at all. Many of the campaigners for women-centred obstetric care, for instance, would probably come into this category, as would many of the women involved in self-help and other support groups (Foley 1985; Shearer 1989; Kitzinger 1990). It is also significant that an increasing number of women are defining health issues in individual terms, focusing on 'life-style' and consumer issues rather than collective action to change the nature of health care. It is important, therefore, to adopt the broadest possible definition of feminism to include a variety of activities unified not by their political label but by their potential for increasing women's autonomy and enhancing their health and well-being.

The remainder of this chapter will examine women's challenge to medicine in more detail. The next section documents gender inequalities in control of the medical enterprise and assesses their impact on women's subjective experiences of health care. The following section looks at male bias in the production of medical knowledge and its relationship to clinical treatment. The final section attempts to identify any changes in medical practice resulting from these analyses and the campaign that they have generated.

WHO CONTROLS WHOSE HEALTH?

At the heart of all feminist critiques of medicine is the recognition that women lack power in formal health care systems. This disadvantages those women who work in the health sector but also has a profound effect on all women using its services. Doctors – the majority of whom are male – continue to exercise a high degree of control over the research and development effort in medicine, the allocation of scarce medical resources and the quality of treatment given to individual women. Despite their greater use of medical services, their numerical preponderance in the health labour force, and their responsibility for unpaid caring, most women still have relatively little say in their own health care or that of their dependants. Thus the organisation of the NHS, like that of most other health care systems, reproduces a wider pattern of patriarchal power. Women make up about 75 per cent of NHS workers, but most control remains with doctors and senior administrators, the majority of whom are men.

In medicine itself women now make up about 50 per cent of the student body but only 23 per cent of hospital doctors and 20 per cent of GPs (NHSME 1992). While these numbers will increase as students move through the system, it is apparent that women do not pursue their careers on equal terms with men. Only about 15.5 per cent of consultants are women and they are concentrated in certain specialisms, most notably paediatrics (24 per cent), anaesthetics (20 per cent), radiology (16 per cent), adult psychiatry (15 per cent) and pathology (15 per cent) (NHSME 1992). Only 3.7 per cent of women consultants are found in surgical specialties (NHSME 1992). While women now make up a higher proportion of senior registrars than they did in the past – about a quarter in 1991 – they still have a long way to go to reach equality. Hence, very few are involved in making key decisions about current and future priorities of medical practice. They are under-represented on professional bodies such as the BMA and the General Medical Council, which regulate terms and conditions of service and professional standards and codes of conduct, and have only a small presence in the Royal Colleges, where major decisions are made about the form and content of medical knowledge (Elston 1981).

The traditional power of doctors in decision making in the NHS has increasingly been transferred to a broader arena as other chapters in this volume demonstrate. However this has not increased the participation of women. The number of women in senior management has risen in recent years, but they still occupy only about 18 per cent of such posts. Over 60 per cent of NHS managers are women, but they are still concentrated at the lowest levels (NHSME 1992).

Membership of the new Regional, District and Family Health Service Authorities also remains male-dominated. Only 10.8 per cent of general managers are women, as are 22.8 per cent of executive members of the authorities, 25 per cent of chairs and 30 per cent of non-executive members (Cairncross *et al.* 1991). Indeed, recent research suggests that the NHS reforms have reduced rather than increased the number of women on these bodies, with a decline from 35 per cent on Regional and District Health Authorities to a figure of 26.8 per cent following the NHS and Community Care Act, 1990 (Cairncross *et al.* 1991). Ironically, then, women's role in decision making may have been reduced still further at precisely the moment when the purchasing role could have been used to articulate their interests more clearly.

The relative scarcity of women in senior positions in medicine and in the management structure of the NHS is in itself the object of feminist criticism. It is a result both of structural obstacles and also of more diffuse factors associated with 'male' occupational cultures (Witz 1992). Hence medicine, like most of the other professions, is in need of major reform to ensure equal opportunities for all. But the implications are, of course, much wider than concern about the occupational advancement of a few women. Women's lack of authority and power also contributes to a situation where female users of the NHS continue to be constrained in the exercise of their own autonomy, as well as risking inappropriate diagnosis and treatment.

It is a central tenet of medical ethics that those receiving care should give their informed consent to it (Beauchamp and Faden 1986). While most members of the profession respect this in theory, the practice varies markedly between doctors and institutions. Individual factors can inhibit the capacity of patients of both sexes to exercise their autonomy – lack of education, a paternalistic doctor, or one who lacks communication skills, for instance. However, research suggests that structural factors such as class, race and gender also affect the exercise of patient autonomy (Faulder 1985; Doyal 1985).

There is growing evidence that women experience particular difficulties both in getting enough information and being able to act on it (Faden 1991; Whitbeck 1991; Holmes and Purdy 1992). This applies especially to black and working-class women, many of whom are given very little time and attention (Cartwright and O'Brien 1976; Doyal 1985). Many doctors appear to be reluctant to let women speak for themselves and many women feel unable to assert their wishes (Roberts 1985; Fisher 1986). Women's own experience is devalued by comparison with that of doctors' expert 'knowledge' and too many doctors are unwilling to admit ignorance or uncertainty (Graham and Oakley 1981). As a result female patients frequently become the passive victims of doctors' ministrations.

For individual women this can be a distressing and demeaning experience and many of the early criticisms of the medical profession consisted of women's accounts of their humiliations and frustrations at such treatment (O'Sullivan 1987). These accounts led some feminists to explore the implications of medical practice for the reinforcement of women's subordination in the wider society. Drawing on themes developed by a number of social commentators, they argued that doctors and other health workers had taken over new areas of women's lives, making them increasingly subject to medical control (Riesman 1983; Miles 1991, ch. 7; Freidson 1975; Zola 1975; Illich 1977)).

Two separate but interrelated aspects of this process have been identified. In the first case, women who are healthy are treated as 'sick' and subjected to medical direction and control. This can be illustrated most clearly in the area of obstetrics, where women are treated 'as if' ill, though most go through an unproblematic process of pregnancy and childbirth (Graham and Oakley 1981). Similar issues have been identified in the context of fertility control, where women who want to determine their reproductive lives are frequently able to do so only with the tacit – and sometimes even explicit – consent of doctors (Petchesky 1986; Gordon 1976).

Medicalisation, in the second sense, has been used to apply to situations where women with problems that are primarily social in origin have them transformed into an 'illness'. More women than men visit their GPs in an attempt to cope with the stresses of daily life (Office of Health Economics 1987). Not surprisingly, most doctors respond with a narrowly medical solution which may (or may not) relieve the symptoms but which certainly leaves the woman herself in the same unhealthy environment. The higher rates of tranquillisers prescribed for women have been widely criticised on these grounds (Gabe and Williams 1986; Ashton 1991).

There is therefore a growing recognition that the (variable) benefits offered by medicine have been bought by women at the price of greater control over their lives. According to its feminist critics many aspects of medical practice encourage women's conformity to social norms that are ultimately damaging to them (Riesman 1983). While this analysis can clearly be applied to the medical treatment of both sexes, it has particular resonance for women. On the one hand, their reproductive needs have drawn them further into the medical arena than men, as have their responsibilities for the care of dependants. On the other hand, the norms to which they are encouraged to conform are ones which reflect and reinforce wider gender inequalities. Thus, medicine has been identified as a significant part of the institutional structure which holds together contemporary forms of patriarchy, affecting women as a group as well as women as individual patients.

Though these are powerful arguments, it is also important to acknowledge the value of recent warnings on the limitations of a crude model of 'professional imperialism' (Strong 1979; Elston 1991). Some of the earlier feminist critiques can now be seen as 'over-determined' in their negative assessment of the benefits some medical techniques can offer women, in their exaggeration of the power of individual doctors and in their assumption of the universality of unremitting sexism among all practitioners. There has also been a tendency on the part of some of these commentators to operate with a conspiracy model of 'nasty' doctors. Instead, we need a more interactive understanding of the relationship between women and their doctors, and an emphasis on the impact of the medical actions rather than the intention of individual doctors (Gabe and Lipshitz-Phillips 1986).

However, this should not be taken to mean that the fundamental problems identified by feminists were not real or that they have now been eliminated. As we shall see, recent research has illuminated more subtle yet apparently intractable aspects of medical sexism. Indeed, it has shown that bias against women may be not just depressing but positively dangerous since it affects not only their feelings but also the quality of the clinical care they receive.

DO WOMEN GET THE TREATMENT THEY DESERVE?

Many women are inappropriately diagnosed and treated by the doctors they consult. Of course, many factors contribute to such mistakes, but male bias in both research and clinical decision making has now been identified as a significant element.

It has long been evident that research priorities tend to ignore specifically or predominantly female problems unless they are connected with reproduction. Dysmenorrhoea, cystitis, incontinence, osteoporosis and nutrition in post-menopausal women have all been cited as problems that worry women a great deal but have received little medical attention (Rosser 1992). Even the menstrual cycle itself has not been extensively researched. Hence we know relatively little about an extremely important aspect of women's normal bodily functioning that also generates a large volume of clinical morbidity (Koblinsky, Campbell and Harlow 1993). The potential importance of such research was highlighted by the recent discovery that the timing of surgery during the menstrual cycle strongly influences how long women with breast cancer will survive (Hrushesky *et al.* 1989).

In both the United States and Australia, women are now beginning to subject this gender bias in research to critical scrutiny. In the USA one in ten women are affected by breast cancer during their lifetime and many are killed by it, but it receives less than 1 per cent of government medical research funds (Freedman and Maine 1993; Brady 1991). Overall only 13.5 per cent of research funding is devoted to health issues of particular relevance to women. Of course this does not mean that all other research is irrelevant to women's needs, but it does give an indication of the low priority accorded to specifically female issues (Kirchstein 1991; United States Public Health Service 1992).

Taking this analysis a stage further, American investigations have also demonstrated that even where health problems affect both men and women, methodological bias has meant that women's interests are not adequately represented. That is to say, few studies of particular diseases have explored the possibility of differences in life history, symptoms and treatment response between the sexes (American Medical Association, Council on Ethical and Judicial Affairs 1991). Researchers working on coronary heart disease, for example, have continued to act as though it were only a 'male' problem, despite the fact that it is the single most important cause of death in post-menopausal women, killing half a million each year in the USA. The Physical Health Study, which demonstrated the effectiveness of daily aspirin consumption in preventing cardiovascular disease, involved 22,071 men and no women, while the sample used in the 'Mr. Fit' study of the relationship between heart disease, cholesterol and life-style consisted of 15,000 men (Freedman and Maine 1993).

AIDS, too, has been treated for research purposes as a predominantly male disease. Though it is now growing as fast among women as among men, there is still very little known about sex differences in its effects. Indeed, the very definition of the clinical entity of AIDS continues to be based on male experience (Denenberg 1990). As a result, women presenting different symptoms from men may be inaccurately diagnosed, and receive less than optimal treatment (Bell 1992).

Most medical research in the United States continues to be done with all-white male samples, unless it concerns a sex-specific problem. Even animal studies are usually performed on male rats. The main arguments used to defend this practice are, first, that female hormonal cycles will 'contaminate' research results and, second, that if drug testing is involved, there may be a risk of damage to an unborn child. While these are clearly important problems, the consequence of ignoring women in research design is that there continue to be huge gaps in our knowledge of women's health and illness. Even more importantly, treatments tested only on men will continue to be given to women without any real assessment of their sex-specific safety or effectiveness. Recent research has shown, for example, that anti-depressant drugs may affect women differently during the various phases of their menstrual cycle. However, preliminary testing excluded women despite the fact that they are major users of the drugs (Hamilton 1985, 1986).

There also appears to be systematic bias in some areas of clinical decision making. Recent evidence from the United States suggests that despite women's greater use of medical care overall, they sometimes receive less effective treatment than men for the same condition. In the case of kidney disease, for instance, gender has been identified as a key factor determining the likelihood of receiving a transplant (Held *et al.* 1988; Kjellstrand 1988). An analysis of US data between 1981 and 1985 indi-cated that a woman undergoing renal dialysis had only 70 per cent of the chance of an equivalent man to obtain a transplant (Held *et al.* 1988). In the age group 46 to 60 women had only half the chance. A major reason for this appears to be that women's contribution to society is judged less valuable than men's (American Medical Association, Council on Ethical and Judicial Affairs 1991).

In the case of cardiac surgery, American men are six times more likely to be given diagnostic catheterisation than women with the same symptoms (Tobin *et al.* 1987). Women also have a higher operative mortality rate than men for coronary bypass surgery and a higher mortality rate at the time of an initial myocardial infarction (Wenger 1990; Fiebach *et al.* 1990). This appears to reflect the fact that the disease is often more advanced in women than in men at the time of surgery or first attack, which itself may reflect a failure to identify heart disease as a serious problem for women.

Evidence has just emerged of similar patterns in Britain. Despite the existence of the National Health Service, men in the South-West Thames Region are 60 per cent more likely than women with the same condition to be offered coronary artery bypass operations or angioplasty (Petticrew *et al.* 1993). According to the authors of the study, doctors may discriminate against women on clinical grounds or they may place less value on the benefit that would be gained by women. They may also be influenced by the way in which many studies of prevention and treatment of cardio-vascular diseases have been conducted exclusively in men (Petticrew *et al.* 1993). This similarity in women's treatment in two very different health care systems is striking, and research is urgently needed to explore other patterns of gender bias in the allocation of clinical resources in the NHS.

In the field of reproductive medicine, the situation is of course quite different, with women (or their bodies) usually the centre of attention. However, as feminists have pointed out, this has not always been an unalloyed benefit. In the case of contraception, for example, the post-war period has been marked by the development of a wide range of new methods. While they have certainly given many women greater control over their fertility this has sometimes been bought at the expense of other aspects of their health and well-being (Bruce 1987; Jacobson 1991). There is clear evidence that many of the most commonly used methods – from the pill through IUDs to the new injectables – are potentially dangerous. The origin of these hazards lies in the research and development process where the agenda has often been dominated by the need to find cheap and effective ways to control fertility, sometimes at the expense of general health. The absence of women's own voices from any part of the process has meant a devaluing of their needs and desires and an unwillingness to take the 'side effects' of contraception seriously. This has forced many women to make hard choices between controlling their fertility and promoting other aspects of their well-being.

In the context of childbirth, too, women have been critical of both the safety and the efficacy of many of the procedures they are required to undergo. At the most basic level there is no evidence that either shaving or the giving of enemas improves the outcome of childbirth for either mother or baby. They cause distress to many women, yet they continue to be required in some British hospitals (Garforth and Garcia 1989). Similarly, there are no data to show that routine episiotomies – what Sheila Kitzinger has described as 'genital mutilation' – do anything to improve either delivery or *post partum* recovery (Chalmers, Garcia and Post 1989).

More seriously, there is evidence that the 'active management' of labour – including chemical induction and electronic foetal monitoring (EFM) – may not only be distressing to the mother but potentially harmful to both her and her child (Chard and Richards 1977). Increased EFM appears to have contributed to the very high rate of Caesarean section in the USA, yet again there is little evidence to suggest that its routine use improves the outcome of labour for either party (Banta and Thacker 1982; Grant 1989; Simkin 1986). Not surprisingly, women have become increasingly concerned that doctors' own professional interests may sometimes be the key factor pushing obstetric innovation.

ARE WOMEN CHANGING MEDICINE?

We have seen that feminist criticisms of medicine have been extensive and that they have included issues relating to class and race as well as gender. However, any attempt to assess their impact on medical practice in Britain faces severe difficulties. Doctors and researchers are only beginning to develop the necessary techniques for systematic monitoring of effectiveness and efficiency in medical care, and qualitative measures of the caring process are still rare. Furthermore, evaluation strategies have rarely identi-fied gender issues as a priority. Even if changes can be identified, precise causality is hard to impute. Hence the last part of this chapter can offer only a brief indication of those areas where medical practice appears to be evolving in a direction broadly consonant with feminist beliefs.

The easiest areas to monitor are women's employment in medicine and management and their representation on the committees that run the NHS. In general practice the situation of women has noticeably improved, with an increase in female principals from 1 in 7 in 1980 to 1 in 4 in 1991. However, serious obstacles continue to exist for those women wishing to achieve their potential in this area of medicine, with many of those who work part-time forced out by recent changes in their conditions of service (NHSME 1992). In hospital medicine the progress of women has been much slower. Strategies such as part-time training schemes have made very little impact on the structures that make it difficult to combine medical work with motherhood or the care of other dependants.

A recent scheme initiated by the NHSME as part of the national Oppor-tunity 2000 programme has set a target of increasing the percentage of women consultants from 15.5 per cent in 1991 to 20 per cent by 1994. In surgical specialties the target rate of increase is from the current 9.7 per cent per annum to 15 per cent by 1994, and a Women in Surgical Training Scheme has been launched in conjunction with the Royal College of Surgeons. There are also plans to increase the proportion of women in general management posts from 18 per cent in 1991 to 30 per cent in 1994, and the number of women members of authorities and trusts from 29 per cent to 35 per cent over the same period.

These are important developments that represent one of the first attempts at a major equal opportunities initiative in the NHS. However, it remains to be seen how effective they will be. Like all policies of this kind, they will be heavily dependent for their success on the willingness of those involved to take them seriously. This is likely to be a particularly acute problem in medicine, where the weight of tradition is substantial. The pressures for change are largely fuelled from outside the profession itself and are therefore likely to be resisted by at least some of the key players.

This potential resistance highlights important aspects of the current organisation and culture of the medical profession. As Anne Witz has argued, the initial exclusion of women from its hallowed ranks and their subsequent failure to achieve equal status with male colleagues have not been the result of an accidental 'misfit' between women's needs and those of the profession (Witz 1992). Rather, they reflect the reality of medicine as an institution that is profoundly 'male' in much of its ideology and practice, which has consistently employed strategies of exclusion on a gender basis (Witz 1992). It is unlikely that these characteristics will be easily challenged.

Women entering the medical profession face considerable pressure to fit in with existing values. Many will not find this a problem, but for those who do, standing out as a 'feminist' can be extremely damaging both to their careers and to their own health (Grossman *et al.* 1987; Lorber 1984; Miles 1991, ch. 5). Women in Medicine was set up in 1981 to offer information and support to female doctors and medical students in the NHS (Women in Medicine 1987). However, the pressures to conform remain strong, and the obstacles to change great.

So have women fared better as users of the NHS? It is difficult to assess whether doctors have responded to their criticisms by treating them with greater sensitivity. Women do report 'bad' experiences more frequently than they used to, but this may simply reflect their enhanced confidence and greater expectations. Attempts have been made to inculcate greater 'gender awareness' in younger doctors through the inclusion of sociology and psychology in the medical curriculum along with more teaching on ethics and communication skills. However, we have no formal evidence about their impact when doctors get into practice. Most older doctors, on the other hand, have had little incentive to change their traditional way of working. Indeed, some women have reported an obvious backlash among doctors who have felt confronted but unconvinced by consumer pressure in general and feminist ideas in particular. The picture therefore remains unclear, with more research needed to give up-to-date information on qualitative aspects of women's relationships with their doctors.

Some practitioners have attempted to improve women's experiences of health care through providing services in a new way, but their success has been limited. Services outside the NHS are few and far between because state funding is rarely available and charges would exclude the neediest women. It is only in mental health and substance abuse that a significant number of projects have been developed, reflecting the paucity and male-centredness of NHS services in these areas (Women in MIND 1986).

Within the health service, primary care has proved to be the easiest arena for innovation, since GPs have traditionally had more freedom in how they organise their services (Webb 1984). Women doctors in particular have attempted to exploit such opportunities, though many have experienced considerable difficulty in changing the traditional relations of hierarchy between doctor and patient and between doctors and other health workers (Eisner and Wright 1984). These initiatives have often taken the form of 'well women' centres and by 1987 over a hundred health authorities claimed to be running such services (Foster 1989). While these have often been improvements on existing provision, most have been limited in what they offer and in the degree to which they have challenged existing models of care (Craddock and Reid 1993).

In the United States and Australia, on the other hand, women-centred services have proliferated widely. In the latter this has reflected the greater availability of federal and state funding, while in the former most developments have been undertaken on a commercial basis. Some of these health centres have offered exciting versions of more holistic care designed to meet women's needs. However, there has been growing concern in the USA that some feminist ideas have been co-opted by mainstream providers in ways that limit their effectiveness (Worcester and Whatley 1988).

Focusing specifically on the issue of informed consent, we can again see improvements in certain areas of the NHS. Attempts have been made in some maternity units to help women to be more active participants in their own labours. Among the most valuable of these initiatives has been the 'link worker' schemes set up to provide advocates for pregnant women from black and ethnic minority communities (Maternity Alliance 1984). The best-known of these, the Hackney Multi-Ethnic Women's Health Project, was set up in London in 1980 (Cornwell and Gordon 1984). Most have been successful in gaining the support of both mothers and NHS workers, but the majority are voluntary initiatives funded outside the NHS making them vulnerable and often marginalised.

In the area of breast cancer, too, there is evidence that some surgeons are beginning to pay attention to the desire of many women to exercise greater autonomy in the context of clinical decision making. For many years, the standard treatment involved a biopsy under anaesthetic followed by whatever treatment the surgeon deemed appropriate. A variety of pressures, including those from female patients themselves, eventually led to a significant reduction in this practice. The two procedures are now separated and many women are able to have a much greater say in decisions about their treatment. This appears to offer not only a more ethical approach but also a more therapeutic one. Research suggests that women who have 'actively' chosen their treatment (or non-treatment) may be better able to cope with the consequences (Morris and Royle 1988).

However, decisions of this kind can be very difficult to make and require considerable time and support. While some initiatives have been set up to offer women help and advocacy they continue to be few and far between. Many are still not offered a real choice and feel constrained to accept whatever may be chosen for them, not just in the case of breast cancer but in other areas of surgery too. Hysterectomy, in particular, is often singled out as a procedure where clinical indications are opaque and uncertainties abound, but women may have little opportunity to express their own desires and perceptions.

Here again, it is worth comparing the partial and contingent changes achieved in the UK with the US and Australian responses to such problems. In Australia, there has been extensive public debate about informed consent leading to the introduction of national guidelines. While this has not gone as far as many commentators would like, it has put informed consent on the political agenda and women have been at the forefront of that process (Hancock 1991). In the United States, too, the absence of effective mechanisms for ensuring consent has caused major disquiet, leading in about 50 per cent of states to the enactment of informed consent legislation relating specifically to breast cancer (Montini and Ruzek 1989). Again, a variety of factors have created these different policies in the three countries. In the United States, for instance, women have become increasingly politicised on the whole issue of breast cancer, while the generally more litigious nature of the society has pushed American doctors towards more formal consenting procedures.

Turning finally to the production of medical knowledge itself, there is little evidence that research practice in the UK has been changed as a result of feminist criticism. Indeed, women themselves have hardly begun to identify the problem. No systematic 'audit' of patterns of spending has yet been carried out and there is little information available about the practices of medical researchers in relation to gender. Again, it is interesting to contrast this with the USA, where the National Institutes of Health recently issued guidelines for ensuring gender equity in government-funded projects. As part of these new procedures, all applicants have to demonstrate that any sex bias in their methodology is necessitated by the research problem itself and would not be discriminatory to any group of potential patients (US Public Health Service 1992).

Over the past decade, British doctors have been under increasing pressure to to carry out clinical audit – to evaluate both new practices and 'old' ones whose effectiveness had previously been taken for granted. Again, gender issues have rarely been included in this process, which has been largely economic in inspiration. However, women have often been at the forefront of criticisms of existing technologies. Radical mastectomies and hysterectomies, as well as many aspects of obstetric technology, have come under particular scrutiny. It seems likely, therefore, that women may be particular beneficiaries of clinical audit. On the one hand, a number of common procedures specific to women may cease if they are shown to be ineffective; on the other, properly executed audit should identify the impact of both biological and social differences between the sexes on treatment outcomes. Indeed, audit is likely to lead in some instances to the 'demedicalisation' that many women are seeking.

A similar coalescence of interests between feminists and other reformers can be observed in the increasing emphasis on the prevention of illness and the promotion of good health. Medicine has been widely criticised for its emphasis on the biological at the expense of the social, on the physical to the detriment of the psychological. This is clearly a concern relevant to both women and men, but it is women who have been especially active in documenting the relationship between gender divisions and patterns of health and illness. There is now a growing literature documenting the ways in which class, race, sex and gender influence women's well-being in a variety of social, economic and cultural contexts (Koblinsky, Timyan and Gay 1993; Smyke 1991; World Health Organization 1992; White 1990). As the limitations of curative medicine are more widely understood women are playing an active part in the campaign to shift the focus of care away from the traditional activities of doctors towards the creation of a healthier society.

Our conclusion must be that there are few instances where feminist challenges alone have been powerful enough to effect major changes in medical practice. However, women's activities have played an important part in the general campaign to transform the culture and organisation of British medicine. Under the 'new' NHS, doctors have been challenged and some of the traditional power eroded. It remains to be seen whether this will lead to the efficient, effective, humane and democratically accountable health care needed by both women and men.

REFERENCES

American Medical Association, Council on Ethical and Judicial Affairs (1991) 'Gender disparities in clinical decision making', *Journal of American Medical Association*, 286: 559–62.

Arditti, R., Duelli Klein, R. and Minden, S. (1984) *Test-Tube Women: What Future for Motherhood?*, London: Pandora Press.

Ashton, H. (1991) 'Psychotropic drug prescribing in women', *British Journal of Psychiatry*, 158, supplement 10: 30–5.

Banta, D. and Thacker, S. (1982) 'The risks and benefits of episiotomy: a review', *Birth*, 9: 25–30.

Beauchamp, T. and Faden, R. (1986) *A History and Theory of Informed Consent*, Oxford University Press.

Bell, N. (1992) 'Women and AIDS: too little, too late?', in Bequaert, H., Holmes, H. and Purdy, L. (eds) *Feminist Perspectives in Medical Ethics*, Bloomington and Indianapolis: Indiana University Press.

Boston Women's Health Book Collective (1971) *Our Bodies Ourselves*, New York: Simon & Schuster.

Brady, J. (1991) *1 in 3: Women with Cancer Confront an Epidemic*, Pittsburgh and San Francisco: Cleis Press.

Bruce, J. (1987) 'Users' perspectives on contraceptive technology and delivery systems: highlighting some feminist issues', *Technology in Society*, 9: 359–83.

Cairncross, L., Ashburner, L. and Pettigrew, A. (1991) 'Authorities in the NHS: membership and learning needs', *Research for Action*, paper 4, Centre for Corporate Strategy and Change, University of Warwick.

Cartwright, A. and O'Brien, J. (1976) 'Social class variation in health care and in the nature of general practitioner consultations', in Stacey, M. (ed.) *The Sociology of the NHS: Sociological Review*, mimeograph no. 22, University of Keele.

Chalmers, I., Garcia, J. and Post, S. (1989) 'Hospital policies for labour and delivery', in Chalmers, I., Enkin, M. and Keirse, M. (eds) *Effective Care in Pregnancy and Childbirth*, Oxford: Clarendon Press.

Chard, T. and Richards, M. (1977) *Benefits and Hazards of the New Obstetrics*, London: Heinemann.

Commonwealth Department of Community Services and Health (1989) *National Women's Health Policy*, Canberra: Australian Government Publishing Service.

Corea, G. (1985) *The Mother Machine*, New York: Harper & Row.

Cornwell, J. and Gordon, P. (1984) *An Experiment in Advocacy: The Hackney Multi-Ethnic Women's Health Project*, London: King's Fund.

Coulter, A. (1991) 'Evaluating the outcomes of health care', in Gabe, J., Calnan, M. and Bury, M. (eds) *The Sociology of the Health Service*, London: Routledge.

Craddock, C. and Reid, M. (1993) 'Structure and struggle: implementing a social model of a well woman clinic in Glasgow', *Social Science and Medicine*, 36: 67–76.

Denenberg, R. (1990) 'Unique aspects of HIV infection in women', in ACTUP New York Women and AIDS Book Group (eds) *Women, AIDS and Activism*, Boston: Southend Press.

Douglas, J. (1992) 'Black women's health matters: putting black women on the research agenda', in Roberts, H. (ed.) *Women's Health Matters*, London: Routledge.

Doyal, L. (1983) 'Women, health and the sexual division of labour: a case study of the women's health movement in Britain', *Critical Social Policy*, 7, summer: 21–33.

—— (1985) 'Women and the National Health Service: the carers and the careless', in Lewin, E. and Olesen, V. (eds) *Women, Health and Healing: Toward a New Perspective*, London: Tavistock.

Ehrenreich, J. (1978) *The Cultural Crisis of Modern Medicine*, Boston: Monthly Review Press.

Eisner, M. and Wright, M. (1984) 'A feminist approach to general practice', in Webb, C. (ed.) *Feminist Practices in Women's Health Care*, Chichester: John Wiley.

Elston, M. (1981) 'Medicine as old husband's tales: the impact of feminism', in Spender, D. (ed.) *Men's Studies Modified*, Oxford: Pergamon.

—— (1991) 'The politics of professional power: medicine in a changing health service', in Gabe, J., Calnan, M. and Bury, M. (eds) *The Sociology of the Health Service*, London: Routledge.

Faden, R. (1991) 'Autonomy, choice and the new reproductive technologies, the role of informed consent in prenatal genetic diagnosis', in Rodin, J. and Collins, A. (eds) *Autonomy, Choice and the New Reproductive Technologies: Medical, Psychosocial, Legal and Ethical Dilemmas*, Hillside, NJ: Lawrence Erlbaum Associates.

Faulder, C. (1985) *Whose Body Is It? The Troubling Issue of Informed Consent*, London: Virago.

Fiebach, N., Viscoli, C. and Horwitz, K. (1990). 'Differences between women and men in survival after myocardial infarction', *Journal of the American Medical Association*, 63: 1092–6.

Fisher, S. (1986) *In the Patient's Best Interest: Women and the Politics of Medical Decisions*, New Brunswick: NJ: Rutgers University Press.

Foley, R. (1985) *Women and Health Care: Self-help Health Groups in Britain*, Southampton: Southampton Institute of Higher Education.

Foster, P. (1989) 'Improving the doctor/patient relationship: a feminist perspective', *Journal of Social Policy*, 18 (3): 337–61.

Freedman, I. and Maine, D. (1993) 'Women's mortality: a legacy of neglect', in Koblinsky, M., Timyan, J. and Gay, J. (eds) *The Health of Women: A Global Perspective*, Boulder, CO: Westview Press.

Freidson, E. (1975) *Profession of Medicine – A Study of the Sociology of Applied Knowledge*, New York: Dodd, Mead.

Gabe, J. and Williams, P. (1986) *Tranquillisers: Social, Psychological and Clinical Perspectives*, London: Tavistock.

Gabe, J. and Lipshitz-Phillips, S. (1986) 'Tranquillisers as social control?', in Gabe, J. and Williams, P. (eds) *Tranquillisers: Social, Psychological and Clinical Perspectives*, London: Tavistock.

Garforth, S. and Garcia, J. (1989) 'Hospital admission practices', in Chalmers, I., Enkin, M. and Keirse, M. (eds) *Effective Care in Pregnancy and Childbirth*, Oxford: Clarendon Press.

Gordon, L. (1976) *Woman's Body: Woman's Right: A Social History of Birth Control in America*, New York: Grossman Publications.

Graham, H. and Oakley, A. (1981) 'Competing ideologies of reproduction: medical and maternal perspectives in pregnancy', in Roberts, H. (ed.) *Women, Health and Reproduction*, London: Routledge & Kegan Paul.

Grant, A. (1989) 'Monitoring the fetus during labour', in Chalmers, I., Enkin, M. and Keirse, M. (eds) *Effective Care in Pregnancy and Childbirth*, Oxford: Clarendon Press.

Grossman, H., Salt, P., Nadelson, C. *et al.* (1987) 'Coping resources and health responses among men and women medical students', *Social Science and Medicine*, 28 (9): 1057–63.

Hamilton, J. (1985) 'Avoiding methodological and policy making biases in gender-related research', in US Department of Health and Human Services (eds) *Women's Health: Report of the Public Health Service Task Force on Women's Health Issues*, vol. II, Washington DC: US Government Printing Office.

—— (1986) 'An overview of the clinical rationale for advancing gender-related psychopharmacology and drug abuse research', in Ray, B. and Braude, M. (eds) *Women and Drugs: A New Era for Research*, National Institute on Drug Abuse, monograph 65, Washington DC: US Government Printing Office.

Hancock, L. (1991) *Women and Surgery: 1990 Conference Proceedings*, Melbourne: Healthsharing Women.

Health Care for Women International (1992) *Special Issue on Lesbian Health: What Are the Issues?*, 13 (2), April–June.

Health Sharing Women (1990) *The Healthsharing Reader: Women Speak About Health*, Sydney: Pandora Press.

Held, P., Pauly, M., Boubjerg, R. *et al.* (1988) 'Access to kidney transplantation', *Archives of Internal Medicine*, 148: 2594–600.

Holmes, H.B. and Purdy, L. (1992) *Feminist Perspectives in Medical Ethics*, Bloomington and Minneapolis: Indiana University Press.

Hrushesky, W., Bluming, A., Gruber, S. and Sothern, R. (1989) 'Menstrual influence on surgical cure of breast cancer', *Lancet*, 2: 949–52.

Humm, M. (1992) *Feminisms: A Reader*, Brighton: Harvester Wheatsheaf.

Illich, I. (1977) *Limits to Medicine*, Harmondsworth: Penguin.

Jacobson, J. (1991) *Women's Reproductive Health: The Silent Emergency*, Worldwatch Paper 102, Washington DC: Worldwatch Institute.

Kerby-Eaton, E. and Davies, J. (1985) *Women's Health in a Changing Society*, Vols 1 and 2, proceedings of Second National Conference on All Aspects of Women's Health, Australian College of Advanced Education, Adelaide, South Australia 4–7 September (no publisher).

Kirchstein, R. (1991) 'Research on women's health', *American Journal of Public Health*, 81: 291–3.

Kitzinger, J. (1990) 'Strategies of the early childbirth movement: a case study of the National Childbirth Trust', in Garcia, J., Kilpatrick, R. and Richards, M. (eds) *The Politics of Maternity Care: Services for Childbearing Women in Twentieth Century Britain*, Oxford: Clarendon Press.

Kjellstrand, C. (1988) 'Age, sex and race inequality in renal transplantation', *Archives of Internal Medicine*, 148: 1305–9.

Koblinsky, M., Campbell, O. and Harlow, S. (1993) 'Mother and more: a broader perspective on women's health', in Koblinsky, M., Timyan, J. and Gay, J. (eds) *The Health of Women: A Global Perspective*, Boulder, CO: Westview Press.

Koblinsky, M., Timyan, J. and Gay, J. (eds) (1993) *The Health of Women: A Global Perspective*, Boulder, CO: Westview Press.

Larbie, J. (1985) 'Black women and maternity services, a survey of 30 young Afro-Caribbean women's experiences and perceptions of pregnancy and childbirth', London: Training in Health and Race.

Lorber, J. (1984) *Women Physicians – Careers, Status and Power*, London: Tavistock.

Lovell, T. (1990) *British Feminist Thought: A Reader*, Oxford: Basil Blackwell.

Maternity Alliance (1984) *Multi-racial Initiatives in Maternity Care: A Directory of Projects for Black and Ethnic Minority Women*, London: Maternity Alliance.

Miles, A. (1991) *Women, Health and Medicine*, Milton Keynes: Open University Press.

Montini, T. and Ruzek, S. (1989) 'Overturning orthodoxy: the emergence of breast cancer treatment policy', *Research in the Sociology of Health Care*, vol. 8, Greenwich, CT: JAI Press.

Morris, J. and Royle, T. (1988) 'Offering patients a choice of surgery for early breast cancer: a reduction in depression and anxiety in patients and their husbands', *Social Science and Medicine*, 26 (6): 583–5.

National Health Service Management Executive (NHSME) (1992) *Women in the NHS: An Implementation Guide to Opportunity 2000*, London: Department of Health.

Office of Health Economics (1987) *Women's Health Today*, London: OHE.

O'Sullivan, S. (1987) *Women's Health: A Spare Rib Reader*, London: Pandora Press.

Petchesky, R. (1986) *Abortion and Women's Choice: The State, Sexuality and Reproductive Freedom*, London: Verso.

Petticrew, M., McKee, M. and Jones, J. (1993) 'Coronary artery surgery: are women discriminated against?', *British Medical Journal*, 306: 1164–6.

Phillips, A. and Rakusen, J. (1978) *Our Bodies Ourselves: A Health Book by and for Women*, British edn, Harmondsworth: Penguin.

Riesman, C.K. (1983) 'Women and medicalisation: a new perspective', *Social Policy*, summer: 3–18.

Roberts, H. (1985) *The Patient Patients: Women and Their Doctors*, London: Pandora.

Rosser, S. (1992) 'Re-visioning clinical research: gender and the ethics of experimental design', in Holmes, H. and Purdy, L. (eds) *Feminist Perspectives in Medical Ethics*, Bloomington and Indianapolis: Indiana University Press.

Ruzek, S. (1978) *Women's Health Movement: Feminist Alternatives to Medical Control*, New York: Praeger.

—— (1986) 'Feminist visions of health: an international perspective', in Mitchell, J. and Oakley, A. (eds) *What is Feminism?*, Oxford: Basil Blackwell.

Shearer, H. (1989) 'Maternity patients' movements in the United States 1826–1985', in Chalmers, I., Enkin, M. and Keirse, M. (eds) *Effective Care in Pregnancy and Childbirth*, Oxford: Clarendon Press.

Simkin, P. (1986) 'Is anyone listening? Lack of clinical impact of randomised controlled trials of electronic fetal monitoring', *Birth*, 13: 219–22.

Smyke, P. (1991) *Women and Health*. London: Zed Press.

Spallone, P. (1989) *Beyond Conception: The New Politics of Reproduction*, London: Macmillan.

Stacey, M. (1985) 'Women and health: the United States and the United Kingdom compared', in Lewin, E. and Olesen, V. (eds) *Women, Health and Healing: Toward A New Perspective*, London: Tavistock.

—— (ed.) (1992) *Changing Human Reproduction: Social Science Perspectives*, London: Sage.

Stanworth, M. (1985) *Reproductive Technologies: Gender, Motherhood and Medicine*, Cambridge: Polity Press.

Strong, P. (1979) 'Sociological imperialism and the profession of medicine: a critical examination of the thesis of medical imperialism', *Social Science and Medicine*, 13A(2): 199–215.

Tobin, J., Wassertheil-Smolter, S., Wexler, J. *et al.* (1987) 'Sex bias in considering coronary bypass surgery', *Annals of Internal Medicine*, 107: 19–25.

United States Public Health Service (1992) *Report of the National Institutes of Health: Opportunities for Research on Women's Health*, Washington DC: National Institutes of Health.

Webb, C. (1984) *Feminist Practices in Women's Health Care*, Chichester: John Wiley.

Wenger, N. (1990) 'Gender, coronary heart disease and coronary bypass surgery', *Annals of Internal Medicine*, 112: 557–8.

Whitbeck, C. (1991) 'Ethical issues raised by the new medical technologies', in Rodin, J. and Collins, A. (eds) *Women and New Reproductive Technologies: Medical, Psychosocial, Legal and Ethical Dilemmas*, Hillsdale, NJ: Lawrence Erlbaum.

White, E. (ed.) (1990). *Black Women's Health Book: Speaking for Ourselves*, Seattle: Seal Press.

Witz, A. (1992) *Professions and Patriarchy*, London: Routledge.

Women in Medicine (1987) *Careers for Women in Medicine: Planning and Pitfalls*, London: Women in Medicine.

Women in MIND (1986) *Finding our Own Solutions: Women's Experience of Mental Health Care*, London: MIND Publications.

Worcester, N. and Whatley, M. (1988) 'The response of the health care system to the women's health movement: the selling of women's health centers', in Rosser, S. (ed.) *Feminism within Science and Health Care Professions: Overcoming Resistance*, Oxford: Pergamon Press.

World Health Organization (1992) *Women's Health: Across Age and Frontier*, Geneva: WHO.

Young, A. (1981) 'A woman in medicine – reflections from the inside', in Roberts, H. (ed.) *Women, Health and Reproduction*, London: Routledge & Kegan Paul.

Zimmerman, M. (1987) 'The women's health movement: a critique of medical enterprise and the position of women', in Feree, M. and Hess, B. (eds) *Analyzing Gender*, London: Sage.

Zola, I. (1975) 'Medicine as an institution of social control', in Cox, C. and Mead, A. (eds) *A Sociology of Medical Practice*, London: Collier Macmillan.

9 The anti-vivisectionist movement and the science of medicine

Mary Ann Elston

INTRODUCTION: ANIMAL EXPERIMENTATION AND MODERN MEDICINE

Living non-human animals are integral, although largely hidden, props of modern health care.[1] Animal experimentation will have been involved at some stage in the development, production or testing of almost all therapeutic and clinical preventive drugs and techniques currently employed in allopathic medicine. Animals stand proxy for humans in the testing of an immense range of products and processes to detect potential damage to human health. Much of this work is mandatory under national or international law. A large part of the curriculum for students of 'basic' medical sciences is derived from research with living animals. Its transmission may involve pedagogic demonstrations or, occasionally, student practicals with live, but usually terminally anaesthetised animals, although the extent of the latter varies between countries as well as between professions.[2] Slightly less contentious, but possibly more extensive today than the use of living animals, is the use of animals specifically bred and killed for their tissues in medical research and education.

Not all animal experimentation is devoted to furthering knowledge with direct human health applications. And the ascendancy of the laboratory-based approach has been neither uncontested nor total within British medicine (e.g. Lawrence 1992). But under the statutes regulating animal experiments in Britain for over a century (Cruelty to Animals Act, 1876, and Animals (Scientific Procedures) Act, 1986) prevention, diagnosis or treatment of disease is the first stated purpose for which scientists may be licensed to perform scientific procedures on animals. The vast majority of the 3.2 million scientific procedures carried out under this legislation in 1991 claim a direct or indirect health promoting purpose (Home Office 1992).

In short, to lead what most people would consider to be a normal life, to engage in normal health and illness behaviour, in an industrialised society like Britain, is to take for granted a large area of co-ordinated scientific activity involving the use of laboratory animals. Whether this situation is a morally justifiable one; whether we should eschew animal experiments and forego any putative health benefits on moral grounds; whether we might in fact be healthier if we did so; whether the same or better knowledge might be (or have been) obtained through alternative methods: these are, for some, important questions. This chapter does not attempt to answer them. Rather, it analyses the tactics and arguments deployed by those who have persistently asked such questions from an oppositional standpoint and the response of those challenged.

The chapter begins by outlining the links between the rise and fall of the anti-vivisection movement and the medical profession's rise in status and autonomy from the 1870s to the 1960s. Against this historical background, the marked revival of anti-vivisectionist activity over the last twenty-five years raises obvious questions, which the chapter seeks to address, about possible connections between the resurgence of public opposition to animal experiments and the themes of this volume: that is, the putative de-professionalisation or proletarianisation of medicine and loss of medical authority in late twentieth-century western societies. The chapter demonstrates how current questioning of animal experimentation exemplifies and draws on the external challenges to medicine described in other contributions. The anti-vivisectionist campaign attempts to open up the 'black box' of medical knowledge and technology right back to its earliest stages. The campaign's efforts have generated a response from the institutions of medical research which reveals some of the tensions facing those who might wish to close up the box again.[3]

A CENTURY OF CONTROVERSY OVER ANIMAL EXPERIMENTS

Opposition to live animal experiments is a central feature of the contemporary 'animal rights' movement. This social movement is particularly strong in Britain, the main focus of this chapter. But parallel movements have arisen in the United States (Lederer 1987; Sperling 1988; Jasper and Nelkin 1992), Australia, the Nordic countries and, to a lesser extent, in other parts of Europe (Ryder 1989). The term 'social movement' is apposite in that the animal rights campaign is a loosely structured 'collective actor constituted by individuals who understand themselves to have common interests and, for at least some significant part of their social existence, a common identity' campaigning for social change (Scott 1990: 6). The contemporary movement, or rather part of it, exemplifies many of the features of so-called 'new social movements' (NSMs). These include calls for major changes in values and life-style (e.g.

conversion to vegetarianism if not veganism) and an emphasis on grass-roots support and direct action (liberating animals from laboratories or damaging butchers' shops) rather than conventional political mobilisation. But as with other contemporary oppositional 'NSMs' (Scott 1990), the movement for 'animal rights' represents a resurgence of long-standing concerns about human–animal relationships as well as manifesting some distinctively new features. This is particularly apparent in the protest against animal experimentation.

The modern idea of animal rights is often contrasted with an allegedly more traditional concern with animal welfare. The latter implies that humans have a duty to treat animals humanely when they make use of them for (morally acceptable) human ends. An animal rights position implies that animals have a moral standing that is in some sense equivalent to that which we accord to humans.[4] Hence animals are never acceptable objects for human exploitation, not for food, sport nor entertainment, not as pets nor in science and medicine. There are, undoubtedly, important conceptual distinctions between 'animal rights' and 'animal welfare' as philosophical positions. But in practice the distinction is often less sharp. And sustained collective action against animal experiments is not new. Nor has it ever been 'merely' about animal welfare (although it has always been about this among other things).

Concern about the morality and utility of animal experimentation dates from the practice's tentative beginnings in ancient Greece (Rupke 1987a). But it was after 1850 that vivisection expanded rapidly, bringing with it major public controversy and collective opposition (French 1975). Ever since, the vivisection controversy has been a vehicle for argument about what animal experiments have come to symbolise: the claims and the power of modern science and of a form of medicine that espouses and legitimates such science.

The Victorian cause

Vivisection was an integral part of the application of the methods and values of experimental natural science to the study of living things that began in Germany and France in the mid-nineteenth century. In Britain, a movement of (largely medically trained) scientists worked to reform the medical curriculum around the new physiology from the 1850s. They shared a vision of what the education of modern medical gentlemen should be and a desire for a secure institutional base for their research activities (Butler 1981; French 1975). They acted under the protective shelter offered by the wider medical profession which thereby demonstrated its growing power and its (at least partial) espousal of the values of science. When sociologists speak of the professionalisation project of medicine employing science as a legitimation (e.g. Larson 1977) or the ascendancy of laboratory medicine as a medical cosmology (Jewson 1976) it is this process that is being referred to. Demonstrably superior healing powers of science-based medicine did not precede the conversion. Rather, science was conceived of as 'a powerful and compelling means of conferring "expert status" upon medicine, thereby consolidating its position as an "autonomous" learned profession' (Austoker 1988: 31). This development was bitterly contested by many Victorians. From the 1870s to the early 1900s, competing reformist and abolitionist anti-vivisection societies proliferated. Some of these survive today, the major English ones being the National Anti-Vivisection Society (NAVS) and the British Union for the Abolition of Vivisection (BUAV). Within and outside these societies were hundreds of activists, mostly upper and middle-class women (Elston 1987). Their weapons were media exposure, petitions, personal lobbying and public meetings. In 1876, only the efforts of the organised medical profession turned a parliamentary bill that would have significantly curbed experimentalists' activities into the much less restrictive Cruelty to Animals Act of 1876. Anti-vivisectionists were especially embittered by what they saw as their betrayal by a medical profession corrupted by the experimental approach (French 1975).

Materialist medicine: disputing its morality and utility

At the heart of Victorian anti-vivisectionists' passionate crusade was not only concern about cruelty to animals. To its Victorian critics, the materialist approach to knowledge that vivisection represented was itself immoral, reducing human beings to mechanical assemblages of cells. Vivisection was the weapon with which causal links between religious faith, moral conduct and physical health were being broken, e.g. through bacteriologists' doctrine of specific etiology. The discoveries of those 'scientific devils' Koch and Pasteur reduced disease to a matter of chance encounter with amoral germs. In the opinion of the doyenne of the Victorian anti-vivisectionist movement, Frances Power Cobbe, this led not to the relief of suffering but to 'hygeiolatry', an obsession with health which itself increased susceptibility to disease. According to her, doctors' socialisation through vivisection was leading them down the slippery slope to experiments on humans (Cobbe 1882).

Moreover, according to its critics, the new medical profession was illegitimately claiming the right to dictate personal morality in the name of health. The anti-vivisectionist movement had strong affinities with other late nineteenth-century movements protesting against doctors' and state arrogation of power in relation to health. These included the movements against compulsory smallpox vaccination, for women doctors and against the Contagious Diseases Acts controlling prostitutes in garrison towns (French 1975; Elston 1987; Walkowitz 1980). Anti-vivisectionism appealed particularly to women on the grounds of their greater dependency on doctors (and doctors' greater economic dependency on them). The movement's rhetoric drew heavily on a metaphor of vivisection as the 'rape of nature', linking contemporary concerns about science and medicine with those about sexual vice. Women were repeatedly invited to identify with laboratory animals, both being victims of allegedly sadistic doctors (Elston 1987).

For most Victorian anti-vivisectionists the question of the utility of animal experiments was secondary to the moral issue. For Cobbe, the idea that an evil scientific method could produce valid results was blasphemous (Elston 1987). But, from the 1880s, experimentalists' claims for the clinical utility of a materialist approach strengthened (Rupke 1987b). By 1900, George Bernard Shaw spoke for many other anti-vivisectionists when he declared that the utility of vivisection could never justify the cruelty (Shaw 1900). But others continued to reject Shaw's implicit concession that the method might ever be useful. Attacks on animal experimentation's medical utility were proffered alongside the moral critique. Vaccinations, as against rabies and smallpox, and anti-diphtheria toxin were particular targets. Alternative approaches to health were often commended, for example, spiritualism (Westacott 1949).

Anti-vivisectionists were a highly visible source of pressure on scientists until the First World War. But after the 1880s, their influence was reduced by the close relationships developing between biomedical scientists, the medical profession and government (French 1975). From 1918, the visibility of anti-vivisectionism declined with the growing success of materialist medicine and the rise in state-sanctioned autonomy of scientists and the medical profession. Medical practice that explicitly shunned the products of animal experimentation became increasingly subject to professional and public censure and alternative medicine was dismissed as 'quackery' (Westacott 1949). From the 1920s to the 1960s, verbal skirmishes with 'anti-vivs' continued to be a taken-for-granted minor occupational hazard for biomedical scientists using animals (see e.g. Austoker 1988; Rose 1987). But the anti-vivisectionist message about animal research was being reiterated by what appeared to be a diminishing, ageing and increasingly eccentric constituency.

Thus the course of Victorian anti-vivisectionism demonstrates both the initial contestation of medical professionalisation in civil society and the profession's subsequent success in establishing itself as *the* cultural authority on matters of health. Yet, looking back from the 1990s, we can ask if this was a contingent and possibly temporary achievement.

LABORATORY ANIMALS' RIGHTS AND WRONGS: REVIVED CONCERNS

The first signs of revival in the anti-vivisection movement were in the mid-1960s in Britain, simultaneously with early moves in what was to become the general animal rights movement (Ryder 1989). This was also just after the thalidomide catastrophe brought the question of drug safety testing to public notice and led to legislation mandating more extensive animal testing of all new ethical drugs in Britain (Paton 1993: 145). Against a sharp increase in the number of animal experiments, the organised anti-vivisectionist movement sought compromise around restrictive reforms and further development of alternatives to living animals (Hampson 1987: 316). But the newer animal rights consciousness, acting almost entirely outside the organised anti-vivisection movement, was turning its attention to laboratory animals in various ways. These included militants' attacks on research institutions and the more peaceful publications of an informal network of philosophers and others in Oxford (Henshaw 1989; Ryder 1989).

In Britain, 1975 marked a turning point, with a series of critical incidents including tabloid revelations that beagles were being used to test the safety of alternatives to tobacco. In the United States, a protest against the use of cats by the American Museum of Natural History in New York in 1976 marks the beginning of the contemporary protest movement (Jasper and Nelkin 1992: 26). Against this background of widespread publicity, two new 'anti-speciesist' manifestos attacking animal experiments were widely reviewed: Richard Ryder's *Victims of Science* (1975) and what became the movement's 'bible', Australian philosopher Peter Singer's *Animal Liberation*, first published in the United States in 1975 and in the United Kingdom in 1976. An active campaign to put animals into British parliamentary politics was launched by a coalition of animal welfare and animal rights groups (Hollands 1980; Ryder 1989: 245–9). On both sides of the Atlantic myriad local and special-cause animal rights groups began to appear from the late 1970s. New formal animal rights organisations were founded such as Animal Aid in Britain, in 1977, and the largest of the new American animal rights organisations, People for the Ethical Treatment of Animals (PETA), in 1980. By the 1980s, the new animal rights consciousness was affecting most of the older, often wealthy animal welfare and anti-vivisection societies. Indeed, Britain's largest animal welfare society, the Royal Society for the Prevention of Cruelty to Animals (RSPCA) (income of £29.9 million in 1991, RSPCA 168th Annual Report 1992), has been riven by internal disputes between moderates and radical animal rightists for much of the last two decades. Policy on animal experiments has been one of the most contested issues (Garner 1993; Ryder 1989).

So, since the mid-1970s, the animal rights movement as a whole has clearly grown in both public visibility and in membership on both sides of the Atlantic. Precise assessment of the growth of active support is difficult because of the very nature of social movements. The three largest organisations campaigning against all animal experimentation in Britain (NAVS, BUAV and Animal Aid) had a total of 47,000 members in 1991 (but with much multiple membership) and a total annual income of £2.5 million (*Research Defence Society Newsletter*, October 1991: 8). Active campaigners now appear to be predominantly young, the rank and file still mainly female, spanning both the class and political spectra (Henshaw 1989; Ryder 1989; Jasper and Nelkin 1992). Outside the core support, there are indications of some public uneasiness about the use of laboratory animals, especially among the young in Britain, according to surveys of public opinion (Durant *et al.* 1989; Lock and Millet 1991).

Like most social movements (Scott 1990), anti-vivisectionism and the animal protection movement generally is split into fundamentalist and pragmatic wings, although changing positions and alliances often cut across the divide. In 1983 two pragmatic reform groups, the Scottish Society for the Prevention of Vivisection (SSPV) and the Fund for the Replacement of Animals (FRAME), formed an alliance with the British Veterinary Association to influence government proposals for what became the Animals (Scientific Procedures) Act, 1986. Their support for this alleged 'Vivisectors' Charter' was opposed by a coalition of fundamentalist groups, including BUAV, NAVS and Animal Aid (Hampson 1987: Garner 1993). This coalition's title, 'Mobilisation Against the Government White Paper', epitomises the transformation of the Victorian anti-vivisectionist societies into radical animal rights organisations.

Since 1986, all sections of the British movement have continued to campaign vigorously in and outside Parliament. Schoolchildren and students have been particular targets, with campaign buses, school visits and campus leafleting directed against animal use in education (including dissection) as well as in research and safety evaluation. Animal rights handbooks aimed at children have proliferated (e.g. Newkirk 1991; James 1992). Infiltration of scientific institutions to expose alleged malpractice has been increasingly attempted, particularly in the United States. Two American instances, the case of the 'Silver Springs monkeys' in 1981 and videotapes made in the University of Pennsylvania in 1984, were significant in generating media attention and inspiring support (Jasper and Nelkin 1992: 31). Particularly in Britain, the activities of the more extremist wing have extended to planting bombs aimed at individuals (Paton 1993: 237–40).

One feature of the arguments modern campaigners used to inspire support when the revival began is notable. It was *not* a challenge to medical research. From the late 1960s to the 1980s, the emphasis was primarily on the moral status of animals. To this was added a sustained attack on the infliction of pain and repeated calls for increased accountability of scientists. Attacks on the validity of the scientific knowledge gained were primarily claims about the difficulties of drawing inferences from data obtained with one species to another species (the problem of species error). According to a leading activist, by attacking the allegedly widespread use of laboratory animals *'not* for strictly medical purposes' (e.g. behavioural research and safety testing of cosmetics) 'it was easier for us to erode the then widely accepted view of animal experimentation as a high-minded medical necessity involving little or no suffering for its non-human victims' (Ryder 1989: 244–5, 250–1, original emphasis). Even if distinguishing between acceptable (medical) and unacceptable (non-medical) research was only a tactical ploy (Duffy 1984: 46), the effect was to leave medical research largely unchallenged. But during the 1980s, and especially after 1986, this changed. Anti-vivisectionist claims about the morality and value of animal experiments for human health were again becoming a central feature of their rhetoric.

HEALTH WITH HUMANITY OR THE CRUEL DECEPTION UNMASKED?

Animal experiments are, so much anti-vivisectionist rhetoric now alleges, not just cruel abuses of animals. They are useless and even damaging to human health, a 'cruel deception' (Sharpe 1988). To the question 'Animals or people – which come first?' raised by defenders of animal experiments, the response has been recently that 'the question is meaningless because vivisection benefits neither animals nor people' (McIvor 1990: 18). Most versions of this critique draw explicitly on sources familiar to medical sociologists.

An early restatement of this condemnation of medical research was the millenarian vision of the corrupt, evil and iatrogenic biomedical establishment set out in *Slaughter of the Innocent* by the controversial Swiss antivivisectionist Hans Ruesch (1983). Among Ruesch's sources is 'Ivan Illich's carefully researched *Medical Nemesis*' (Ruesch 1983: 285, citing Illich 1976). (This book was a key influence on the more general radical critique of medicine that developed from the mid-1970s.) When first published, Ruesch's views were widely criticised within the animal rights movement, as a counterproductive distraction from the general moral arguments. But from the mid-1980s, the critique of medical research spread across the movement. The BUAV launched a 'Health with Humanity' campaign in 1988 (BUAV n.d.; McIvor 1990). NAVS has revised and reissued many of its old pamphlets attacking medical research. Much is made of any support for the anti-vivisectionist cause by doctors (e.g. Coleman 1991: 111; *Outrage*, 70, Oct./Nov. 1990: 3). Two fundamentalist organisations for doctors have appeared in Britain since the late 1980s but, according to pro-research sources, their membership is small (*RDS Newsletter*, Oct. 1991; Jan. 1992). One recent survey indicates that most British doctors believe animal research to be of value (*BMA News Review*, June 1993).

The challenge to the morality of modern medicine

There are two main strands in the renewed attack on the morality of modern medicine, both new versions of old themes. One is the idea of the corrupting, desensitising influence of the practice of vivisection, destroying the natural and healthy 'squeamishness' of the neophyte through intense pressure to conform (e.g. *Outrage*, Aug./Sept. 1990: 9). This may lead to 'the "cut, burn, poison" approach' to patient care and could be a step towards experiments on humans (McIvor 1990: 9). The literature is again full of invitations for humans to empathise with animal victims, especially in the eco-feminist critiques of medical research which posit a natural affinity between women and animals (e.g. Caldecott and Leland 1983; Collard 1988).

Scientists are described as self-seeking individuals motivated by 'mere curiosity' and career advancement, blinded by their socialisation and their vested interests from adopting non-animal alternatives. From here it is but a short step to a condemnation of the institutions of medicine and bio-medical research, reiterating much of the Marxist-influenced political economy critique of the pharmaceutical industry as profit- rather than need-driven (e.g. Sharpe 1988). The 'soft' targets of universities and medical research charities have recently been accused of being morally and scientifically bankrupt and wasters of the public's money (e.g. Langley 1990). All research institutions are condemned for their 'closed doors' as indicative of there being something to hide.

The other strand in the moral argument is to draw distinctions between acceptable and unacceptable categories of research within the medical field. Here the question of human culpability for ill-health is crucial. A link between human conduct and health that materialist medicine allegedly ignores is once again being asserted in defence of animals. To make animals suffer for our own misconduct, where behavioural change would eliminate the problem, is especially unacceptable. Thus the (human) 'victim-blaming' approach that has become widespread in health promotion policies since the 1970s (Crawford 1977) is given a further twist by anti-vivisectionists.

Research into the effects of tobacco or alcohol is condemned by the whole movement. But, for some, all those conditions where epidemiology has indicated the theoretical possibility of prevention by behavioural or social change are unacceptable. Thus, on the basis of epidemiological statements that up to 90 per cent of the variance in some cancers' incidence can be statistically accounted for by known social, behavioural and environmental risks, it is claimed that all animal experiments in cancer research are immoral. Cancer research charities are then condemned for their alleged neglect of health education, epidemiology or clinical research (Langley 1990).

The 'facts' about modern medicine?

Alongside the critique of the morality of animal-based medical research is a renewed emphasis on its uselessness. Indeed, controversial doctor and journalist Vernon Coleman declares that 'Like most modern anti-vivisectionists I prefer to argue against vivisection on scientific and medical grounds' (Coleman 1991: 31). Again there are two main themes: revising the celebratory history of medicine and a strong thesis about the problem of species error. The first theme sets up a contrast between what 'people have come to believe . . . that were it not for animal based medical research we would still be experiencing the appalling level of ill health which was common in Victorian times' and 'the facts [which] may come as a surprise' (BUAV n.d.: 4).

Some of these 'facts' may be of less surprise to medical sociologists or even to most doctors and medical students, based as they are on the academic literature of the 'efficacy debate', notably the work of Thomas McKeown (e.g. 1976). For example, the second edition of Singer's *Animal Liberation* includes a new section on this literature (1990: 88–92). A widely cited British source, Sharpe's *The Cruel Deception* (1988), commends sociological sources such as Doyal (1979) and the Black Report on Health Inequalities (DHSS 1980). From the (undisputed) premise that the massive decline in mortality from many infectious diseases experienced by western countries since 1800 preceded the introduction of specific chemo-therapies or immunisations, inferences are made about the value of such animal-derived interventions once they became available. For example, Singer's revised text concludes that 'any knowledge gained from animal experimentation has made at best a very small contribution to our increased lifespan; its contribution to improving the quality of life is more difficult to assess' (1990: 91). Many other opponents, for example Ruesch (1983), would not grant even this much credit to animal experimentation.

With the aid of a catalogue of modern medicine's iatrogenic effects and a pessimistic picture of increasing ill-health resulting from modern life, a wide spectrum of medical interventions is drawn into the anti-vivisectionists' critique of the effects of animal experimentation. The animal rights journal *Turning Point* is typical with its regular 'Bitter Pills' feature on reports of harmful side effects and failings of prescribed medicines. As well as promoting life-style changes, the 'gentler' approaches of 'alternative medicine' are widely held to hold greater promise for human health (e.g. Hall 1985; Langley 1990). Here we have another old theme being reiterated but with new meaning because of the growth in support for alternative medicine since the mid-1970s (see Saks this volume).

Much of the blame for the ineffectiveness of modern medicine is attributed to the false method employed in its development – the animal model. 'The fact is that animal experiments tell us about animals and not about people' (BUAV n.d.: 4). Differences between species are said to lead to the adoption of therapies that are, in fact, ineffective or even dangerous for human use, while potentially useful ones are lost. The result, according to Coleman, is that, far from advancing human health, '*animal experiments kill people*' (1991: 1, original emphasis). What is required instead of animal-based research is 'REAL science: the study of human beings and human disease' (NAVS 1987: 1). Or, as 'the simple (but often overlooked) truth is that no matter how many animal tests are done the first two or three generations of people who use a new drug or technique are the real guinea pigs', so people should be the primary subjects of medical research (LIMAV/Coleman 1991). Preferred methods of medical research include clinical observation studies, epidemiology, trials using human volunteers, post-marketing surveillance of therapies and more use of 'alternative' techniques, such as those using human tissue cultures.

There is a paradox here. Among the 'key ontological underpinnings of the new ethical orientations to animals are notions of [human–animal] kinship and interdependence' (Benton 1991: 8). Animal rightists have long accused animal experimenters of inconsistency: of invoking human–animal closeness in pressing the case for the utility of animal models in research for human benefit while denying such closeness when attempting a moral justification for using such models (Ryder 1975; Singer 1975). But in recent 'health with humanity' arguments, many contemporary antivivisectionists appear to be doing the converse.

Not surprisingly, the HIV/AIDS epidemic has attracted considerable attention in the movement's literature. Its growing death toll is taken to symbolise the failed promise of medicine. Because human conduct is implicated in the transmission of HIV, animal-based research is widely held to be unnecessary and immoral (e.g. McIvor 1990). To search for a vaccine is cruel, unnecessary and doomed to failure (Sharpe 1988: 56). The difficulty of reproducing AIDS symptoms in as close a relative as the chimpanzee is taken to confirm the weakness of animal models. To cause suffering to members of such a sensitive species, endangered in the wild, is condemned across the movement. For some critics, the HIV/AIDS epidemic demonstrates the dangers of using non-human primates in research for human health. Some anti-vivisectionists favour the 'Green monkey' explanatory account of the origins of HIV; that is that the virus originated in a species of African monkey and has somehow crossed the species barrier, becoming cruelly virulent in the process. For Sharpe (1988), this underlines the difference between species and the dangers posed by breaching the boundaries between them.

Others, including NAVS and Coleman (1991: 66), have explicitly promoted the view that the HIV virus has spread from and perhaps was actually created in the research laboratory. Unacknowledged mixing of viruses, through blind arrogance or negligence, could, according to NAVS, have produced a new retrovirus exported around the world by the trade in laboratory animals. If so, when transmitted to humans through (allegedly widespread) laboratory worker carelessness, this new retrovirus has proved to be a 'biological time bomb'. This is, according to the authors of *Biohazard*, just the tip of an iceberg of laboratory-induced disease. Biomedical laboratories are alleged to be a major threat to health for all who work and live near them, carrying 'the same dangers as nuclear research (if not more so)' but being even more secretive and less accountable (NAVS 1987: 71).

Why the shift in focus?

Most modern anti-vivisectionists, like their predecessors, probably still see their campaign as primarily a moral one. Many might still argue, as did Shaw in 1900, that attacking the utility of an immoral method is not the central point (e.g. Singer 1990: 92). This chapter does not claim that attacks on medical research have become the sole platform of modern anti-vivisectionism. But there are many reasons why the animal rights-influenced contemporary movement has returned to more traditional anti-vivisectionist concerns with medicine.

One factor may be simply the rediscovery of the movement's history as younger animal rightists have taken over the anti-vivisection organisations. In Britain, the critique of medical research clearly gained momentum when the campaigning groups needed a fresh focus after new legislation in 1986. But, faced with the institutionalised pervasiveness of science and medicine, it may be hard to achieve radical change in the use of animals by appeal to moral principles alone (cf. Benton 1993). Legitimations that appeal to scientific authority may carry some force, even for a movement opposed to one institutionalised form of such authority. If animal experiments can be shown to be useless or even damaging for human health a major defence of the practice is removed and self-interested grounds for public opposition provided. The renewed attack on medical research from anti-vivisectionists has clearly gathered momentum and ammunition from the other contemporary challenges to medicine discussed in this book. Medicine is attackable in the 1990s in a way that it was not twenty years ago.[5] But, even if now challengeable, the authority and strength of the institutions of medical research are, of course, quite different now than a hundred years ago.

MEDICAL RESEARCH'S RESPONSE TO THE ANTI-VIVISECTIONIST CHALLENGE[6]

For much of the last century, responses by either individual medical researchers or institutions to public campaigning against animal experimentation were relatively low-key. There are many reasons for this, not least that those engaged in medical research may have other priorities. Between the 1920s and the 1970s, to have responded vigorously might have seemed to give the challenge undue credence and invited further unwanted attention. With the rise of the Animal Liberation Front's terrorist campaign from 1972, reluctance to 'stick one's head above the parapet' is an understandable response by scientists. Even after animals had been placed on the parliamentary political agenda in the late 1970s, the bio-medical research community in Britain initially concentrated on securing 'bureaucratic accommodation' with realistic reformers rather than on public campaigning. This reflects the characteristic British style of public policy making through seeking negotiated consensus between 'insider groups'. In the much more openly adversarial political culture of the United States, the scientists' response was much more publicly aggressive from the start (cf. Gluck and Kubacki 1991). This is in part because American scientists are still contesting the principle of government regulation of animal experimentation itself, a principle British scientists have worked under since 1876 (Elston 1992).

But, of course, even in Britain there have been moves to engage public opinion in support of animal research, especially during the peaks of anti-vivisectionist challenge, in the 1880s (Rupke 1987b), in the 1900s and in the last decade. In 1908, the Research Defence Society (RDS) was founded specifically for this purpose and has published many pamphlets extolling the contribution of animal experiments to human health (e.g. RDS 1908). In fact, from the 1950s to the late 1980s, the RDS worked primarily as an 'insider group', mainly representing graduate researchers, especially in academia. But during the long negotiations leading up to the Animals (Scientific Procedures) Act in 1986, the RDS ran a national advertising campaign. Distinguished pharmacologist Sir William Paton published a book-length defence of animal experiments emphasising the practical benefits (Paton 1984). At the same time the Association of the British Pharmaceutical Industry established the Animals in Medicines Research Information Centre (AMRIC) to inform the public about the use of animals in the pharmaceutical industry.

But a much more active public campaign on the part of British medical researchers and their organisations has developed from the late 1980s. Besides producing new educational material, researchers have been encouraged to 'go public' in the mass media and before lay audiences, above all in schools. The RDS has taken on a much more public profile. In 1990 the British Association for the Advancement of Science (BA) launched a Declaration on Animals in Medical Research, which supports the case for animal experiments in biomedical research while urging scientists to respect animal life. A similar resolution was adopted by the American Association for the Advancement of Science (AAAS) in 1990 (Paton 1993: 221). The BA Declaration had been signed by 'nearly 1000 eminent doctors, scientists and organisations' a year later (*RDS News*, Summer 1991).

In 1991, the major medical research funding charities launched the Research for Health Charities Group. Its objectives include increasing public understanding of the role played by animals in medical research as well as encouraging good research practice among its members (*RDS Newsletter*, Jan. 1992). The British Medical Association (BMA) agreed to mount a campaign 'informing the public of the importance of animal experiments in the fight against disease' after a 'lively debate' at its 1992 Annual Representative Meeting (*RDS Newsletter*, July 1992). The voice of the patient is also being raised, through Seriously Ill for Medical Research (SIMR), founded in 1991 (*Hope*, SIMR Quarterly Newsletter 1, July 1991), and its much larger American counterpart Incurably Ill for Animal Research (iiFAR) (Jasper and Nelkin 1992: 134).

Behind the developing response in Britain lies a widespread view within the medical research community that the animal rights movement has been winning the public debate 'by default', aided by the mass media's interest in controversy and hence in the protest movement. The response needs to be seen in the context of the British scientific community's general concern about public understanding of science and future recruitment of scientific workers (e.g. Royal Society 1985). Recruitment is a particularly pertinent issue in biomedical research because of the concern about animals among the young.

These organised moves are, then, in part, a reaction to the success of the pro-animal movement in integrating some of its concerns into public (including scientists') consciousness and political life in Britain. Biomedical scientists and their institutions have had to learn new strategies for responding to direct action and mass media attacks. But the upturn in overt response from the research side followed after the animal rights movement's shift to attacking the utility of medical research. This may be a sign of confidence as much as of concern. It is not just that scientists may feel more confident debating claims about science than about moral philosophy. Rather, in the current social climate, medicine and science cannot claim exclusive authority in moral debates. But if a dispute centres on claims about 'scientific facts', specialist expertise can be invoked to try to close off controversy (cf. Michael and Birke 1994).

Thus what the scientists' side widely refers to as 'the battle for (the) hearts and minds' of the public is currently being waged. The battle is most intense in the classroom but is also being fought in all forms of the mass media, especially the local press. (Both sides use mailing services to place correspondence across the country.) Counter-claims about the contribution of animal experimentation to medical progress are the dominant theme in the scientists' response. For example, corrective accounts are given of oft-repeated anti-vivisectionist allegations about the role of animal tests in the thalidomide disaster or the isolation of insulin, or about species error. The importance of social factors for increases in life expectancy in the past and the role of behavioural factors and prevention are all explicitly recognised, perhaps more so now than a decade ago. But many of the inferences made by anti-vivisectionists are rejected as invalid. For example the implication that (animal-based) bacteriology made no contribution to public health's success in controlling infectious diseases in the late nineteenth century or that all cancers and heart disease can be blamed on the victim's behaviour is disputed (e.g. Paton 1984, 1993).[7]

There is a high level of public consensus among the biomedical research community about the broad content of the message about medical research. But, at least in Britain, there is much less agreement about how to transmit that message (e.g. discussions in Botting 1992). Such disagreements are only one aspect of the internal debate about animal use now taking place within the research community. Some researchers call for forceful proselytising, often looking to clinicians to carry the message with more public credibility than 'boffins' could. This group often cites with approval the American approach, for example the glossy campaign material of the American Foundation for Biomedical Research, which deploys images quite as emotional as any anti-vivisectionist propaganda (Jasper and Nelkin 1992: 133).

Others see aggressive campaigning or 'knee-jerk' defences as unwarranted or potentially counter-productive. They call for more opening up of laboratories, at least to the press if not always to active opponents. The need for constructive debate with the pragmatic animal rights and welfare groups, who concede that animals have been useful in past medical research, is stressed.

Interestingly, as the volume of 'pro-research' educational material has increased since the mid-1980s, there have been changes in style. The presentation of 'both sides' is increasingly incorporated into the structure of pamphlets and videos with less reliance on 'authoritative' voices alone. For example, AMRIC's 1993 video for schools, *Life on the Line*, takes the form of a class project investigating the topic, not, as in previous ones, a voiced-over documentary or a famous scientist's view. This shift in format partly reflects the importance placed on material that can be used by teachers. But it also suggests a recognition that it may not be possible to settle the debate by appeals to the authority of science and medicine alone or even desirable to try. The research community appears to be learning that, to use Wynne's phrase, scientists' 'body language' – how they put their message across – may be as important as its content in influencing public response, especially among young people (Wynne 1991: 119).

CONCLUSION

This chapter has demonstrated how, in disputing the value of a key route to knowledge, the anti-vivisection movement explicitly challenges the claims of medical research to scientific rationality, technical prowess and moral probity. Anti-vivisectionism has undoubtedly had some impact, albeit intermittently, on medical research in Britain over the past century. The contemporary movement has achieved public recognition of some of its concerns. Its pressure was a major factor bringing about new legislation regulating animal experimentation in Britain (although the fundamentalist wing had virtually no influence on the law's contents). The response from biomedical researchers is itself being influenced by shifts in the status of medical research. It is too soon to assess the impact of this counter-campaign, whatever its style. But it is certainly achieving a higher public profile for the pro-research side.

Returning to the more general themes of this book, it is clear that the level of support for anti-vivisectionism in general and the focus of its claims have varied with the strength of other challenges to the social and cultural authority of medicine and medical research. Lay perceptions of doctors and their work have probably never taken the form of blind faith nor, indeed, of total scepticism. Rather, medical sociology has documented a complex mixture of the two, the balance shifting pragmatically according to particular contexts (e.g. Calnan and Williams 1992). But there is good reason to think that, in general, the scales may have tipped towards scepticism since the 1970s (Elston 1991). In the last twenty-five years, public knowledge and concern about the risks and limitations of modern medicine has been increasing, alongside more general questioning of expertise and professionalism (Scott *et al.* 1992).

This is one product of what Giddens calls the 'reflexivity of modernity' (1990: 36). The arguments about health and medicine deployed by the contemporary anti-vivisection movement demonstrate the reflexivity of modern knowledge about medicine very vividly. The debates about medicine within academic social science and medicine become the basis of an external critique of the utility of medicine which seeks to penetrate to the heart of the expert system itself. Evidence of the fallibility of scientific knowledge, of disagreement between medical scientists, of false trails, all these are taken by critics as evidence of the need for distrust of medical science. Yet the anti-vivisection movement, in giving its supporters a social identity, is itself, in part, an 'adaptive reaction' to any growing distrust of medicine (cf. Giddens 1990: 134, 137).

So implicit trust in both the individuals who practice medicine and the underlying system of knowledge may have been weakening. Does this point to a radical deprofessionalisation of medicine? Or even to a post-modernist eclipse of scientific medical authority (cf. Bakx 1991)? If so, does this confirm the animal rights movement as a 'New Social Movement', a qualitatively new kind of oppositional movement ushering in a general transformation of capitalist or modernist society (e.g. Crook *et al.* 1992)?

It is impossible to give definitive answers to these questions, but my position tends towards a qualified 'no' to all of them. Certainly, there is much that is new about the animal rights movement but there is also sufficient continuity with the past, at least in relation to anti-vivisectionism, to suggest that building a grand theory of social change on its 'newness' might be foolhardy. There is also much that fits with the changes identified by deprofessionalisation theorists (e.g. Haug 1988). Medical research's claims may have become more challengeable. But the continued appeal to scientific authority and the importance placed on 'real' medical research by the anti-vivisectionist movement suggests that the post-modernist cultural world is still some way off. More generally, what deprofessionalisation and post-modernist cultural theories neglect is the institutionalised permeation of everyday life by biomedical science, a permeation that is normally invisible until we have reason to mistrust it. As set out in the beginning of this chapter, embedded into the structure of our taken-for-granted routines is this abstract system of knowledge and technology that relies on, among many other methods, the use of living animals. The revival of the anti-vivisectionist movement may have made us more aware of this reliance but it has not radically changed it.

ACKNOWLEDGEMENTS

Research for this paper was undertaken as part of the Science Policy Support Group/Economic and Social Research Council programme 'The Changing Culture of Research' and funded by ESRC award number Y305253003. An earlier version was presented at the British Sociological Association's Annual Conference in 1991.

NOTES

1 The terminology in the controversy I am outlining here is contentious. I shall use 'animal' to refer to non-human creatures only, except where special emphasis is called for. Those working with laboratory animals reject the term 'vivisection', with its literal connotation of cutting open living creatures, as too emotive to apply to the vast majority of scientific procedures carried out on animals today.

2 Students of human and veterinary medicine generally have much more direct exposure to animal experimentation than those in so-called paramedical fields such as physiotherapy. Perhaps because of more restrictive legislation, British students are, in general, much less likely to actually perform experiments than American ones (Smith and Boyd 1991: 233).

3 The term 'black box' has been adopted within the sociology of science from its use in engineering to refer to technologies that can be treated as uncontroversial, predictable input/output systems without consideration of their internal mechanisms (e.g. Latour 1987).

4 The term 'animal rights' is being used here to refer to the contemporary movement in general. Not all the philosophers associated with the movement employ the philosophical concept of 'rights' and, for some purposes, it is important to distinguish between 'animal rights' and 'animal liberation' segments of the movement.

5 Activist Richard Ryder expressed this view in an interview with the author in 1992.

6 In addition to published sources, the following section draws on interviews with 120 persons engaged in work involving laboratory animals, from animal technicians and bench scientists to directors of funding bodies and government officials, and observation in research settings and professional meetings. The focus of this necessarily brief discussion is on the public response of the biomedical research community to the high-profile radical animal rights challenge. It does not cover the ongoing debates about the use of animals generally within the research community or the less public dialogues about laboratory animal welfare between animal researchers and more pragmatic reformers.

7 McKeown explicitly recognises both these points (1976: 156–75).

REFERENCES

Austoker, J. (1988) *A History of the Imperial Cancer Research Fund 1902–1986*, Oxford: Oxford University Press.

Bakx, K. (1991) 'The "eclipse" of folk medicine in western society?', *Sociology of Health and Illness*, 13: 20–38.

Benton, T. (1991) 'Biology and social science: why the return of the repressed should be given a (cautious) welcome', *Sociology*, 25: 1–29.
—— (1993) *Natural Relations: Ecology, Animal Rights and Social Justice*, London: Verso.
Botting, J. (ed.) (1992) *Animal Experimentation and the Future of Medical Research* (Proceedings of the Conference held at the Royal Society, London, 26 April 1991), London: Portland Press.
British Union for the Abolition of Vivisection (BUAV) (n.d.) *Health with Humanity*, London: BUAV.
Butler, S.V. (1981) 'Science and the education of doctors in the nineteenth century: a study of British medical schools with special reference to the development and uses of physiology', unpublished Ph.D. thesis, University of Manchester.
Caldecott, L. and Leland, S. (eds) (1983) *Women Reclaim the Earth*, London: Women's Press.
Calnan, M. and Williams, S. (1992) 'Images of scientific medicine', *Sociology of Health and Illness*, 14 (2): 233–54.
Cobbe, F.P. (1882) '"Hygeiolatry" and "Sacrificial Medicine"', in Cobbe, F.P. (ed.) *Peak of Darien*, London: Williams & Norgate.
Coleman, V. (1991) *Why Animal Experiments Must Stop: And How You Can Help Stop Them*, London: Green Print.
Collard, A. with Contrucci, J. (1988) *Rape of the Wild*, London: Women's Press.
Crawford, R. (1977) 'You are dangerous to your health: ideology and politics of victim blaming', *International Journal of Health Services*, 7: 663–80.
Crook, S., Pakulski, J. and Waters, M. (1992) *Post-Modernization: Change in Advanced Society*, London: Sage.
Department of Health and Social Security (DHSS) (1980) *Report of the Working Group on Inequalities in Health* (Black Report), London: DHSS.
Doyal, L. with Pennell, I. (1979) *The Political Economy of Health*, London: Pluto.
Duffy, M. (1984) *Men and Beasts: An Animal Rights Handbook*, London: Paladin.
Durant, J., Evans, G.A. and Thomas, G.P. (1989) 'The public understanding of science', *Nature*, 340: 11–14.
Elston, M.A. (1987) 'Women and anti-vivisection in Victorian England, 1870–1900', in Rupke, N. (ed.) *Vivisection in Historical Perspective*, London: Croom Helm.
—— (1991) 'The politics of professional power: medicine in a changing society', in Gabe, J., Calnan, M. and Bury, M. (eds) *The Sociology of the Health Service*, London: Routledge.
—— (1992) 'The "animal question" in the British science press: the case of *New Scientist*, 1970–1991', in Hicks, E.K. (ed.) *Science and the Human–Animal Relationship*, Amsterdam: SISWO.
French, R.D. (1975) *Antivivisection and Medical Science in Victorian Society*, Princeton: Princeton University Press.
Garner, R. (1993) *Animals, Politics and Morality*, Manchester: Manchester University Press.
Giddens, A. (1990) *The Consequences of Modernity*, Cambridge: Polity Press.
Gluck, J.P. and Kubacki, S.R. (1991) 'Animals in biomedical research: the undermining effect of the rhetoric of the besieged', *Ethics and Behaviour*, 1 (3): 157–73.
Hall, R. (1985) *Indefensible Treatment*, London: Corgi.
Hampson, J. (1987) 'Legislation: A practical solution to the vivisection dilemma?', in Rupke, N. (ed.) *Vivisection in Historical Perspective*, London: Croom Helm.

Haug, M. (1988) 'A re-examination of the hypothesis of deprofessionalization', *Milbank Quarterly*, 66 (Suppl. 2): 48–56.

Henshaw, D. (1989) *Animal Warfare: The Story of the Animal Liberation Front*, London: Fontana.

Hollands, C. (1980) *Compassion is the Bugler: The Struggle for Animal Rights*, Edinburgh: MacDonald Publishers.

Home Office (1992) *Statistics of Scientific Procedures on Living Animals 1991*, London: HMSO.

Illich, I. (1976) *Medical Nemesis*, New York: Pantheon Books.

James, B. (1992) *The Young Person's Action Guide to Animal Rights*, London: Virago.

Jasper, J.M. and Nelkin, D. (1992) *The Animal Rights Crusade: The Growth of a Moral Protest*, Chicago: Free Press.

Jewson, N. (1976) 'The disappearance of the sick-man from medical cosmology, 1770–1870', *Sociology*, 10: 225–44.

Langley, G. (1990) *Faith, Hope and Charity?*, London: BUAV.

Larson, M.S. (1977) *The Rise of Professionalism: A Sociological Analysis*, Berkeley: University of California Press.

Latour, B. (1987) *Science in Action*, Milton Keynes: Open University Press.

Lawrence, C. (1992) 'Experiment and experience in anaesthesia: Alfred Goodman Levy and chloroform death, 1910–1960', in Lawrence, C. (ed.) *Medical Theory, Surgical Practice: Studies in the History of Surgery*, London: Routledge.

Lederer, S. (1987) 'The controversy over animal experiments in America, 1880–1914', in Rupke, N. (ed.) *Vivisection in Historical Perspective*, London: Croom Helm.

LIMAV (League Internationale Médecins pour l'Abolition de la Vivisection)/Coleman, V. (1991) *Why Animal Experiments Must be Stopped*, Arbedo: LIMAV.

Lock, R. and Millet, K. (1991) *The Animals and Science Education Project, 1990–91*, Birmingham: University of Birmingham School of Education.

McIvor, S. (ed.) (1990) *Health with Humanity: The Case Against Using Animals for Medical Research*, London: BUAV.

McKeown, T. (1976) *The Role of Medicine: Dream, Mirage or Nemesis*, London: Nuffield Provincial Hospitals Trust.

Michael, M. and Birke, L. (1994) 'Animal experimentation: enrolling the core set', *Social Studies of Science*, 24: 81–95.

National Anti-Vivisection Society (NAVS) (1987) *Biohazard: The Silent Threat from Biomedical Research and the Creation of AIDS*, London: NAVS.

Newkirk, I. (1991) *Save the Animals: 101 Easy Things You Can Do*, London: Angus.

Paton, W. (1984) *Man and Mouse: Animals in Medical Research*, Oxford: Oxford University Press.

—— (1993) *Man and Mouse: Animals in Medical Research*, new edn, Oxford: Oxford University Press.

Research Defence Society (RDS) (1908) *Experiments on Animals: Pamphlets Issued by the Research Defence Society, February–August, 1908*, London: Research Defence Society.

Rose, S. (1987) *Molecules and Minds*, Milton Keynes: Open University Press.

Royal Society of London (1985) *The Public Understanding of Science*, London: The Royal Society.

Ruesch, H. (1983) *Slaughter of the Innocent*, Klosters: Civitas (first published New York: Bantam Books, 1978).

Rupke, N. (1987a) 'Introduction', in Rupke, N. (ed.) *Vivisection in Historical Perspective*, London: Croom Helm.

—— (1987b) 'Pro-vivisection in England in the early 1880s: arguments and motives', in Rupke, N. (ed.) *Vivisection in Historical Perspective*, London: Croom Helm.

Ryder, R.D. (1975) *Victims of Science: The Use of Animals in Research*, London: Davis-Poynter (second edn 1983, London: National Anti-Vivisection Society).

—— (1989) *Animal Revolution: Changing Attitudes Towards Speciesism*, Oxford: Blackwell.

Scott, A. (1990) *Ideology and the New Social Movements*, London: Unwin Hyman.

Scott, S., Williams, G. and Thomas, H. (eds) (1992) *Private Risks and Public Dangers*, Aldershot: Avebury.

Sharpe, R. (1988) *The Cruel Deception: The Use of Animals in Medical Research*, London: Thorsons.

Shaw, G.B. (1900) *The Dynamitards of Science*, London: London Anti-Vivisection Society.

Singer, P. (1975) *Animal Liberation: A New Ethic for our Treatment of Animals*, New York: New York Review of Books (British edn 1976, London: Thorsons).

—— (1990) *Animal Liberation*, second edn, New York: New York Review of Books.

Smith, J. and Boyd, K. (eds) (1991) *Lives in the Balance: The Ethics of Using Animals in Biomedical Research*, Oxford: Oxford University Press.

Sperling, S. (1988) *Animal Liberators: Research and Morality*, Berkeley, CA: University of California Press.

Walkowitz, J. (1980) *Prostitution and Victorian Society: Women, Class, and the State*, Cambridge: Cambridge University Press.

Westacott, E. (1949) *A Century of Vivisection and Anti-Vivisection*, Rochford, Essex: C.W. Daniel.

Wynne, B. (1991) 'Knowledges in context', *Science, Technology and Human Values*, 16 (1): 111–21.

10 Epilogue

The last days of Doctor Power

Gareth Williams, Jonathan Gabe and David Kelleher

Dr Power sits hunched over his desk. He looks unhappy and lost in thought. A threat of litigation from an aggrieved patient has arrived in his mail, a journalist from the local newspaper has just phoned about rumours of unrest among the staff, and he has been informed by his Chief Executive that the Mainchance Purchasing Consortium is going to buy its specialist assessment facilities from another hospital down the road.

A Stranger enters his consulting rooms and a conversation begins to develop. . . .

Stranger: You say you have done so much for your patients. So why do all these people challenge you? Why are they criticising what you are doing?

Dr Power: I really don't understand. I have been working in the health service for thirty years. The improvements that have taken place – they would have been unimaginable when I first qualified. Hospitals have better equipment, drugs and surgery are safer and more effective, services are more efficient . . . although, of course, there are now more internally and externally imposed constraints. . . .

Stranger: What constraints are those, Dr Power?

Dr Power: Oh, you know, nurses going on about the nursing process, working to a budget, clinical directors breathing down your neck, directives from the Secretary of State every other week, patients quoting chapter and verse from their Charter . . . we have no autonomy any more, and less authority.

Stranger: Don't you think that part of the problem is that the improvements you mention have been perceived to be more for the benefit of doctors than the people they treat?

Dr Power: They have certainly made our work a lot easier and safer, but of course there have been benefits for our patients too . . . more accurate diagnosis, more effective treatment, a more comfortable therapeutic environment.

Stranger: I'm sure that's true, but for many years there have also been voices telling us that patients are not treated as people. Many of these constraints you refer to could be seen as attempts to rectify that situation.

Dr Power: I think most of our patients are satisfied . . . there are always a few for whom nothing is right, and those few patients sometimes complain a lot! . . . Always telephoning the Community Health Council. In a busy hospital it isn't always easy to be polite. The main thing is to get the patient well.

Stranger: But you have to admit that people are often satisfied almost in spite of what you do for them. It is the warmth and kindness of doctors and nurses, when they have the time, that most impresses itself on people, not the machinery and the drugs. And it is rudeness and arrogance that upsets people even when the treatment has been 'a success'.

Dr Power: Patients would soon become dissatisfied if we did not diagnose accurately and treat quickly . . .

Stranger: I'll grant you that, Dr Power, but it doesn't really answer the question about what it is that people are looking for, and what makes the process and outcome of care a satisfactory one from their point of view. Do you think you are providing people with what they want?

Dr Power: I know what the patient needs. All that matters to me is that patients come in ill and in pain, and they leave feeling better – better than they did when they came in, anyway. Of course there are more people complaining and taking out negligence claims now . . . the Patient's Charter, the demands from purchasers, the lack of resources, a more litigious society, medical disaster stories on television have all created a situation in which complaints are more likely. All these changes undermine our authority and raise unrealistic expectations in patients. But in general . . .

Stranger: How can you say 'in general'?

Dr Power: Because I know what my patients think. I know them and they know me . . .

Stranger: In what sense do you know them? Isn't one of the criticisms of doctors that they only look at the pathology and not at the person? And

I'm sure that most patients feel far too vulnerable to speak their minds to you . . .

Dr Power: I'm not sure that they want me to know them personally, and anyway, to get to know them too personally is not helpful when you are trying to focus on the symptoms they present. As for speaking their minds, I can assure you I get plenty of that these days . . .

Stranger: You keep on talking about getting people well, and dealing with the illness or the condition as if it were something to be isolated and removed. Surely most of what you deal with now is chronic disease, often in old people with multiple problems, for whom there is no prospect of cure.

Dr Power: Cataract operations and hip replacement surgery can transform patients' lives, once we can get a bed for them, but . . . I suppose you are right. We can't cure many diseases, but we can make patients much more comfortable than they would otherwise have been.

Stranger: Such modesty is admirable. But it seems to sit rather oddly alongside the enormous power and influence that doctors have managed to acquire. Don't you think that the heart of the matter is that people just don't trust doctors and medicine any more, what with all these scandals about drug side effects reported by *Panorama* and other television programmes . . .

Dr Power: I can't believe that's true. Of course there have always been people who have been envious of our status and critical of our authority. There have always been patients who have complained that their rights have been infringed or that their health has been damaged. . . . Anyway, now *you're* talking about people 'in general'. . . . How do *you* know?

Stranger: Of course it is difficult to say that people in general no longer trust doctors, but there is evidence that things have changed significantly in the last decade or so.

Dr Power: What evidence?

Stranger: Well, for example, complaints about the NHS are at record levels. The Health Service Ombudsman upheld more than half the huge number of complaints he received last year. There's evidence of slapdash medical record-keeping, lax handling of complaints by doctors and NHS managers, and poor doctor–patient communication. Then there are the criticisms from women's health groups about male doctors failing to give sufficient priority to women's everyday health problems. In addition, we have had many years of a Conservative Government whose approach to health policy has involved an assault on the foundations of the NHS and the power and privilege of the professionals working within it. Doesn't all that tell us a great deal about what people really think?

Dr Power: These complainants never take account of resources . . . we just don't have enough time to devote to proper record-keeping, for example. And as for politics, it's got nothing to do with what the electorate thinks about the health service, let alone doctors as a profession. Unlike teachers and social workers, we have always been regarded with respect, if not awe, by our patients. They know that we, unlike the politicians and the bureaucrats, have their interests at heart. We spend time with them when they are least able to help themselves, unlike politicians, who seem to be interested in people only when they *can* help themselves, or just before an election.

Stranger: There is no doubt that doctors are more liked than politicians. They are probably regarded with more affection than bank managers and garage mechanics too! Perhaps part of the problem in this discussion is that we are conflating the Health Service and the medical profession.

Dr Power: Without us there would be no NHS . . .

Stranger: That is certainly true, but it is also true that there would be no NHS without nurses, without cleaners and without porters . . .

Dr Power: Well, that is self-evident, but the point is that you can find a cleaner or porter anywhere, but skilled surgeons and physicians are a rare breed . . .

Stranger: No doubt that is why you are paid so much. . . . But isn't it the case that it was because of doctors' own interests that the NHS always contained within itself the seeds of its own destruction? Don't you think that the stuffing of the consultants' mouths with gold has turned out to be something of a Trojan horse?

Dr Power: What do you mean, Stranger?

Stranger: All I mean is that it is difficult for you, the doctors, to claim that you have the patients' interests at heart when you have been so manifestly adept at protecting and enhancing your own.

Dr Power: Well, we are not doing charity work! It is a modern professional activity, highly skilled, and deserving of adequate remuneration and resourcing. . . . When you consider the length of our training and the long hours we work I don't think you can conclude that we are overpaid. And anyway, our attempts to ensure our autonomy and authority *are* in the interests of our patients. Without proper procedures for registration and training, without decent salaries and terms and conditions, we wouldn't attract good people, and wouldn't be able to control the quality of the service. We would be no more than quacks!

Stranger: I'll concede that. But look at the numbers of people who are flocking to 'quacks' working outside the medical profession . . .

Dr Power: People have always been duped in that way. Whatever we do for people, there are those who will be dissatisfied and seek help elsewhere. They usually come back when they are suffering the consequences of one or other miracle cure.

Stranger: That may or may not be the case. I am not making a point about numbers – though almost one in seven of the population now go to alternative practitioners. Nor am I disputing the fact that some of those practitioners cause damage. Instead, I am trying to get you to talk about what needs there are, and the extent to which modern medicine seems to be able to meet them. If it cannot, it is not surprising that so many challenges to the profession exist. It is clear that people feel there is something they need that is not provided by doctors. What is it?

Dr Power: I just think that people have come to have unrealistic expectations, as I said before, fuelled by all this political meddling in the NHS, and the ridiculous stories peddled quite irresponsibly by media people such as that Rantzen[1] woman. . . . They expect their GP to have all the answers, and when he doesn't they want to be referred immediately to a hospital of their choosing. These are unrealistic, especially now, with fundholding practices taking priority. They expect to be cured, which is often impossible. They expect to be treated courteously, which is difficult in a busy, under-resourced clinic. They demand the best in the way of drugs and rehabilitation, which is increasingly difficult to provide. They want a better quality of life, which is hardly within our gift . . . and so on, and on . . .

Stranger: But if those expectations are unrealistic, what, in fact, do people treated in the health service by doctors have the right to expect?

Dr Power: They have the right to be seen by a doctor, and to have the best treatment available.

Stranger: But if the doctor is not able to help, or if the best treatment isn't available, or if it takes a considerable amount of time for the patient to be seen, or if the treatment doesn't improve quality of life . . . what is the point in seeking help from a doctor? All you seem to do is provide drugs for people, whatever the problem.

Dr Power: It is not our fault if patients expect a pill for every ill, and a pill that works at that. They are the consumers who make demands on us, not we on them . . .

Stranger: Oh come on, Dr Power, it is not as if pills and potions have been brought into existence, *de novo*, by the demands of frightened, vulnerable patients! Don't you think that your cosy relationship with the pharmaceutical industry has something to do with it? And anyway, it is a gross misrepresentation to say that patients expect a pill for every ill. Indeed, that is just what they don't want. What they want is something – a pill, a word of a advice, a relationship – that will enable them to feel better and to live more fully.

Dr Power: But that really is not our job. We are trained to deal with things that go wrong with the organism. We really cannot be expected to put everything else right as well!

Stranger: That is perfectly true, but one might expect at least a greater sense of professionals working in harmony for the good of the patient, rather than competing for status and control. . . .

Dr Power: We try and work as a team of course. Despite our ups and downs I try and maintain a good relationship with those working under me . . . the nurses, the physios, the OTs. They know what I want and they usually get on with the job. . . .

Stranger: But isn't that part of the problem? Doctors generally see other professionals and their patients as being good when they are being compliant, rather than encouraging a climate of equality with a genuine sharing of perspectives and knowledge . . .

Dr Power: What do you mean, Stranger?

Stranger: What I mean is what I referred to earlier as being the heart of the problem: a loss of trust. By that I do not mean to suggest that people think that doctors are always on the make. I am referring to something more profound. What we are talking about here is not simply an attack on doctors. We are witnessing the most recent manifestation of what has been happening for at least a century: the questioning of objectivity and the undermining of authority. There has been a loss of faith in expert systems. The turning to alternative medicine, the rise of self-help groups, the anti-vivisection and women's health movements, the growth of litigation – all are surely related to this. People are disillusioned with experts and professionals, a sentiment that right-wing politicians have of course used to justify cutting services. But the response of doctors cannot be inward looking and elitist. They cannot be forever harking back. Unless the medical profession tries to create shared goals with the public, with purchasers, with other professionals . . . they will become an irrelevance . . .

A nurse runs into the room. 'Doctor! Come quickly! The "Chief" (Chief Executive) has had a heart attack.'

'I'll be right there,' the doctor replies.

The nurse dashes from the room and the doctor leans back in his chair. He turns to the Stranger and smiles. As he gets up and, unhurriedly, heads for the door, he turns. 'An irrelevance?' he asks, and closes the door quietly behind him, happy and self-possessed once more.

Dr Power arrives at the scene and moves slowly, without expression, to the covered body of the dead man. His hand hesitates momentarily over the sheet. He pulls it back, and a shock of recognition runs through him as he finds himself gazing down on the contorted face of the Stranger.

ACKNOWLEDGEMENTS

We would like to thank Eva Elliott, Susan Pickard and Jennie Popay for their helpful comments. Any literary or sociological shortcomings are, of course, the authors' alone.

NOTE

1   This refers to Ms Esther Rantzen who is a well-known media personality on British television.

Index